TO REASON WHY

TO REASON WHY

Denis Forman

Pen & Sword
MILITARY

First published in Great Britain in 1991 by André Deutsch Limited
Reprinted in this format in 2008 by
PEN & SWORD MILITARY
an imprint of
Pen & Sword Books Ltd
47 Church Street
Barnsley
South Yorkshire
S70 2AS

Copyright © Denis Forman, 1991, 2008

ISBN 978 1 84415 792 1

Printed and bound in Great Britain
By CPI UK

Pen & Sword Books Ltd incorporates the Imprints of
Pen & Sword Aviation, Pen & Sword Family History, Pen & Sword Maritime,
Pen & Sword Military, Wharncliffe Local History, Pen & Sword Select,
Pen & Sword Military Classics, Leo Cooper, Remember When,
Seaforth Publishing and Frontline Publishing

For a complete list of Pen & Sword titles please contact
PEN & SWORD BOOKS LIMITED
47 Church Street, Barnsley, South Yorkshire, S70 2AS, England
E-mail: enquiries@pen-and-sword.co.uk
Website: www.pen-and-sword.co.uk

To Olga Wigram
in belated response to
a request she made of me
in June 1944

AUTHOR'S NOTE & ACKNOWLEDGEMENTS

The earlier chapters of this book are based substantially upon my recollections of the events of half a century ago. Conversations reflect the spirit and context of the times as accurately as memory will allow. Some events are translated in time or place to permit the story to flow more easily, but never, I hope, to the detriment of a true picture. From October 1943 onwards the accounts of military operations are underpinned by official war diaries or other contemporary documents.

I would like to thank Nan Taylor for her work in obtaining original copies of the many documents quoted; Sir Paul Bryan, John Pateman and my brother Michael for checking their recollection of events in Shetland and Italy against mine; David Barbour for his research into several regimental matters; Gaynor Johnson for transcribing a virtually illegible manuscript into the neatest of typescripts; and my wife Moni in her invaluable role as consort.

DF

The illustrations between pages 102 and 103 and pages 186 and 187 are all from Sir Denis Forman's personal archive, except the two photographs of the Sangro front which are reproduced by courtesy of the Imperial War Museum. The maps were drawn by Adrian Yarborough.

At the end of the book are appended a number of documents concerning Lionel Wigram's report on the Sicilian campaign (including the report itself) and the consequences for Lionel Wigram of that report; two accounts of Lionel Wigram which appeared in the press after his death; and an article from *The Times*, 3 March 1951, on the origins and influence of battle schools. There is also a list of military abbreviations and their meanings.

MILITARY ABBREVIATIONS

A/A, ACK-ACK	Anti-aircraft	GSO (I II, III)	General Staff Officers (operations) I Lieutenant Colonel, II Major, III Captain
ADMIN	Administration		
AFHQ	Allied Forces Headquarters		
AMN	Ammunition	HE	High Explosive
AP	Anti-personnel	HLI	Highland Light Infantry
ART, ARTY	Artillery		
ATK, A/TK	Anti-tank	HQ	Headquarters
BN	Battalion	HRS	Hours
BDE	Brigade	HS	House
C IN C	Commander in Chief	HY	Heavy
CMDS	Commanders	I/C (2 I/C)	In Command (Second-in-Command)
COMD	Command		
CO	Commanding Officer	INC, INCL	Including
CONCS	Concentrations	INSTR	Instructor
COY	Company	IO	Intelligence Officer
COMNS	Communications	JUNC	Junction
CQMS	Company Quartermaster Sergeant	KOSB	Kings Own Scottish Borderers
		L/CPL	Lance Corporal
CSM	Company Sergeant Major	LMG	Light Machine Gun
		LOB	Left out of battle
DDMT	Deputy Director of Military Training	LT COL	Lieutenant Colonel
		ME	Middle East
DIV	Division	MED	Medium
DMT	Director of Military Training	MGGS	Major General General Staff
FD	Field	MG (34, 42)	Machine Gun (German machine gun Mark 1934 and Mark 1942)
FDL	Forward Defensive Localities		
FM	Farm	MO	Medical Officer
FUP	Forming-Up Place	MRTR, MTR	Mortar
GHQ	General Headquarters	MT	Motor Transport
GNL	General	NCO	Non-commissioned Officer
GP	Group		
GRD	Ground	OCTU	Officer Cadet Training Unit
GS	General Staff		

OFFR	Officer	RWK	Royal West Kents
O Group	Order Group	SMLE	Short Magazine Lee
OP	Observation post		Enfield (Rifle)
OSDEF	Orkney and Shetland	SUPP	Support
	Defences	TG	Tommy Gun
PL	Platoon	TMC	Thompson Machine
PON	Position		Carbine
PTE	Private (soldier)	TPT	Transport
Q	Quartermaster	TPS	Troops
RD	Road	TSMG	Thompson
RECCE	Reconnaissance		Sub-machine
REGT	Regiment		Gun
RLY	Railway	WD	War Department
RTO	Railway Transport	WO	War Office
	Officer	W/Set	Wireless Set

CHAPTER

1

THE OLD HIGHLAND RAILWAY ran a stopping train on Saturdays from Fort William to Glasgow leaving at ten in the morning, and one day in August 1938 I was peering through its grimy windows at the dappled bulk of Ben Nevis. I felt a little shopsoiled, a combination of hangover, lack of sleep and muscular exhaustion caused by an excess of dancing. It was the end of the Highland Ball circuit and I had done Perth, Inverness, Portree and Fort William. The day before I had run in the sprints at the Gathering (soon to be called the Highland Games) and then danced all night.

We had been a party of sixteen – all parties were of thirty-two, sixteen or eight, so that reels could be danced 'in party'. There was social advantage and some grandeur in a party which could field two sixteensomes. Hostesses who were of limited means or of weaker drawing-power had to be content with a single eightsome. After dinner in the cave-like dining room of a nearby castle we had gathered at the Station Hotel in Fort William and danced from 10 p.m. to 7 a.m. – Dashing White Sergeants, Petronellas, Hamilton Houses, Flowers of Edinburgh and, as things speeded up, the Duke of Perth and Speed the Plough, and between each pair of set dances there were reels, eightsomes followed by foursomes, which gave the men a chance to show their mettle in a brief moment of solo exhibitionism.

As the night wore on the party moved towards a state of almost manic exhilaration, the men hoching and hooting as they leapt and capered (bad manners at staider gatherings), the girls stamping and clapping the wilder excesses of the male dancers with little cries as if they were in sexual crisis. There was, however, little romance in the air: for one thing the men sweated so profusely that they were forced to change their dress shirts once, twice or even three times in a night, their doublets or Prince Charlie jackets became dark and slimy and little drops

1

of sweat sprayed out from the fringes of their kilts as they swung and twirled.

There was the traditional pause at 2 a.m. for supper, and after that we switched from whisky and champagne to beer, all of which we had sweated out by the time we sat down to breakfast. It was the general opinion of our party as we walked by the sea shore waiting for the train, that we had on the whole danced better than any other party, and this view was said to have been confirmed by the elderly but discriminating jury which lined the walls, some of them sticking it out until the bitter end.

Indeed, as we struggled up past Spean Bridge, the group of six in our compartment mused complacently on the success of the night.

'Charlie was just terrific,' said one. 'Did you see his Snatchers?' (a particularly difficult and fast reel step).

'Wizard show,' said another, 'just wizard.'

'Rory McDonald [a man from another party] was sick on the stairs,' said a malevolent Campbell, 'then he passed out on the floor of the gents and lay there for an hour.' There were noises of assent. Many people had seen Rory lying under the row of washbasins. No one had helped him to his bedroom. This was part of the Highland Ball ethic. If you made an exhibition of yourself you had to bear the consequences.

'Charlie said he had two whole bottles of Glen Grant alongside the usual stuff,' said the Charlie fan, 'and he never turned a hair. Danced as dainty as a cat.'

'Wizard dancer,' said the other, 'just wizard.'

'Wasn't Tim [Tim Wright, the most favoured dance-band leader] just terrific?' asked the third. 'He gave us three encores for the last eightsome. Never done that before.'

'Wizard,' said the appreciative one, 'just wizard.'

But the stuffy smell and heavy upholstery of the old Highland first-class compartment (with its woven mat on the floor, fish-net luggage racks and huge leather strap to lower and raise the window – which would never budge) began to do its work. Eyelids began to droop and breathing became regular and heavy.

Next to me, a pretty London girl's jaw sagged and a little trickle of saliva began to run down her chin. I thought how ashamed she would be when she woke up. Opposite me sat a plain girl with a harelip, sister to an equally plain boy. She was not asleep and

2

neither was I, and with characteristic indifference to the comfort of the rest of the party she began arguing with me again about the matter of the pound.

'You must take it back. Honestly you must.'

'Why should I? The McLeans gave me five pounds to cover all expenses and I took it out of that.'

'But you must have spent more than five pounds on extra drinks for the party.'

'What I spent on drinks is none of your business.'

'I could easily have travelled third class.'

'The five of us here in this compartment and you sitting alone at the other end of the train. A likely scene.'

'Mummy will be furious when I tell her.'

'Too bad. She's not my mummy.'

'But I simply can't let you pay. It isn't honourable.'

The pretty girl on my right stirred in her sleep and wiped the spittle off her chin. 'For Christ's sake,' she said. 'Don't be so *provincial*. I'll give you a pound each if you'll stop this bloody argument and let me sleep.'

Just then the train pulled up at Tyndrum and there was a boy on the platform selling papers. On the front page was the news of Munich.

So that was it. It wouldn't be long now. For some time I had known that war with Germany was inevitable. Most of the world in which I moved hoped wishfully that the threat would go away, and acted accordingly, but a few of my Cambridge friends shared my conviction; indeed some of them were in part the cause of it. There was Peter Keuneman, son of a distinguished Indian judge, a communist and mature beyond the ken of most of the childlike ex-public school population of Pembroke. It was he who had laid out for me lessons to be drawn from the relentless progress of Hitler and had projected his moves into the future – to the conclusion that another world war was unavoidable. The laws of international politics, he said, were as harsh as those of Greek tragedy; the difference was that their application was real, and affected our lives.

Then there was James Morton, who was training to be a fighter pilot in the university squadron and who knew a great deal about the relative strengths of the two sides' armed forces. He was a quiet and mainly private man, and we would

3

sit together far into the night while he sucked his pipe and we contemplated the huge and terrifying discrepancies between the German war machine and ours.

'You see, old man,' he would say, 'I don't give much for the motivational rubbish, the Youth Movement and Strength Through Joy, but the flying clubs are real: nearly a thousand of them turning out trained pilots by the cartload. We have six auxiliary squadrons with piss-poor instructors. While the bloody young Krauts have all got their heads down over navigational maps of Kent our chaps are buggering about playing rugger and getting pissed.'

There was practical evidence, too, from Joe Klein, the Czechoslovakian javelin-thrower in the Cambridge athletics team. His parents and his sister, who had come to a May Ball, knew the *Realpolitik* of living under the German threat; and there was Harry Rosenberg whose Jewish relatives were desperately trying to escape and make a bolt for the West.

The war was like a leaden weight, slowly but surely pressing down on the froth and folly of our lives, sometimes making them seem like a dance of death. It was coming, it was horrible and it was going to take me, and a million others, into its maw.

I opened the carriage door and felt the stale breath of the old world puff into my face.

'There's news in the paper,' I said, chucking it at the two young men next to the windows. They looked at it sleepily.

'Seems good news,' said one.

'Good old Chamberlain,' said the other.

'He's been conned,' said I. The plain girl puzzled over the paper for a moment.

'Mummy says there won't be a war,' she said, 'and even if there is Graham will be all right because his is a reserved occupation.'

'What about the rest of us?' said I.

'For God's sake,' said the pretty deb, 'will you all stop TALKING? I'm trying to get some sleep.'

'There's going to be a war,' I said.

'Will you please SHUT UP,' she said and turned her face into the dusty upholstery.

Jim Rheilly, our loquacious chauffeur, met me at Beattock station.

4

'It was great,' he said as he drove me home to Dumcrieff. 'There was Mr Chamberlain, all the foreigners had tried to quell Hitler and our Mr Chamberlain walks into his office and just tells him off. No further territorial ambitions. Eh?' And he laughed in his delight. 'He tellt him he couldna win.'

'Do you think Hitler will stick with it?' I asked.

'He's got tae,' Jim replied. 'He signed the paper didn't he? He canna go back on that can he?'

When I got home the mood was much the same. 'You have a very wonderful man as prime minister,' said my mother.

'I've always said there was a lot of good in Hitler,' said my father.

'Have you read what Winston had to say?' I asked.

'Winston is an ass,' said my father.

'This will give Hitler just what he wants,' said I. 'A few months to get things sorted out, to get his aircraft production going and when he's ready he will strike.'

'But he has signed a treaty with Mr Chamberlain,' said my mother. 'No one would ever trust him again if he broke that.'

'I don't think that would trouble him too much,' said I.

Nor was the war uppermost in the minds of the community of Pembroke College, Cambridge. There was speculation as to whether the first boat could hold its place, being (as was widely known) the lightest first boat on the river. I was pressed to play in the Cuppers and, though loath to break my athletics training, eventually succumbed. I read a pretentious paper to the Martlets on modern music which no one understood. The debating society was split between two factions, one standing for more serious and cleaner debating, the other for even more filthy and flippant debating.

The senior tutor attended a debate in which I led for the filthy faction and afterwards said to me, 'That was an eloquent and wholly abhorrent performance,' to which I replied, 'Counsel does not always believe in the cause he advocates.'

'I have an idea,' he said, 'that your heart was in it.' And indeed, in my case perhaps as a reaction to the oppressive religious régime of my youth, and in others simply as a continuation of their public-school habits, we did talk in an extraordinarily scatological style. After myself and Jesus Palmer (so named because he preceded practically every sentence with the word), Harrovians were the most foul-mouthed; one of these, James Campbell, who today adorns the list of Honorary Fellows of Pembroke, kept The Book, with his brother Colin. In The Book was recorded every poem, every song, every rhyming squib or limerick that passed one single test – was it sufficiently obscene?

Hardy annuals like 'Eskimo Nell' and 'The King's Piece' had several alternative versions annotated in scholarly manner by the Campbell brothers, giving the date of composition, authorship where known, and the occasion of any notable performance. Thus the 'Ball of Kirriemuir' must have had well over fifty verses added to the statutory dozen which formed the authorised version for performance at Caledonian Club dinners.

Sometimes our minds turned to more serious matters, such as boredom. One night a Trinity Hall man boasted that his college had in it the most boring men in the university. This was more than we at Pembroke could stomach. We maintained that in the matter of boredom Pembroke had resources which no other college could match. The debate grew heated and ended in a challenge: three bores would be selected by each side and matched at a sherry party given on neutral ground. The bores themselves had to be entirely innocent of what was going on, but the promoters were at liberty to coach them into being even more boring than they were.

For the best part of three weeks we thought of little else. My man, the Pembroke Number One, could whistle a chord, and the intensity of the boredom induced by his explanation of this phenomenon made him, I thought, a certain winner. But I left nothing to chance, going to the music schools and looking up every reference to whistling, columns of vibrating air and the Pythagorean definition of harmonic intervals, and reading the results to my man so that his analysis and explanation of the *coup de siffleur* became even more lengthy and tedious.

The match was started by gunfire – a mistake, for it startled the bores and some of them took time to settle down, particularly the Pembroke Number Three, who had been trained on the Assyrian Tribes. In the end it was a pushover due to the devilish cunning of the Pembroke promoters. We had studied the form of the Trinity Hall bores and discovered by careful enquiry how best they could be diverted from their topic and become quite amusing conversationalists. Thus their Number One, a hefty rugger player,

6

was stopped in his tracks halfway through a dissertation on Welsh Disestablishment by being asked what happened after the last Varsity match dinner, when he had gone to urinate oblivious of the fact that he had not removed a french letter from his penis and thus fell into a state of drunken panic, thinking his bladder was swelling up outside his body. This anecdote put paid to the Trinity Hall claim that he was a top-class bore. Similarly, we found that their Number Two had shot his father's dog by mistake on a grouse moor, an arresting incident, and their Number Three had met Mussolini.

It was all over in half an hour. The Trinity Hall men took it very well and agreed to join us in a petition to the Blues Committee to award a blue, or at least a half-blue, to members of a team in a bores match between Oxford and Cambridge. The secretary's reply was brief and to the point: Gentlemen and Bores, You must be mad. Yours sincerely.

Meanwhile I was making other plans. Alongside the conviction that war was imminent, I felt a burning anger at our refusal to accept the fact that to win it we and the French had to adjust our national outlook and become professional about the practice of war itself. I read Liddell Hart in the *Illustrated London News* with avidity, and everything I could find about the Spanish Civil War. I went to a lecture by Tom Harrisson, who had commanded the International Brigade, and quizzed him mercilessly. I met veterans from Spain when ski-ing in Austria and in a labour camp I organised in the summer. It seemed to me that the two new weapons which were going to dominate the next war were the JU-87 and the MG-34, the dive-bombers and the rapid-fire, light and reliable machine gun – the ultimate evolution from the founding father of the line, the Maxim. I knew that our old Vickers, although slow to move, was a valuable basic weapon, that the Lewis gun was obsolete and the Bren untried. There was not yet any evidence about tanks. What else could I do about the war?

I had no difficulty in deciding. The infantry was still the central core of any army. They were at the heart of the battle, and I knew that the German infantry would be light years ahead of us in their weaponry, training and military professionalism. I had to join the infantry.

In my zeal for a better and more up-to-date army I snobbishly despised the Territorial Army, whose officers were mainly the sons

7

of landed gentry, whose troops were gardeners, gamekeepers and labourers and who went to camp, I thought, to get away from their wives and have a good booze-up. It is true that the feudal and amateur element in the Territorials may have inhibited a proper study of warfare in peacetime, but I was later to learn the advantages in action of a countryman's knowledge of field sports, and of the strength of morale in close-knit units made up of kinship and common culture. But at the time the Territorials were not for me.

I admired the tradition of dash and derring-do of the Highland regiments. The Guards were too posh and although Lowland regiments might have great qualities they were a drab lot when compared to the Highlanders. Also, as president of the Caledonian Club, where my function was to arrange Highland Balls, eat dinners and drink whisky, I had many friends who were destined for Highland regiments and one or two for the Argyll and Sutherland Highlanders. I would join the Argylls as a private soldier the day war broke out and become an officer cadet as soon as possible.

Meanwhile life at Pembroke continued to be all gas and gaiters, with short periods of anxiety caused by the proximity of exams. I remember a group of a dozen Pembroke friends drinking coffee in Tullivers Café after Hall one night in May when, after the usual scatological review of the day's news, Peter Scott (destined for the Colonial Service) said, 'Well I don't suppose it matters much if we get through the exams because in a couple of years' time we will all be bumped off in this war.'

'There's not going to be any bloody war,' said Philip Langridge, a relaxed rowing type. 'It's all sabre rattling and bullshit.'

'Don't see what we can do about it either way,' said Peter.

'Jesus,' said Palmer, 'you should see what Foreskin is at.' (An unpleasant nickname which I shook off on going down from Cambridge.) 'He's so shit-scared he's reading up everything he can lay his hands on about war. He plans to be a fuckin' general so fast he'll never have to fight.'

'The politicians will fuck it up for sure,' said Peter Withycombe, a huge blond discus thrower. 'They don't want to break treaties, they don't want to stand up to the Axis and so they dither on.'

'Jesus, man,' said Palmer, 'Hitler and Mussolini are all set to give them the bums' rush just when they want to.'

'If they stood together and stood firm . . .' started Peter.

'Jesus, politicians – what the hell do you expect of them anyway?' interrupted Palmer. 'They are all crap. Jesus, anyone who believes in politics needs his head read.'

'A lot of people in Europe didn't believe in politics,' said Peter Keuneman, 'until politics came in through their front door. You lot are the same. You are pig-ignorant and will only believe in politics when the bombs begin to drop, which they will, probably next year.'

'Jesus man,' said Palmer. 'Make it two years and give us a chance to beat fuckin' Oxford on the track.'

'You really think, Peter, that war is a certainty and so soon?' asked Peter Scott.

'This year or next,' said Keuneman. 'Absolutely for certain. And with it the great class struggle between left and right . . .' Here his voice was drowned by Bronx cheers, the banging of coffee cups on saucers and shouts of 'Kamerad' and 'Keuneman for pope,' concluding with a rendering of the 'Red Flag' to wholly inappropriate words. In 1939 it was not easy to sustain a serious political discussion in Pembroke College.

In June, just before my final exams, I contracted a streptococcal infection of the throat and was whisked off to the Evelyn Nursing Home with a high fever. I had failed Part I of the classical tripos the previous year and had taken an ordinary degree course in Rural Economy in my last year, with the long-term intention of buying back Craigielands, my first Scottish home, and running it as a model estate. Now, by missing the final exam, I was awarded an aegrotat, thus eventually gaining the distinction of being the only MA Cantab who had never passed any exam. Once on my feet again, I pursued the Cambridge Appointments Board for a job to fill in time until the war began.

'Forman', said the official, clearly a failed don; and again, reflectively, as he ruffled through my papers: 'Forman'. He tried not to show his disdain at my appalling academic record and clutched at one or two straws. 'You won the headmaster's essay prize at Loretto?' he said.

'I was the only entrant,' I replied.

'You won a number of awards for Bible reading both in Pembroke and in Pembroke-endowed livings,' he said. 'Was the competition strong?'

'No,' I said. 'There were two Irish and one Tynesider and the panel couldn't make out whether they were reading from the Old Testament or the New.'

'Ah,' he said. 'Ah. But you got a scholarship to Pembroke?'

'It was an athletics scholarship,' I said. 'My father played rugger for Cambridge and an eccentric don called Comber endowed a set of rooms for the sons of his "family", that is a group of young men who were frightfully good at games. That is the scholarship I got.'

'I see,' he said, and then again, very slowly, 'I see ...' He looked up brightly and said, 'Then it will have to be commerce.'

Three weeks later I had a job selling soap for Hedleys. When this news reached the ears of my old headmaster at Loretto, Jim Greenlees, he wrote me a letter:

> Dear Denis,
>
> I cannot contemplate the prospect of an ex-head-boy of Loretto becoming a soap salesman. I am coming down to Cambridge and would like you to dine with me on Thursday.
>
> Yours ever,
> Jim

It was an awkward dinner. Jim wanted me to follow the traditional Loretto line: go west, or east, or somewhere abroad in Jardine Mathieson or Balfour Williamson and work hard, live cleanly and come back a rich man. His father-in-law was Lord Cargill of Burmah Oil, he would talk to him, also with Gourlay MacIndoe, John Ross and others (he reeled off a list of resounding Scottish names). I said I didn't want to go abroad. The war would soon be with us and I wanted to be in the UK when it broke out. He said thoughts about the war should not affect my career decisions. To get him off my back I agreed to attend any interview he arranged, but left the University Arms still with a distinct preference for selling soap.

A week later I was interviewed by Lord Cargill's representative in Finsbury Square. I said I did not want to live abroad, and the interview ended quickly. This resulted in a furious letter from Jim, saying I was ruining my chances of a good career.

> Now look here, what you have got to face is, that there is no position which you will get abroad which will allow you to come home under twenty years. When you go out you will be twenty-two; when you come back you will be forty-two, and if you do come back as one of the heads

of the firm you go out with, you will be a person in a big position in London at once. If you stay in this country in business, you are not in the least likely to make a big position for yourself unless you have extraordinary luck which you cannot gamble on inside twenty years; and I doubt very much your making a position such as you would have if you rose to be one of the senior directors of the Burmah Oil Company or McNeill's; but it means facing the fact that you have got to get down to really hard work, putting the business first and doing the work out there, because there is no short road.

Beggars can't be choosers, he said. No, I thought, but they can be soap salesmen.

The next interview, with Gourlay MacIndoe of McLean Watson (Far Eastern Importers and Exporters), was more positive. I could do six months in Holland to learn the language and lightering business, then opt for six months in Liverpool or go straight to Batavia, which was my ultimate destination. I would be living all found in Amsterdam and my pay would be twice what Hedley offered. The war would be on by then, I thought, and accepted. I had an ecstatic letter from Jim, congratulating me on my sound good sense. The danger of an entry in the *Loretto Gazette* after my name, 'Sells soap for Hedleys', had been averted.

In Amsterdam I was billeted in De Laressatstraat with two other young men, one Dutch and one Swedish, in the home of a family with three girls named, astonishingly, Wim (pronounced Vim), Pea (pronounced Payer) and Gits (pronounced Yits). Father we never saw, mother had two occupations: cooking and ensuring that Vim, Pea and Yits saw plenty of the young gentleman lodgers. In neither was she successful. Breakfast was potato pie, black bread, cheese and apfelstrudel; lunch much the same, although there was sometimes cheese and fish in the pie, and dinner was potato and cabbage soup, potato scones, cheese, black bread and apfelstrudel. Between these meals the office staff were fed snacks: *Koffeetaffel*, which consisted of a choice of potato pie, black bread and beetroot sandwiches and apfelstrudel. And they aren't even at war yet, I thought, and slipped off in my lunch hour to Wyn and Fockink for a raw herring and a nip of Aquavit.

There was little warmth in the forced commingling of the sexes. We were pushed out on our six bicycles early on a Sunday morning, and good manners forced us to associate for most of the

11

day. The girls were uncommonly plain: Wim had halitosis, Pea flat white pimples and Gits black teeth. All three had a strong Dutch cheese body odour. The Dutchman and I shunned any frolics with them despite giggling entreaties, but the Swede tried to lay all three in turn. We thought he must be a sex maniac or suffer from some obscure Swedish perversion.

The office work was purest routine – listing how cargoes from sea-going ships should be, had been or ought to have been, broken up into various lighter-loads which were then dispersed all over northern Europe. In the office it was generally thought that war would begin soon and that the Germans would walk in and take over. Political and military considerations were not much discussed, rather how German occupation would affect the business (badly) and domestic life (not much). In the lodging house political discussion was forbidden for fear of arousing passion. But among ourselves I found the Swede a convinced anti-Nazi, the Dutchman a prospective collaborator and the girls thoughtless and witless. They rather hoped they would have soldiers billeted on them, preferably officers, rather than just common civilians like us.

I found a different world of opinion through music. At night I worked as a wine waiter in a nightclub, the Lido, and got to know the band so well that when the cellist slipped off for his break I stood in for him. Although hardly able to play the cello, I could just hold a simple oom-pah bass line, particularly if there were plenty of open notes. Two of our band played in the Concertgebouw orchestra – the Concertgebouw was only a few hundred yards away from the lodging house – and I met members of the orchestra (and once the great Mengelberg himself) in a nearby café. These men, mostly Jewish, were terrified at the prospect for themselves, their families and for Holland as a nation. They saw the end of their independent liberal state approaching and felt they faced living in a province of Germany, with all that meant. There was one safe house, an all-night drinking club called Der Pakkist, where anti-Nazis could talk without fear of betrayal and there I would go after the Lido closed to listen to multilingual discussions of the *Realpolitik* of northern Europe. French, Flemish, Dutch, German and English alternated as the discussion went on through the night – sometimes a debate on racial theory, sometimes military history, sometimes on the characters of the Nazi leaders, but always reflecting an atmosphere of fear, sometimes bordering on panic.

As August wore on and the Polish crisis deepened, the streets of Amsterdam began to fill with troops. There were soldiers on the trains, and often one soldier standing behind the conductor on the trams. Why, I thought, why? To arrest suspicious passengers? To take over all transport on a command? To impress the population? I never could decide, but the military presence increased steadily, as did the state of panic of the population at large. On 30 August it was clear that the game was up, and I was wondering what I should do when I got a note asking me to see my boss at seven o'clock that night.

He was sitting at his desk in his shirt sleeves wearing a green celluloid eyeshade that made him look like a croupier. 'Good evening, young man,' he said. 'I have a proposal to make to you that will serve your very good interests. The war will start tomorrow. Perhaps the next day. The Germans will invade France and Belgium, perhaps Holland. In a short time, perhaps a few months, they will overcome. They will march to Paris. To the Hague. To Amsterdam. Perhaps to Denmark. Europe will be German.'

'What will happen then?' I asked.

'Hitler will take his time. He has a great war machine. The greatest ever known. But it will take time to invade England. Perhaps six months.'

'What then?'

'England will be defeated. It will become German.'

'What about the Americans?'

'The Americans will do nothing, perhaps nothing at all. They will talk.'

'What is your proposition?'

'I have a boat sailing for Batavia tomorrow. Even if the war breaks out it will get safely through. I offer you a passage to Batavia. There you will be safe, perhaps very safe. The war will not reach Batavia. Of course, if you wish, you can go back to England. But that would be very foolish. Perhaps suicide. Not in your good interests at all.'

When I left the office and walked back I saw troops bivouacking all round the Concertgebouw. There was a signals truck outside our door.

13

The next morning as I bade farewell to Wim, Pea and Gits – actually going so far as to give each a smacking kiss – I realised I wasn't well. On the packet from the Hook the ship's doctor gave me aspirin and took my temperature. It was 103. I made my way through crowded trains and densely packed Liverpool Street and Euston stations to Beattock. An hour later I was in the Moffat Cottage Hospital. As I went into the operating theatre I went to sleep. When I woke there were spots of blood on the ceiling of my private room, coughed up in a spasm after the removal of my tonsils. At the end of my bed was my sister Sheila; she was trying to tell me something. Great Britain was at war with Germany.

CHAPTER

2

MY PLANS FOR JOINING THE ARMY went only slightly wrong. Instead of joining the Argylls as a private and becoming an officer cadet, I was drafted to an Officer Cadet Training Unit at once and then joined the Argylls. The final posting from the OCTU was said to depend upon one's rating on passing out: the top ten were certain to get to the regiment of their choice, the bottom fifty to be posted to various English regiments at that time regarded as the pits. This was almost certainly untrue but it was one of those clever strategies dreamt up by sergeants, the more keenly to motivate their charges. No cadet could dismiss it from his mind – there might be something in it. My OCTU was sited at Dunbar, only twenty miles from Loretto School, where I had previously spent five freezing years. This experience was to stand me in good stead, for our company of one hundred and twenty young men was billeted through the winter of 1939–40 in two barn-like hotels on cliffs which caught the full force of the wind from Siberia. The hotels were not heated and the room temperature hovered around freezing. Outside it was generally well below.

Although inexperienced and incompetent in the business of fighting, the British army of the 1930s excelled in the matter of training. Foot drill in the barrack square was treated with almost religious reverence as a high art. Although the methods used were not much like those associated with other arts – consisting as they did of bullying, threatening, humiliating and terrorising the participants – as the months wore on we became a superb performing troupe and assembled on the drill square with a thrill of pleasurable anticipation. We knew we were beginning to put on a good show and on the call of 'ON your right marker FALLIN' we stepped out with chins up and a spring in our step like ballet dancers entering for a great third act divertissement. Weapons training demanded dexterity of hand and limb and accuracy of eye, and became a pure joy for a proficient performer.

15

The bren gun was as familiar and fitted the body as comfortably as an old sporting gun, and one moved one's fingers over one's rifle as instinctively and almost as lovingly as over one's current girlfriend.

Route marches, welcome in such weather because they kept the circulation going, were sustained in a wonderfully dogged rhythm. I soon found that the British army marched at a metronome mark which, alas, did not match the tempo of the classical allegro. There were no first movements of the Beethoven symphonies that would fit it, but nearly all the adagios worked with a crotchet to each left-right. The scherzos and the quicker finales went well to a minim to each left-right, but the finale of the Seventh and Eighth dragged and the choral finale of the Ninth went at the hell of a lick – no great disadvantage, as I then thought. The most perfect tempo was accorded the second movement of the Second and the Fifth symphonies, and it was with great chagrin that, in the middle of one of the more sublime passages, I heard the sergeant shout 'You horrible men, you bloody ragged lot – SHOUT IT.' At which a modulation from E flat to F major might be interrupted by the cacophony of the well-known

> I had a good job but I LEFT
> I had a good job but I LEFT
> Now don't you think I was perfectly RIGHT
> I had a good job but I LEFT

Motor Transport (MT), learning to drive a fifteen hundred-weight truck, bren carrier or motor bike on the sand dunes, was cold, but tactical exercises were colder. Lying on the slopes of Doon hill in the small hours of the morning with rifle at the ready, icy particles wounding the cheeks and limbs freezing, was a common experience. Some of our softer brethren resorted to charcoal hand-warmers, silk underwear and Whisky Mac, but the tougher element, of which I was one, scorned such sybaritic practices.

There was no comfort awaiting us on our return to barracks. The showers were cold or at best tepid; the wind whistled under the three boards which lay on two stumpy trestles to form a bed. Three blankets were the regulation issue and these, together with one's greatcoat, were hopelessly inadequate, so every cadet went to bed in two sets of long Johns, two army shirts and many with the lower portions of their legs in their kitbags.

Yet there was moral comfort in the spartan life and in the ownership of so few things. At bed inspection every single item in one's personal estate was on display, for one's toilet (razor, shaving brush, toothbrush and soap); for dining (mess tin, mug, KFS); one's total wardrobe (greatcoat, spare battle-dress, two pairs long Johns, two shirts, socks made of a sort of grey wire, spare boots); and one's personal armoury of rifle and bayonet. I was intensely proud of my bed as laid for inspection and spent many hours honing my scabbard and boots. There were various theories as to the best method of doing this; some used methylated spirits and 'burned off' to give a superficial surface skin, others tried lacquer paint, but I stuck to the traditional method of boning in blacking with a toothbrush handle and then honing the surface for several hours. Similarly, some kept the creases in their battle-dress trousers by sewing the two sides together, but this was generally regarded as the sort of thing suitable only for the lower orders such as the Service Corps. Most of us ironed a thick dressing of soap into the apex of the crease with a dab of chewing gum at the knee and the ankle.

In the classroom and later in the field my great joy was maps. The *Manual of Military Reading* was the first textbook I committed to memory (before the end of the courses I could recite most of the standard manuals by rote – always excepting the *Manual of Military Law* – and indeed I set several pages of *Small Arms Training* to music as a duet for alto and bass which was much in demand at canteen sing-songs), but when one became really fluent at map reading a new world was opened up. At first I travelled by map only around East Lothian, but soon my ambition grew. I traversed the Caledonian Canal, climbed Ben Nevis and became thoroughly familiar with Lochinver and Ullapool. From Scotland my mind turned to the theatres of war, but alas there were few large-scale maps available of France and those I could obtain from Scottish Command were of such poor quality as to be virtually useless. I began to realise that a unique example of British genius was to be found in the one-inch Ordnance Survey map (or 1:50,000 as it is today).

If reading a map was pleasure, making one was bliss. I started with the class near the seashore, using the Union Jack method, but after a day or two of this nothing short of triangulation would do.

17

With the help of a friendly instructor, I began, for the first time, to discover what a glorious tool trigonometry could be, revelling in sines, co-sines and tans, and entered the enchanted realms of the surveyor's art. Much of my free time during daylight hours was spent mapping the town of Dunbar. For the first time in my life I was learning what I wanted to learn. Schoolwork had held no attraction and I had slithered through the statutory exams with the help of natural intelligence. At Cambridge I doubt if I spent as much as an hour a day studying Classics, and was ashamed but in no way surprised when I flunked the exam. I did study agriculture with relish in my last year, but I regarded this more as a hobby than a discipline and much of it I knew already. But now I had a body of knowledge I could grasp and assimilate in its entirety and I revelled in the opportunity.

There was only one snag. The OCTU course was well designed, the commandant was excellent and the instructors were more than adequate, but we were being trained for the wrong war. We had the wrong weapons – the old SMLE rifle of World War One, instead of the Czech automatic rifle or the tommy gun; the bren gun, a fragile and hysterical creature compared to the sturdy MG34, the pathetic little two-inch mortar, which lobbed toy bombs a few hundred yards, and the anti-tank rifle, which could be seen only as a bad joke. It was inordinately heavy, difficult to fire and incapable of penetrating the latest German armour (my hatred of the anti-tank rifle was justified when I found that in the field more of them lay at the bottom of rivers or dumped in ditches than were in active use).

One also had to doubt the relevance of square-bashing to modern warfare. The idea that drill formations appropriate to the Battle of Waterloo would be used in the war that lay ahead was faintly ridiculous. Similarly, the many hours devoted to the construction of trenches, including meticulous measurements for parapets and firing bays and detailed instructions on how to revet in sandy soil, seemed a little out of proportion. Either we would be ensconced in some huge complex of concrete such as the Maginot Line, or we would be digging foxholes, as they did in Spain.

These thoughts were often aired in the few moments of leisure allowed us. We were accorded two weekend leaves during our twenty-week course, otherwise we had to entertain ourselves locally. The canteen with its wooden forms and trestle tables was useful only for satisfying our animal needs for food and drink. The management had made a gesture to our status as officer cadets in making available two of the reception rooms in our hotels as sitting rooms, but since there were only some forty seats for one hundred and twenty cadets, they tended to be crowded, especially since Clanzer McDonald when drunk would frequently disembowel armchairs and sofas for bayonet practice, yelling all the while 'I'll get ye – ye bloody papist.' He got drunk every Saturday night and was called Clanzer because of his habit of saying when checked 'Always done that way in my clan, sir.'

But for the élite who played golf and could afford five pounds there was the membership of the Dunbar Golf Club with a cosy clubroom, a well-stocked bar and a variety of snacks on sale. I couldn't play golf and couldn't afford five pounds, but Claude Carter paid my subscription for me, being very rich and needing someone to listen to lengthy accounts of his sexual exploits. These were numerous and occupied every moment of his waking life when not on parade. There were about seven or eight girls he was pursuing in Dunbar, one in Spott and another two in Haddington. He was heavily oriented towards virgins and appeared not to care what a virgin looked like so long as she was the real McCoy. He was in the orderly room more than once as a result of his unpunctuality, caused by the imperative nature of his sexual activities, and once on a route march he was left lying behind a dyke trying to decide with the help of binoculars which members of a gang of female field workers were virgins. He was so rich that he had a car garaged with the father of one of his one-time virgins and this was an enormous asset. He complained, however, that the car was ill-formed to accommodate the sexual act in any other than a perfunctory and constricted fashion, and talked about purchasing a better model with a passenger seat which would flatten out and allow full rein to his artistry. Above all, he deplored the cold weather, which put *al fresco* dalliance out of the question, and longed for the advent of summer. After leaving Dunbar I lost touch with Claude except that on the first of May for many years I received from him an elegant little card inscribed 'Ditch Fucking Begins'.

The reason I endured the endless saga of Claude Carter's sexual adventures was that when his mind could be diverted from his main preoccupation, he could lash the British army and its idiot complacency with excoriating wit. So too could Mo de Mier, the son of an Argentinian diplomat, by our standards an old man approaching the age of thirty, a sophisticate who had seen guerrilla warfare in Spain and whose sexual experiences (his guide and partner had been an uncle of evil repute) made those of Claude Carter sound like the romps of a country bumpkin.

It was most agreeable on a Saturday night to sit in the golf club parlour drinking brandy and ginger ale and reviling in violent terms the pigheadedness and blind obstinacy of the British High Command. I wanted to write a paper on the subject, have it signed by a hundred officer cadets and send it to Scottish Command. The others thought this would be mutiny and we would all be cashiered before we were even commissioned and, anyway, sex was more interesting.

As the course neared its end, the other topic frequently canvassed in the golf club parlour and elsewhere was who would get the sword of honour. This was a misnomer. There was no sword and precious little honour in passing out first and certainly none of the melodrama surrounding the event at Sandhurst, with cadets fainting and horses climbing steps before an adoring audience of women in Ascot hats. But I decided I would get it, and I did, so one bleak March day with the sleet driving across the Castle parade ground, I passed the company out to their several destinations. My sister Sheila came to watch the parade, and she cried; not, I thought, because she believed I would be killed but out of sisterly pride. Before I left Dunbar I knew I had got my posting to the Argylls. Not to the 8th, where my friends were and which was in France, but to the 8th's sister battalion, the 11th, which had recently been formed. But first I had to go to the depot at Stirling.

Stirling Castle, occupying one of the key strategic positions in Scotland, had probably seen more battles, more bloodshed, more treachery and more royal chicanery than any other pile of stone north of the border. The fabric had been left untouched since the seventeenth century; the anteroom was in a stone tower where we sat in front of a one-bar electric fire in a monumental fireplace with an aperture twelve feet across and eight feet high. We dined in a mediaeval hall with the regiment's battle honours (flags to you and me) on poles high above our heads. As we tackled our tepid Brown

Windsor I turned to the commandant in charge of the castle and looking at the array I said to him lightly: 'Interesting isn't it that all the regiment's battle honours were gained in defeats; Balaclava, Corunna . . .'

'Get on with your soup, Forman,' said the commandant. So I wended my way to my bedroom, twenty feet by fifteen, with water running down the walls, arrow-slit windows, a single folding iron bedstead, a mat three feet square, a chair of laminated wood, my kitbag and valise and tin trunk in the middle distance and everywhere else nothing but damp grey stone. It was just under a quarter of a mile to the nearest flush lavatory.

I stayed at the depot for a week, changing my clothes. There were ten different standards of dress, from denims at the bottom to the kilt and jacket, badger sporran, Sam Browne and all at the top. But they weren't called by the names of what you wore. Denims were called Fatigue Order; the kilt with battle dress, top boots and puttees was called Company Parade Order; battle dress with trousers was called Field Order. So one had to learn that catalogue of orders by heart, for one had to change at least seven times a day, often within a break of ten minutes. There were two other young subalterns, one of them an unthinking rugger player from Merchiston School, who was desperately keen on all the wrong things, and the other the scion of a noble Scottish family who carried his own horn spoon in his pocket to eat his morning porridge. Once I went into his bedroom and saw on a linen drugget on a side table all his silver toilet gear with embossed initials, including a hand mirror and lip salve.

Our duties, apart from perpetually changing our clothes, were not taxing. We inspected a lot: rifles, consumable stores, men's teeth and feet, pots in the kitchen, but never what seemed in much greater need of inspection – namely the leaking roofs and stinking drains. When not inspecting or acting as orderly officers, we performed fatigues. A fatigue was when the quartermaster had dumped a thousand coils of Dannert wire in the wrong place and twenty men had to hump it to another place, which in the fullness of time would be discovered once again to be the wrong place. We had a daily period of instruction on regimental history (for which we had to change into Regimental Order), and after evening mess we had a series of talks from the CO on regimental traditions, which again mainly concerned changing clothes: what

21

to wear when the colonel of the regiment took a parade, how far from the knee the kilt hose should be, what garter flashes were permissible and how to maintain your badger sporran (it had the complete head of the wretched animal on the forward flap) in tip-top condition.

One night after mess I said to my two companions, 'I don't see how changing clothes will help us to win the war.'

The Merchistonian flared up in a fury. 'Ye'd be better if ye did what ye were tellt and belted up,' he said. 'You and yer bloody college ways – ye've nae respect for the regiment.' I looked at the other one. He was gazing out of the window with a haughty detached air and moved his head slightly to one side in a non-committal gesture.

The next day I went to see the adjutant. 'When am I going to get my posting?' I asked.

'Hard to say,' he replied. 'Scottish Command are capricious.'

'But my battalion are only ten miles away at Doune,' I said. 'Why can't I join them? They need subalterns.'

'Can't leave without a posting,' said the adjutant. 'Never done.'

'Suppose I spent the day with my battalion,' I said, 'and came back here for evening mess?'

'Irregular,' he said. 'Quite irregular. Not done.'

'How long could it be?' I asked again. 'A day? A week? A month?'

'Impossible to say,' he replied. 'Could be tomorrow. Could be three months. Scottish Command are capricious.'

'Three months!' I said. 'Not three months?'

'McKerrow was here for four months,' said the adjutant, 'Before he died, poor fellow.' To hell with McKerrow, I thought, and walked briskly down to the Golden Lion. I sat by the telephone for an hour, ringing up everyone I knew or had contact with in Scottish Command. Jim Johnstone, the GSOII and a Dumfriesshire neighbour, was my best hope.

'It's absolutely crazy, Jim,' I said. 'Here am I in Stirling Castle, constantly changing my clothes and ten miles away my battalion is crying out for a subaltern to train the troops to fight the Germans.'

'Don't push it, old boy,' he said. 'Don't push it. Half the officers in the command want a posting, don't like their CO, want to get near the wife, or more often away from the wife. My desk is snowed under.'

'Jim,' I said. 'Do you remember the otter?' There was a pause.

Once as a boy out on an otter hunt I had dislodged an otter from a particularly secure cranny to the great delight of the hunters if not the otter. Jim had been standing near me and everyone mistakenly gave him the credit for a particularly daring feat. I had kept quiet.

'I remember the otter,' he said.

'Applegarth Bridge?' I said.

'Applegarth Bridge it was,' he said.

'Do your best?' I said.

'Don't push it, old boy,' he said. The next day my posting came through.

I walked into a commandeered hotel sitting room in Doune. It was the anteroom to the mess of the 11th Argylls. Three figures were sitting round the one-bar electric fire. One of them stopped biting his nails and rose lazily to his feet. 'How d'ye do,' he said looking at me disdainfully. 'Just from the depot?' Had I met him in civilian life I would have cast him as the secretary of a down-at-heel golf club with his clipped moustache and carefully cultivated military bearing. He had a lieutenant colonel's pips up. I gazed at him in disbelief. Could this be the CO, Colonel Frank Elliot who won the MC on the Western Front in World War I at the age of nineteen? Whose courage and daring on the North West Frontier had earned him the nickname of Frontier Frank? Indeed it had to be so, and it was clear that sitting in Doune training raw recruits was not at all to his taste. A second officer, a major, had got to his feet unsteadily, a burly fellow with curled handle-bar moustaches and the swarthy complexion of an Italian ice-cream seller.

'Slayter,' he said. 'You Forman?' I nodded assent.

'Baker Carr,' he said, indicating the recumbent figure in the third chair, who did not stir. I looked more closely at Major Baker Carr. A pink gin dangled perilously in his right hand, half of which he had spilled down the front of his tunic: he was drunk. It was just after noon.

'Luncheon twelve thirty,' said the colonel. 'Headquarters officers,' and, returning his gaze to the one-bar electric fire, resumed the attack on his nails.

'You Highlander?' asked Major Slayter.

'Dumfriesshire,' I said.

'Ah, Lowlander,' said he. 'Blow the pipes?'

'Only the chanter, sir,' I said.

'Dance?' he asked.

'Yes, dance,' I replied. 'Danced for Loretto in 1936.'

'Officers' dancing every morning half an hour. Blow for it myself. Pipe major instructs dancing. Ten minutes after reveille. Kilt and bare feet,' he barked.

'Very good, sir,' I said.

'Just from the depot?' he asked, and when I nodded, 'Did two years there myself.'

'As CO?' I inquired politely.

He bridled. 'As a matter of fact as Q,' he said. 'Been abroad?'

'Only Europe,' I replied.

'Not Africa?' he asked.

'No, sir.'

'Africa ten years myself,' he said. 'Never in Africa?'

'Never once, sir,' I replied.

'Ah,' he said and turned his attention once more to the *Daily Sketch*.

I sat down and observed this unholy trio and my heart sank. My God! These were the three officers I would look to for guidance, instruction and inspiration. I thought of Hitler's shock troops, of the qualities the German army looked for in officers of field rank, of the campaigns in Poland and Finland. I found it difficult to see these three as effective figures in the firing line, and indeed I was soon to discover that Frankie, Baking and Bobo, as the trio were known, were universally regarded as figures of fun.

After lunch I saw the adjutant Pat Patterson and realised at once who ran the battalion. He was a diminutive Glasgow accountant with a bright eye and a quiet wit and there were no flies on him. I was posted to A company in Callender. The company commander was Mike Kenneth, whose brother was married to my old friend James Campbell's twin sister Helen. I felt I was nearing my target.

The daily régime of the battalion at that time consisted mainly of three things – fatigues, route marches and weapons training. The fatigues were mainly concerned with the domestic economy of the unit: shovelling coal, shifting stores, or with local defence – erecting, God knows why, barbed wire obstacles around

24

the telephone exchange and the police station. Sometimes, in the clan tradition of the Highland regiment, an old boy would ask if we could spare some troops to dig ditches and clear woods on his land; if he were known to be 'a first-class chap' (which they nearly all were), these were usually granted. The Jocks (as troops in a Highland regiment were called) were of two kinds, one lot recruited from the Gorbals and Glasgow's gangland, many of them just out of prison, the rest proud slow-speaking West Highlands farm workers, gamekeepers, fishermen, pushed into the army by their employers and accepting military service as a natural part of life.

My company commander, Mike Kenneth, was courting a girl in Bridge of Allan and as soon as parade was dismissed at 4.30 p.m. he jumped on to his motor bike, a huge Norton, and sped away, to return some twelve hours later to the room I shared with him, bringing in powerful gusts of Chanel No. 5. Indeed, the perfume so impregnated his battle dress that the Jocks could smell it on parade next morning and used to make loud sniffing sounds like dogs scenting the breeze for game. 'Mike,' I said to him one day, 'why don't you strip off your battle dress top before getting down to work with Pam?'

'Too cold,' he said. He was suffering from the same problem as Claude Carter. It was only the first of May.

As the summer of 1940 warmed, I found some relief in weapons training. I made my platoon the best in the company, in the battalion and, they claimed, in Scottish Command. I pestered the COMS for live ammunition and organised inter-company contests on the rifle range, but supplies were limited and we had no proper issue of weapons, the whole company having to make do with SMLE Mark II rifles from World War One, one Lewis gun and one defective two-inch mortar.

As the Allied retreat gathered momentum I read the newspapers avidly, and would ring up friends closer to the realities of life for their views on what might happen. On the night of the French capitulation there was a gathering of officers at Battalion HQ. Frankie, Baking and Bobo crouched over the radio, the rest of us in a respectful semi-circle behind. What a moment, thought I, these two great nations for ever at each other's throats, the pendulum swinging now to Germany. Will we have the guts to fight on? I doubt it. What would occupation be like? If we do fight on, how long will it take for Hitler to strike? If he does strike, how can we possibly resist his mighty war machine with battalions led by Frankie, Baking and Bobo and a Home Guard armed with pikes and sickles? As the news of France's total collapse came to an end, Frankie, realising that something was demanded of him, turned his head to the ring of officers and said: 'So the Frogs packed in. And a bloody good thing too.'

CHAPTER

3

L ATER IN THE SUMMER OF 1940 the battalion headquarters moved to Speyside, finally settling in Gordon Castle near Fochabers. This capacious building – the frontage was a quarter of a mile long – housed about one half of our number, the rest were billeted in the village. I elected, for good reasons, to make my billet in the head gamekeeper's house, where there was room for my batman too.

With the battalion all together, there were full-strength parades on the huge gravel carriage sweep in front of the castle. Frankie was in his element, loving as he did the trappings of military glory, and against the advice of Pat the adjutant he decided to take one parade on horseback. The horse fouled his boots before he had even mounted and the whole parade was held up until they had been restored to spotlessness; just as he was about to dismiss the parade the horse saw a stray dog and charged across the park, scraping Frankie's bonnet off on one of the lower branches of a great oak tree.

Fatigues and weapons training continued but there was something new: field training, at first only at company level. We attacked farms, defended woods, dug trenches in waterlogged peat and generally lay about for many hours waiting for the enemy, be it Northland or Southland, to attack us. These activities were so remote from reality and so intensely boring that I went to Pat with a proposal. We had by now become sparring partners – I always attacked the battalion training routine, he always defended it.

'Pat,' I said, 'what exactly is our strategic role?'

'To defend the coastline from enemy invasion between Banff and Nairn,' said he. 'You know that. Next?'

'About fifty miles,' I said. 'And we're all here at Gordon Castle. What would happen if the Germans landed a patrol at Portnockie?'

'We would immediately attack and destroy it.'

'How would we get there?'

'Forty men in our four fifteen-hundredweight trucks, the rest by McGuffy's buses from Elgin.'

'How long would it take to get McGuffy's buses here?'

'About an hour.'

'How would we know there had been a landing?'

'Information from civilian sources. The coastguards and the police.'

'Pat,' I said. 'There are dozens of miles of coast with no coastguards and no police. What we need is a mobile patrol. I have an MG. The AA in Inverness has four road patrol motor-bikes and sidecars. We could requisition them. And you would spare us a couple of bren guns and two of the Nortons.'

Pat looked thoughtful. 'Us?' he said.

'I would command it.'

'Don't push your luck,' said Pat.

I got half of what I wanted. The battalion set up two mobile patrols. Mine consisted of one motor-bike, one rifle; one battered sports car, driver (me), binoculars, pistol, batman passenger, rifle; two AA yellow motor-bikes and sidecars, one bren gun, ammunition, rations and the defective two-inch mortar. I commanded one patrol, Hamish Fraser Campbell the other, and during the dusk and dawn of each autumn day we would drive up and down the coast, peering into the gloom with our World War One binoculars and listening intently for the sound of guttural German voices. We never found a German and indeed they did not make any landings save one, when a submarine deposited a single spy on a beach near Cullen. He gave himself up to the police about four hours later and we didn't hear about it until he was safely in Inverness jail.

When not on patrol my main preoccupation was the organisation of the huge Gordon Castle sporting estate for the benefit of the mess. About half a dozen of us formed a syndicate to shoot the two grouse moors, the several hundred acres of partridge-driving country and of pheasant coverts which surrounded the castle; we would also fish the salmon and sea trout beats on the Spey and the brown trout fishing in many lochs. We had five keepers, the Jocks acted as beaters, the batmen as loaders and the cookhouse provided the hot meals. It was sport on a princely scale, and with safe guns from our own and neighbouring battalions, and a judicious number of local gentry, we slaughtered a huge number of innocent birds, including capercailzie and blackgame.

The best sport of all was when three of us rose before dawn and set off with my host, the head keeper whose name was Ridell (although a dignified and unbending figure, inevitably known as Jimmy Ridell), together with his boy, to one of the small lochans in the woods near the sea. As dawn broke duck flew in from the tidal saltings where they had been feeding, and when twenty or thirty had settled the boy showed a flag and flighted them; we, the guns, perhaps a hundred yards away, shot them as they reached tree-top height and showed black against the flush of dawn in the sky. For the rest of the shoot I do not remember the scale of the bags, but I do recall that from one shoot we returned to breakfast with over a hundred duck between the three of us, all shot within forty-five minutes.

Although great claims were made about wild boar and tiger, Frankie, Baking and Bobo did not shoot domestically and thus were a little shifty about what might have been regarded as a deficiency in their performance as officers and gentlemen. I thought they might turn against the shoot and referred my fears to Pat. He thought they were groundless. Frankie had sent half the battalion to dig peat for a laird who was a distant cousin of someone. On the shoot the Jocks were getting valuable field experience. As to the direct costs of transport and goods, these were perfectly properly charged against hospitality to adjacent landlords. He thought perhaps we should pay for our own cartridges.

The mess consisted of some twenty-four officers, including the unholy trio of field rank. About one-half had been Territorials, either in the Argylls or the London Scottish, the rest were either promoted from the ranks or jumped-up officer cadets like me. We were a convivial lot and hard drinking was the order of the day. This began at about six when parade was over and continued unabated until after dinner when the general company would either burst into song or dance to Pipe Major McCallum's music until the small hours, or depart like a flock of starlings to the Gordon Arms in Fochabers.

Whatever the programme for the common herd, Frankie, Baking and Bobo always stuck to the same routine. Before dinner they sat round the huge fireplace and drank pink gin. After

29

dinner they sat even closer to the fire and drank whisky – Baking, only because he was too drunk to know whether it was before or after dinner, sometimes persisting with pink gin. At eleven o'clock Frankie would rise unsteadily to his feet, say 'Gennelmen you may retah', and stumble over a chair to the anteroom door where he was met by his batman and conducted to bed.

Baking would have passed out by then, his great moon face with its ridiculous Charlie Chaplin moustache lolling over the side of his armchair, mouth sometimes open and tongue hanging out like a knackered horse; on occasions a small pool of urine would form on the floor by his dainty boot-and-tartan-trews-clad heels. When the pool formed early, before Frankie had retired, he would call the mess sergeant, wave his arms, indicate Baking and say 'Major Baker Carr wishes to retah', upon which the mess sergeant, with help from batmen, would raise the sodden and inert Baking from his seat and deposit him on his bed.

Not so Bobo. As soon as the other two had departed, he roused himself and indicated his desire to join the fun with the young-sters. Sometimes he had a sort of rutting season, usually lasting a week or so, when he would pass the anteroom roaring 'I WANT A WOMAN. WHERE CAN I FIND A WOMAN?' No one ever volunteered to help him in this quest and he had no car, so his rutting week was one long agony of unfulfilled desire. The nearest he got to satisfaction was in turning the pages of the tabloids and jabbing his thumb down on the breasts of any well-endowed female form, uttering a sonorous sexual grunt at each thrust, then firmly and decisively pinning his thumb on the lady's crotch with a howl of triumph. This seemed to tire him out and he too would soon be led off to bed, sometimes whimpering and crying a little. A plan was hatched to place an appropriate picture of Queen Mary before him when he was at this exercise; if he defiled her with his thumb, he would be reported for *lèse-majesté* and cashiered; but it came to nothing.

Early in the winter the battalion began to train for a major three-day exercise which would involve all troops in north-east Scotland. Frankie became very jumpy; he lectured his officers in tones which alternated between panic and braggadocio, depending upon the time registered on his whisky clock. We were to remember we were Argylls; the Pathans came into it a great deal – they were wily enemies; compared with them the Black Watch (our

30

Southland opponents) were an inferior regiment and a pushover; we had a good team; they had poor leadership (and here he would run over the character defects of the other COs in the formation); we were to get our men fit, see they kept their bowels open and above all do nothing to annoy the umpires.

By now I had handed over the mobile patrol to a newcomer and was in the first flush of commanding a platoon in the field. I trained them carefully to shine in an army exercise, which – although it had little to do with training for war – was a game worth playing in itself. I taught them how to fling themselves spectacularly to the ground, how to howl imprecations at the Boche during the frequent bayonet charges (no one I met throughout the war ever encountered a bayonet charge, but they were a persistent fantasy in the minds of the High Command), how to talk loudly and keenly about the tactical points at issue when umpires were within earshot, to smoke only when I told them it was safe to do so and to keep their faces very dirty at all times.

On the day all went swimmingly. Act One was a long advance up a valley through enemy snipers. My platoon led the advance guard, brilliantly, bravely and in a fashion that would have wiped us all out had the bullets been real. Act Two was night attack. My platoon laid the tapes for the battalion advance, using cover cleverly despite heavy shellfire and two machine guns in enfilade. At dawn I could see my umpire in animated conversation with a group of senior umpires: things were going well. Act Three was a set piece attack. My platoon, with casual disregard of danger (and the enthusiastic support of two umpires who gave away very few casualties), penetrated the enemy's left flank and circled back towards the centre. By now we had four umpires, two of them of field rank, clearly willing us on to the final coup: the capture of the opposing battalion's headquarters from the rear. I decided to give them their money's worth. Under cover of smoke I rehearsed my O group (section commanders and platoon sergeant) and when it cleared I was ready for my final oration. Lying behind a grassy knoll, I raised my head and in a voice which carried clearly to the gaggle of umpires I delivered the orders for an attack in terms of the time honoured formula – In Italy Mussolini Always in Action (Information, Intention, Method, Administration, Informative Any Questions).

'INFORMATION [I cried]: The enemy are over the crest

31

of that hill eight hundred yards to our front occupying an area from the fir tree on the left to the pylon on the right; they are approximately forty in number and comprise enemy battalion headquarters. They are likely to be armed with two LMGs and rifles only . . .' My oration continued in polished army jargon up to the any questions, when two brisk, intelligent pre-planned questions were asked. Out of the corner of my eye I saw the umpires scribbling furiously appreciative notes, and I thought to myself: what a pantomime! In real life I would probably have shouted to the sergeant: 'Donald – see those buggers on the skyline? Stay here and cover us. I'll get after them with the rest – let's go.' Or words to that effect.

The attack was successful. The enemy counterattack was repulsed. At night we consolidated. At dawn the exercise was over. Before we had returned to Gordon Castle there were stories flying around of brilliant junior leadership by a subaltern in the 11th Argylls. Two days later there was a full scale post mortem in Huntly town hall, attended by company commanders and above. Pat told us I was to go too. The general conducting the post mortem said that one of the lessons learnt from the exercise was the importance of initiative and dash at platoon leadership level. We had seen an example of brilliant junior leadership, etcetera. He then called on one of the umpires to give a blow-by-blow account of the exploits of my platoon, with great emphasis on the sagacity, quick judgement and disciplined responses of its leader, and above all on the clarity and force of his verbal orders. It was like a school prizegiving. As I left the hall I realised I must be the most disliked man in Scottish Command.

Next morning Frankie sent for me. As I waited outside his office I reflected that this was likely to be a happier visit than my last. On that occasion a civilian guest at the Gordon Arms had complained that he had been wakened at 3 a.m. by singing coming from the kitchen; on investigation, he had found two officers and a half-dressed woman singing obscene songs, very loudly. (The two officers were Mike Kenneth and me, the half-dressed woman Pam, now Mike's Chanel-No-5-loving wife, who had also been woken up by the noise and had joined us in her dressing-gown).

'This is a bad show,' Frankie had said.

'Yessir,' said I.

'Never sing filth in front of a woman,' Frankie said.

'Nosir,' I replied.

'Never be seen with an undressed woman in public,' said Frankie.

'Half-undressed woman,' said I.

'Half-undressed woman,' said Frankie. 'People talking. Bad for the battalion.'

'Yessir,' said I.

'Bad show,' said Frankie.

'Yessir,' said I.

This time it was different. 'Cup of tea?' said Frankie.

'Thank you, sir,' said I.

'Good show,' said Frankie. 'Rattling good show.'

'Thank you, sir,' said I.

'Good for the regiment,' said Frankie. 'Good for the battalion.' (He meant good for me, Frankie.)

'"A" company,' said Frankie.

'Yessir?' said I.

'Going to give you "A" company,' said Frankie. 'Take over from Captain Forsythe Tuesday.'

'Thank you, sir,' said I.

'Captain,' said Frankie. 'Promotion to captain.'

'Thank you, sir,' said I.

'Rattling good show,' said Frankie.

'A' company did not know what had hit them. The luckless Forsythe, who had been carted off to the Recce Corp to make room for me, had been an easy-going ex-Territorial, whose belief in a comfortable life had been greatly appreciated by his men. Now they were up at all hours, chivvied, inspected, punished for idleness, lectured on The Fighting Spirit and subjected to quite the most arduous training schedule in Scottish Command.

'The men greatly admire their new company commander,' panted Sergeant Major Blair as he ran next to me on a route march which I was conducting at the double, 'but if you will take a word of advice, sir, don't push it, sir.' But push it I did. There were seldom less than half-a-dozen Jocks confined to barracks, one of the subalterns was reported to the CO for idleness and the stores' corporal court martialled for fiddling the books. I found that I was generally known among the Jocks as the Beefer, because I was continually finding fault: dirty brasses here, a badly rolled gas-cape there, an idle movement on parade, an ill-trimmed moustache. After a month of this treatment the Jocks had each lost half a stone or more in weight, they moved much faster, they walked erect. I began to be inordinately proud of them, while they, after an initial period of intense hatred, began to tolerate me as an amiable maniac who could run ten miles carrying eighty pounds on my back and set Battalion Part 1 Orders to music for company concerts.

Meantime my company had moved under canvas in a sandy pine forest near Orton House, a few miles from Gordon Castle. There was an added dimension to my life because Polly McDonald took a house in nearby Nairn, where she settled with two small children, a nanny and a large brown poodle called Vigée le Brun. Polly was the wife of a Cambridge don and we had met through the Caledonian Club because Polly was the university's leading Highlander – Catholic, fey and with a Celtic temperament often at war with the restraints of English upper-class life. We loved each other in a happy and carefree fashion, untroubled by her domestic and marital duties and by my preoccupation with military affairs. Each night, as soon as parade was over, I jumped into my crumpled MG and drove the fifteen miles to Polly, returning just in time to shower and shave before reveille.

Polly had high connections within the Highland regiments, especially the two quasi-private armies, the Atholl Highlanders and the Lovat Scouts, which were then being formally integrated into the British army. She had cousins and uncles in positions of power and knew a wide scattering of generals across the length and breadth of Scottish Command and south of the border. I pestered Polly to use her influence and her very considerable charm to persuade one of these to get me a posting to active service. I had had my fill of Frankie, Baking and Bobo. I drafted letters for her to send, and was under the impression that they had been sent until I found a bundle of them under a cushion.

'So you didn't send these letters?'

'Darling,' she replied, 'I would have been mad to send them. They might have taken you away from me. But I didn't want to spoil your warrior fantasies.'

'How sweet of you not to send them,' I said. It was a happy relationship and lasted for many years.

Sergeant Major Blair, the monitor of my standing with 'A'

34

company, confided to me during another route-run: 'The men admire ye greatly, sir.'

'Why, sergeant major?'

'Because ye're intae yet wee caur and away all night and rin about a' day wi nae sleep,' he replied.

Indeed lack of sleep was a problem, and my habit of falling asleep as soon as I sit down in a moving vehicle dates from that period.

One day Pat sent for me. 'What the hell are you doing to "A" company?' he asked.

'Just getting them sorted,' I said.

'The other companies don't like it.'

'Nothing to do with them,' I said.

'I had Jock and Willie in here yesterday,' said Pat. 'They're afraid it might spread. Frankie is getting interested. Efficiency might become compulsory.'

'In this battalion that's impossible,' I said.

'I'm sending you on a course,' said Pat. 'Company commanders at Scottish Command. Four weeks. Make it five with a bit of leave. And when you come back for Christ's sake don't push it.'

The company commanders' course was like Dunbar again with three pips up. Most of the students were ex-Territorials, some in their mid and late thirties, some like me much younger, and a few professionally interested in winning the war. This group used to gather in a knot around the bar in the anteroom and drink malt whisky far into the morning. There was an elderly man who had been second master at Gordonstoun and a close friend of Otto Hahn; an ex-journalist from the *Glasgow Herald*; a young don from St Andrews University; the rich son of a whisky baron and three or four others. We constantly discussed German infantry tactics, their use of armour, their weapons and their morale, and deplored our inferiority in every field and in particular the woeful inadequacy of our training.

It was during one of these late night sessions that I first heard the words 'battle school'. A young instructor, a major, had returned that day from the 47th Division's battle school, initiated by General Utterson Kelso, and we listened spellbound as he told us of an entirely new military philosophy. The instructors talked of nothing but beating the Boche and winning the war, everyone had to be fit, all training was carried out at the double, live ammunition was used in exercises and fired very close to the students to get them accustomed to its sound, there were lectures on the psychology of fear and on motivation, and there was a formidable assault course with casualties so high that an ambulance stood by. Even if no one was hurt it had a helpful role as intimidator. Some of the instructors had rhinoceros hide whips and threw bulls' blood in the faces of the students. The whole conduct of minor tactics was being radically reformed: no more time-wasting O groups, just a shout of Right Flanking, Left Flanking or Pincers. The chief instructor was a tremendous fellow called Wigram.

There were also films, German films; he had brought a dirty and worn 16 mm print of one called *Victory in the West* for us to see. We saw it that night – six of us in a deserted classroom. It dispelled the euphoria arising from the news of the battle school. The power of the Wehrmacht, the impact of the propaganda and the efficiency of both induced in all of us a sick fear in the pits of our stomachs and a mood approaching despair. When the lights went up, we sat motionless for several minutes, until Jock Wilson, the journalist, shouted out in an RSM's manner:

'Those wishing to commit hara-kiri – to the latrines, and spare the anteroom carpet.'

The effect of the film and the excitement over thoughts of the battle school kept me awake all night. Next day we seized the précis and notes from Hector Johnston, the battle school graduate, and had them roneoed by a friendly orderly-room corporal. Now the evening's discussion took an entirely new form. Hector recounted all he could remember of each period of instruction and we listened open-mouthed and quizzed him mercilessly. We left Edinburgh promising to keep in touch with one another but each privately determined to get to a battle school as soon as possible.

On my return to the battalion I went straight to see Pat. 'I would like to put in for a course at the 47th Division battle school,' I said.

'Christ,' said Pat. 'Just back from a four-week course in Edinburgh and wants to go on another. You should try the travel agency in Nairn.'

'Pat, it's serious. I must go,' I said.

'Do you know that the average incidence of courses for officers in this battalion is 0.45 per annum?' Pat asked. 'You aren't even

36

in 47th Division.'

'They take attachments from other formations,' I said, and embarked on an eloquent account of the phenomenon that was going to revolutionise the British army. Pat listened patiently for five minutes and then pushed a sheet of paper across his desk. I saw my name on it and began to read.

'You're on the advance party with me,' said Pat. 'We embark for Shetland at 0400 tomorrow morning. There will be an issue of mountain warfare clothing in half an hour.'

'There are no mountains in Shetland,' I said.

'No,' said Pat, 'but there is weather.'

4

THE SHETLAND ISLANDS gave us a dismal reception. Our horrible little packet battered its way through the storm to Lerwick and a series of low buff-coloured ridges came into view through the driving rain. Nor did Shetland improve on closer acquaintance. Treeless, featureless except for scattered settlements of sad slate-roofed cottages, dripping with water and whipped ceaselessly by gales, those insignificant excrescences of peat and rock, lying between the grandeur of the West Highlands and the dazzling white slopes of Iceland, made up perhaps the most wretched terrain available to a unit of the British army.

We settled into a village of Nissen huts, a dispiriting form of architecture which, when camouflaged, faded into the dreary landscape like an organic part of the land mass they stood on.

Our job was to guard the airfield at Sumburgh Head, a strip of sand between two towering cliffs at the south end of the island, although how we were supposed to bring down enemy aircraft with hand-held bren guns I do not know. A squadron of Beaufighters was stationed at Sumburgh; they could reach the Norwegian coast 180 miles away, spend ten minutes harassing the Germans, and return home post-haste. Alas, if they encountered an enemy plane, if they loitered or if (as was not unknown) they lost their way, they dropped into the North Sea, sometimes in full view of their colleagues' look-out post on the top of Sumburgh Head. Some hit the cliffs on the way in: on the hill north of the airstrip, where our Nissen huts crouched, there were several carcases of crashed Beaufighters. When the first squadron was used up, they sent in a second. This was more than flesh and blood could stand. I tackled Frankie, not in the mess but more formally in the orderly room.

'Permission to express a view, sir.'

'Go ahead.'

'I propose that the battalion should initiate a complaint through OSDEF (Orkney and Shetland Defences) to the War

Office. RAF wasting scant resources, planes and men being lost unnecessarily.'

'None of our business. If the boys in blue want to kill themselves and smash up their planes they're welcome to do it. Bloody fools.'

'Complaint might lead to inquiry, sir.'

'Might also lead to one hell of a bollocking. Always keep out of inter-service rows.'

'Complaint might get us better ack-ack, sir.'

'Might also lead to change in command of this battalion. Anything else?'

'No, sir.'

As I left the Orderly Room thinking mutinous thoughts, Pat called me over.

'Posting,' he said.

'Where to?' I said.

'Six months' garrison duty at the depot,' said he.

'Bugger that,' I said, but he had a twinkle in his eye. 'Come on Pat, where is it?'

'Battle school at Barnard Castle. Your Shangri-La. One month's course.'

Once again lobbying had paid off. I had kept in touch with the company commanders' group from the Edinburgh course, many of whom had now been to Barnard Castle. I had written to Major Wigram, now the chief instructor of the GHQ battle school, of whom I had heard so much, unofficially and – by all canons of military behaviour – improperly. He had replied saying that he could do nothing from his end, that it was up to me. So the trick had been turned by Pat, my old otter-hunting friend Jim Johnstone and another Dumfriesshire neighbour, now GSO I at OSDEF.

After dinner on the first night at Barnard Castle, the programme informed us there would be an opening address by the chief instructor. The first aspect I saw of Lionel Wigram was his back as he strode down the central aisle to the podium. An officious major from the Green Howards had spent some time previously ascertaining that he was the senior officer and barked out 'Parade – Parade Shun.' No one quite knew exactly what posture to adopt when sitting in a cinema. Some stood up, others sat gazing fixedly to the front with their arms pinned to their sides. Lionel turned

39

and addressed the class.

'Sit down and relax,' he said. 'We don't want any of that bullshit here.'

I looked at him keenly. The most striking feature of his broad, unmistakably Jewish face was a pair of large thick-rimmed spectacles which magnified his eyes, augmenting their natural powers of penetration (which were considerable) to an almost frightening degree. He had a tall brow and a cap of thick black hair parted just off-centre; there was an ample nose, a mouth turning downwards in a bow when in repose, and finally a determined chin. He was of medium height, broad and sturdy, with urban legs, slightly bowed, his feet distinctly splayed. In his body movements he looked like a man from behind an office desk, as indeed he was, having already proved himself a brilliant young lawyer.

As I looked at him behind the lectern I thought what a desperate struggle he must have had to train his body to run long distances, climb ropes and storm through Dannert wire. Yet everyone told me that he was the fittest man in camp and, although not blessed with any degree of manual dexterity, he had practised the drill for rectifying a fault in a bren gun for two hours every night until he was as slick as any weapons-training instructor.

Lionel opened with a philippic against the Germans. Politically evil, socially vile, their leaders with characters gross and distorted, power-mad, brutal and sadistic, they stood for all a decent democratic community loathed and despised. The opening blast was delivered with such passion and such obvious sincerity, it transfixed us all. We had never heard a senior soldier talk like this before. He was almost talking politics, which was a forbidden subject, and he was showing emotion, a thing never done.

He then went on to trace the history of the German military *Zeitgeist* from Clausewitz through World War One, the testing ground of the Spanish Civil War and the victories in Poland and in Western Europe. It was the most formidable war machine the world had ever known; but not so formidable if one could overcome its reliance on fear, by far its most powerful weapon. German warfare traded in psychology first and fire-power second. The dive-bomber, the shattering noise of the Minnenwerfer, the green tracer fired from the MG 34 and 42, these were the weapons of fear; once fear was overcome their effect was only slightly more than our own admittedly outdated weapons. He spent a little

40

time on the anatomy of fear, then moved to a more general study of morale, and from there into the best way to induce the right battle attitude. Physical fitness had to be the starting point; confidence in one's body and then confidence in the tactics used against the enemy. All field training, all tactical training had to pass the practical test – would it work under fire, in heavy rain, with troops who have had no food and no sleep for thirty-six hours?

Lionel spoke for less than an hour, and when he finished there was some dialogue with the more pushy students on the course. I did not hear it because I was in a state of exaltation. I had heard the first positive and credible assessment of the British army's task since I had become a soldier. Perhaps we had a chance of winning the war after all.

Next morning the attack on our bodies began. The early assault courses and cross-country runs – sometimes carrying up to 100lbs of equipment – were designed to show how unfit we were. Once we had been reduced to a proper sense of humility, our bodies were carefully built up from day to day by a blend of training in endurance, dexterity and agility. As the weeks passed, even the puniest of the students, and the most timid, were throwing themselves from high walls and thrashing their way through barbed wire with cheerful abandon. Live ammunition whizzed through the air and thunderflashes spluttered and banged all around. Our instructors were all officers – no NCOs, which was a change – and they constantly reminded us that we were working against the enemy, the unspeakable Boche, and not just taking exercise for the good of our health. Bulls' blood and leather whips had disappeared from the battle-school menu, but in some of the older instructors this spirit lived on.

Between gruelling bouts on the assault course we saw German propaganda films (powerfully made in the tradition of Leni Riefenstahl and deeply frightening), Russian propaganda films (innocent and simplistic to a degree, all the lessons of Eisenstein and Pudovkin forgotten), training films from many countries, and finally the ridiculous and shaming British propaganda film, *The Lion Has Wings*. We saw newsreels too, and could compare the empty bombast of the British news with the cool incisiveness and terrifying assurance of the German weekly account of the progress of the war.

There were lectures on battle psychology in which the instinctive

41

motions of fear were examined – bending double with hands thrust into the crotch to protect the genitals (an invariable first reaction to close shellfire); protecting the eyes, a second instinctive move; muscular tremor brought on by fear; instant diarrhoea induced by terror, and so on. Methods of coping were discussed: how to counteract and to pre-empt fear by building up the collective courage bank, by the judicious use of alcohol, never forgetting the importance of a hot meal and a dash of cold water on the face. These things were pondered, as were the realities of what our weapons could do rather than the claims made for them in the military manuals. Rifles were not much good except in the hands of a sharpshooter. Tommy guns were better. Bren guns were thoroughly unreliable so always have the maximum number possible, both in attack and defence. Borrow from reserve troops if you can (a heinous sin against military tradition). Don't carry the two-inch mortar unless you also have a decent quota of bombs, say twenty; but this is far too heavy a load for a platoon moving fast, so leave the mortar behind. If you can't get the anti-tank rifle on to someone's truck, chuck it away. And so on; in the field too, a common-sense approach towards tactics soon swept away Mussolini – no longer Always in Action in Italy – with shouts of 'Right Flanking', 'Pincers' or 'Stay and Cover'. We were breathing the fresh air of common sense and rationality for the first time and hope was beginning to rise within us like yeast.

Towards the end of our time we were given a questionnaire asking for an evaluation of the course. Lionel sent for me.

'You are critical of the use of the word "hatred" and don't seem to understand the importance of motivation,' he said.

'I think I do,' I said, 'but it can't be right to try to whip up a hatred of the Germans. That's childish.'

'I hate the Germans,' said Lionel, fixing me with his lion-tamer gaze. 'Does that mean I am childish?'

'I know that personal hatred of the Germans is real for you. But for many of us it isn't.'

'Is that because I am a Jew?'

'Partly, yes. If a person has a member of his family killed or tortured, he will hate the people who did it. In a way the Jews are a family and they have personalised their hatred for the whole race of Germans. That doesn't make sense to me.'

'Does that mean we can't motivate non-Jews as highly as Jews?'

'Absolutely not. I hate Nazism, the Nazi creed, the Nazi leaders just as much as you do, perhaps more, but I can't personalise that into hating the men opposite me in a German platoon. They are good soldiers and probably quite decent people.'

'Fighting for a filthy and despicable régime?'

'Yes; many of them not by choice.'

Lionel frowned and sat silent for some time. 'Then should a Jew be instructing Anglo-Saxons?' he asked.

'Yes. You are the most effective anti-Hitler weapon this army has got and the battle-school movement could affect the fortunes of war. Your class of hatred is your own affair. I am only saying that for most Brits, bulls' blood, rawhide whips and messages of personal hatred don't work. And it is not rational for a military unit to hate the soldiers on the other side. Some of the best troops have been mercenaries who were so professional that they won without believing in any cause at all. Sometimes they changed sides for higher pay.'

Lionel sighed. We sat in silence for some time.

'I'd like to talk again,' said Lionel. The interview was over.

He did talk to me again the next day, and the day after that. He was not concerned with the morality of preaching hatred, but only with the most effective means of motivating troops. I told him of the deep scepticism of the British soldier, tales such as those about Germans eating Belgian babies in World War One never had a chance. Any atrocity story (and he had told many) would be treated with suspicion unless it was supported by irrefutable evidence. Hearsay was not enough. People suspected that because of his passion he was prone to believe the worst. No doubt the worst was often true (we had heard tales of slaughter in the Polish ghettoes), but unless it was believed it was no good. He asked if he should then conceal his passionate hatred of all things German. I said no – his opening address had been powerful and moving because of it, but he should not expect others to share his feelings. Passion could not be taught. We were not to meet again for over two years, but in the intervening period this was a recurrent theme in the letters we wrote to each other.

When I got back to Shetland I was put in charge of a new company, 'E' company, designed to train new recruits and to refurbish some of the old lags who congregated in the cookhouses and orderly rooms scattered over the administrative extremities of the Shetland mainland. Cooks who had been excused boots for years suddenly had to march twenty miles a day; jailbirds fresh from Barlinnie had to run up hills and stand in the sea up to their waists; clerks, white-faced from their typewriters, found live bullets whistling round their ears. Generally, a hard time was had by all. No form of recreation whatsoever was available to the troops in camp apart from crouching in their huts and playing brag or the occasional session of housey-housey (bingo to civilians) organised by the CSM. So it was that some of the Jocks began to live fantasy lives. The section commanders in No. 1 platoon drove about in large American limousines which could be heard changing gear all over the camp, and, if one were close enough, one could eavesdrop on the conversation between the car's proprietor, usually a gangster, and his chauffeur, a coloured man from the deep South. On one occasion Corporal Meek's Oldsmobile collided with Corporal McFarlane's Cadillac, and for three days they had to take taxis which pulled up, as they fell in on the parade ground, with a squeal of brakes and a stream of invective. Corporal Dow, on the other hand, ran a brothel populated by the girls in No. 1 section who would pirouette and show off their charms to any likely client on payment of a cigarette. But by far the most pervasive form of make-believe concerned horses.

No. 2 platoon started it by hitching their horses to a rail outside the cookhouse before going in for a meal. Then, before touching any food, they would take a piece of bread out to the horse, and in bad weather they would rub it down and cover it with a rug before they ate, whistling through their teeth, groom-fashion, all the while. The number of horses increased until every member of No. 2 platoon was mounted. Each horse had a name and a character and some were bought and sold between owners at a high price, on one occasion a particularly handsome blue roan changing hands for twenty Players. Then the horse craze began to spread to other platoons so that we had to erect a second hitching rail next to the first, then a third. By now it had become clear that the horses were owned by cowboys, and in the evenings in the huts spurs were being polished and dubbin was being applied to saddles.

One day when Frankie was visiting 'E' company he said 'Why are those men walking like that?'

'They are carrying saddles, sir,' I said.

'Saddles? Saddles?' said Frankie. 'I don't see any saddles.'

'They are not real saddles, sir. The men pretend they are cowboys and have horses. Look, there is Corporal Meek watering his horse just over there.' Sure enough, Corporal Meek was offering his horse a bucket of water with one hand while gently stroking its neck with the other.

Frankie gave me a queer look. We went on to inspect the cookhouse. By ill luck the two Shetland ponies we used to cart away the camp rubbish had defecated on the cookhouse path.

'Horseshit,' said Frankie, now really perplexed.

'Yes, sir,' I said. 'The men tell me we had some cattle rustlers ride through the camp last night and that must be their spoor. Our horses never come beyond the cookhouse rail, sir.' Frankie stood undecided, turning over the horse dung with his ash plant.

'Horseshit,' he said again. Then after a moment's reflection: 'Don't want to hear anything more about horses, understand?'

'Yessir,' I said, and as I said it we both heard the penetrating whinny of a stallion seeking its mate.

'Sar'nt major,' I said, 'please see the men keep their horses under control until the CO has left.'

'Very good, sir,' said the CSM and cantered off behind a row of Nissen huts.

But among the men the fantasy continued, and from time to time reality broke in, as when Corporal Meek shot dead Private Murdo's pinto (named Dumbo); a real hole was dug for the wretched beast, the fantasy carcase was dragged in, deposited and subsequently covered up. The chaplain refused, however, to conduct any part of the funeral service over the animal's remains or even to utter a prayer for the departed.

Halfway between fantasy and reality lay the matter of bestiality. It was of course inhumane to keep several hundred vigorous heterosexual young men cooped up in Nissen huts for months on end. Outside of Lerwick, where the available women could be numbered on the fingers of two hands, there was only one compliant female, elderly and ugly, who lived in a lonely hut on top of a peat bog. When the troops were at liberty there was often a queue twenty yards long standing outside her door, but the daintier members of 'E' company spurned this opportunity.

45

Sex-starved as they were, some saw temptation in the grubby little Shetland sheep, and, to the great delight of all Argylls, a private in the loathed Highland Light Infantry was court martialled and found guilty of indulging himself with a black-faced ewe. From then on, whenever two contingents of the rival regiments approached each other on the road, the Argylls, as soon as they were within earshot of the HLI, would break into a chorus of baa-a-as and meh-eh-ehs, swelling to a grand climax as the two bodies of troops passed each other. At first the HLI endured this humiliation in sullen silence, but soon the glorious (to them) news spread that the butcher at Boddam, who had some fourteen dogs hanging around his shop, most of which could loosely be described as Shetland collies, had complained to the Argyll CO that a member of the battalion had been caught interfering with one of his smaller and prettier dogs. The man at first denied it, but when the MO confirmed that on two occasions he had asked for an anti-tetanus injection, after being bitten by a dog, his fate was sealed. Now, when the two regiments met, the sheep-noises of the Argylls were drowned by yapping, snarling and howls of outraged pain from the HLI. Even in Lerwick, when members of the different regiments met on leave, animal noises would break out, often making the night hideous and sometimes leading to fisticuffs.

A more serious diversion was heralded by the put-put-put of the single-stroke diesel engines of Norwegian fishing-boats. These carried men, women and children, and farm animals too, from the fjords around Bergen to the safety of Shetland. Since they could not make the whole distance under cover of darkness, they were still within range of the German planes when dawn broke. For this reason, foggy weather brought them over in numbers, and many were sick and some wounded. We rushed a patrol down to the beach for each arrival and boarded their vessel. If they were in good enough nick, we directed them on to Scalloway where Donald Howarth ran an operation subsequently made famous by his book *The Shetland Bus*.

If required, we took the wounded ashore and ran them to the battalion hospital. Sometimes our Intelligence Officer would conduct an urgent de-briefing. The courage and determination of the Norwegians in tackling the arduous trip across the North Sea, and their relief on reaching our shores, served to keep our minds tuned to the realities of the war and for a time sheep, dogs and horses were forgotten.

The demise of 'E' company when it had completed its training was marked by a dismal event. Brigade HQ arranged a passing-out competition between the training companies of the Royal Scots and the Argylls. Both units would be bused to Lerwick for the day and chosen champions from each would compete on the firing range, on the drill square, in tactical exercises, and finally in a fifteen-mile route march across country.

Any prospect of the battalion gaining credit or the reverse in a public competition threw Frankie into a ferment of anxiety and he visited 'E' company every day, also entering into a tetchy dialogue with his opposite number in the Royal Scots, deciding a set of elaborate ground rules and a points-scoring system for each event. He quizzed me anxiously about our chances. I assured him that in all the team events we were in good form, but the route march presented a problem. We had up to a dozen Excused Boots on our strength who could not manage fifteen miles. Bisset, a cook corporal, was notoriously soft-footed, having worn nothing but plimsolls for years. Provided the MO was allowed to designate men unfit pretty freely, or if we could count a quota of weaklings, we might have a chance. Frankie immediately embarked on a series of heavy negotiations with the Royal Scots CO; after several planning sessions, involving both adjutants and both company commanders as well, it was agreed that a quota of ten be excluded.

On the day of the contest it was blowing a gale, as usual, and as we herded the men on to the trucks in the half-light, we had a message from Brigade. They had heard of the exclusion deal between the COs and were outraged. Every man must march. This was heavy news. We peeled Corporal Bisset's plimsolls off his feet and set to work on a peculiarly unpleasant green fungus which grew between his toes. We cut a hole in a pair of boots to accommodate Private Kelly's bunion; we bandaged weak ankles and put Elastoplast round groggy knees and hoped for the best.

The early rounds of the contest went well enough and we were about Even Stevens when the time came for the route march. The two companies formed up back to back in front of a wooden platform upon which were seated the brigadier, the two COs and various other dignitaries. The two forces were

47

to follow a circular course marching in opposite directions. The start was not auspicious. The Royal Scots swung away in great style whistling 'Scotland the Brave'. As my company passed the platform, Corporal Dow dived under the trestles and vomited, very loudly, just underneath where the brigadier was sitting. As he ran to catch us up he dropped his rifle in a puddle and I knew it was not going to be our day.

Sure enough, we had scarcely gone four miles when Bisset's feet began to swell and he trailed off behind, letting out despairing little yelps. It was at that point that CSM Emmerson came into his own. He detailed two strong men to half-carry Corporal Bisset until we reached a road junction, where a fishmonger's van was drawn up. Bisset was bundled into the back of the van which then took off and passed us. As the two contingents met (with the van well out of sight), Lance corporal McGaultey threw a cowpat at the leading rank of marching Royal Scots and was immediately put on a charge. The cowpat was dry and failed to spread and adhere as he had intended. It was, however, a gesture. From now on the van was to be seen again at every road junction, and by the time we neared the saluting base there were seven men inside.

'We will never get away with this, sergeant major,' I said.

'Contingency plan, sir,' he replied. 'Van disappears, sir. No count of numbers at the end of a march.'

I was uneasy. I rallied the ranks as we approached the brigadier's platform, but it was clear we faced defeat. The Royal Scots had swung into view a full five minutes earlier, still jauntily whistling 'Scotland The Brave', and now they barked and yelped quietly at my mob as they went by. But worse was to come. The fishmonger, although a friend of CSM Emmerson and helpfully inclined, was as thick as a plank. He had misunderstood instructions and as we fell out the van pulled up in full view of the brigadier and his party and the dishevelled crew of crippled Argylls emerged from the back. I saw Frankie put his head in his hands.

Some time later I approached him to make my apologies. He was sitting hunched up on a knoll of heather, with his back to the gale.

'Sorry about that, sir,' I said.

Frankie did not look up, but after a moment of sullen silence 'Shit,' he said. 'SHIT.'

'I have some information, sir,' I said. Frankie sat immobile, repeating 'Shit' under his breath.

'The Royal Scots, sir, got wind of brigadier's mood late last night and transferred all their Excused Boots to other companies at 0800 this morning.'

It took some minutes for the message to sink in. Then a broad smile broke out across his face. 'Shit,' he said again, but now the word was no mere exclamation of annoyance but a description of the CO of the Royal Scots. 'That little man,' (Frankie measured five feet nine inches in height, the Royal Scots CO perhaps five feet eight and a half) 'That little man is a SHIT.' And he rose vigorously, rehearsing in his mind the report to Brigade which would restore the honour of the 11th Argylls.

CHAPTER

5

A YEAR IN SHETLAND SEEMED AN ETERNITY. During the long dark winter I had campaigned relentlessly for an OSDEF battle school. I sent memos to Frankie and Pat quoting General Paget, who was now the patron saint of the movement and C-in-C Home Forces. I got little support from them: they saw a battle school as a threat to their best officers, several of whom made it known they would be off like a shot if the opportunity offered. I had more luck with Brigade where I had an ally in John Pateman, the GSO III (Training), who had taught me at Loretto and who, unlike the majority of the teaching staff, was young, intelligent and very agreeable. His boss was Brigadier Fraser, a wiry hunting type approaching fifty years of age, a clubman, a Grenadier Guards officer and a landowner who moved in circles whose chief reading matter was *The Field* and *Country Life*. Alas for him, there were no horses in Shetland, no country houses and no trees. He regarded war-time soldiering as a sort of *Boy's Own Paper* adventure which he tolerated with whimsical good humour. He had some natural impediment in his throat which he tried constantly to clear, without success.

Brigadier Fraser took a fancy to me when I told him about the cowboy fantasy and asked me from time to time to play bridge at Brigade headquarters, where he would greet me with the words 'Urrgumph. How do the deer and the antelope play today?' and I would regale him with the news that a blacksmith's shop had just opened and that last night the new sheriff had been shot dead in the saloon. One day I was driving with him in his staff car to join an exercise some thirty miles away in the north of the island.

'Why don't you start a battle school here, sir?' I asked.

'Battle school?' he said, 'Whassat?'

I told him about battle schools and I could see he particularly liked the bit about thunderflashes and live ammunition.

'Fireworks, eh?' he said. 'Urrgumph.'

'Indeed, sir, a night exercise at Barnard Castle looks like a Brock's benefit night.'

'Henry [the officer commanding OSDEF] would have to approve it,' he said. 'He would make it an OSDEF affair. Henry would grab it.'

'But even if he tried to do that, sir, if it were sited in Shetland you would be lord of the manor. It would be seen as your school.'

'Urrgumph,' said Brigadier Fraser, and again 'Urrgumph.'

He went thoughtful for twenty miles. As we passed the spectacular rocks of Mavis Grind, I waved my hand at them. 'Those rocks, sir, if we had a battle school . . .'

'Don't push it, Forman,' said the brigadier. 'Urrgumph.' And he went to sleep.

Some months later Pat sent for me. 'What have you been up to?' he asked.

I looked back at him with wide innocent eyes. He pushed a piece of paper across the table. OSDEF was going to start a battle school. A working party was to be set up to recommend establishment, site, syllabus, etcetera. Frankie was being asked to release me to serve as one of its members.

'Frankie's angry,' said Pat. 'He told me to reply that he can't spare you from essential training duties.'

'Cutting peat?' I asked. 'All last week a hundred men of my company were cutting peat. Twenty men moving stores for Q that had been put in the wrong place. Essential training duties?'

Pat gazed at me unmoved.

'Listen,' he said. 'I'll ring Jimmy at OSDEF and tell him to pay no attention to Frankie, on one condition.'

'What condition?'

'That you will not take one single officer nor one single NCO from this battalion for your bloody battle school.'

'Postings have nothing to do with me,' I said. 'Brigade matter.'

Pat didn't deign to reply. He just kept looking at me.

'OK,' I said, 'so long as I remain a major in this battalion I will not plunder.'

'But if you became commandant you would be seconded from us,' said Pat. 'Rank of lieutenant colonel, independent and equal to Frankie. Then you could pinch anybody. "I will not steal" – no qualifications.'

51

'You're a hard man, Pat,' I said. 'I am sure we could come to an understanding,' and I took out of my pocket a piece of army-grey paper upon which were written the names of the battalion's best young officers and NCOs. Pat lit a match, held it to the corner of the paper and watched it burn. 'No qualifications,' he said. 'None.'

I thought for a moment. 'Urrgumph,' I said, using the brigadier's throat-clearing noise in the affirmative mode.

'Urrgumph,' said Pat in a way that confirmed the deal was agreed.

So it was that I set up shop at Voxter, midway up the Shetland mainland in a little village of Nissen huts surrounding the only stone-built house for many miles. My first decision was that no officer would sleep in the stone-built house; it would be reserved for the MO, hospital beds, first aid, laundry, de-lousing of clothing and other functions which made the first call on dry space in any well run battle school. Next I recruited the staff.

As chief instructor I was given one Major Menday, a half-crazy racing driver who would go anywhere, dare anything, strong as an ox, extrovert, the sort of man who would have leapt into the ring at a fairground boxing booth and knocked out the champion with his first blow. The four officer instructors were Dick – a scholarly man, urbane, prematurely bald and with the spare physique of a mountaineer; Hay – a huge Glaswegian recently raised from the ranks, with a sad labrador always at his heels, morose, dogged and with an indomitable will to achieve whatever task was set him; and Norrie Cardigan – a colourful character from the Dundee hinterland, a fiddler with a huge repertoire of Scottish tunes, a schoolmaster by trade, a joker and the commander of the Royal Scots company which had mortified us on the day of the training company competition; finally, there was my younger brother Michael, whom I 'claimed' (under some quaint army tradition probably dating from Tudor times) from the KOSB where he had been a Territorial officer before the war.

With this body of men I began to amass ammunition, weapons, a demonstration platoon and NCO instructors, and to work out the first essential of any battle school, the assault course. Our assault course was formidable, starting with an ascent up a naked cliff, passing through all manner of obstacles, including a pool of liquid mud, and ending with a three-hundred-yard walk through the freezing water of the voe or fjord, chest-high, weapons carried above the head and live .303 bullets whipping up the sea all around.

Brigadier Fraser was delighted. He came to see us often and asked innumerable questions. We found this a bit of a drag so when he visited us on the great opening day to see the demonstration platoon go round the completed assault course, we stood him on a knoll in the centre of a meticulously calculated fire plan. First a burst of bren gun fire whipped through the heather in front of him and when he instinctively drew back a second burst struck some rocks just behind his head. Then, while the firing continued on fixed lines, down came the two-inch mortar bombs, smoke, very close, and clearly visible through the earlier patches of smoke, high-explosive bombs perhaps one hundred yards away all round. But as the smoke engulfed the whole party, the explosions came nearer and nearer and thick and fast until some of the bangs seemed to be only twenty yards away, as indeed they were: not caused by mortar fire, but by half-pound slabs of guncotton which Sapper Fleming had buried in the peat and was now detonating with relish from his hideout a quarter of a mile away.

By now we could see through the writhing smoke that most of the HQ party were on their knees protecting their faces from flying shrapnel, which was in fact nothing more than heather roots and peat. As the smoke cleared the brigadier drew himself up to his full height. He rocked backwards and forwards for a few moments.

'Urrgumph,' he said, and again 'Urrgumph. Good show, Forman. Good – urrgumph – show.'

As he hobbled to his staff car, his GSO II drew me aside. 'Don't . . . do . . . that . . . again,' he said.

'Well,' I said, 'if the brig wants to know what we are doing, we have to let him see it, don't we? And if he continues to visit us daily, he is bound to get involved in live ammunition exercises from time to time. Indeed I did want to warn you to give us previous notice of his movements, otherwise it's quite likely that his car coming up one of these roads may . . .'

'Don't . . . do . . . it . . . again,' said the GSO II.

After that the brigadier visited us less frequently and always gave us two days' notice, and whenever he approached anywhere near the battle school, he sent two motor-cycle outriders in front.

So now the courses began, thirty officers and NCOs at a time. Extremely alarmist reports had been spread by the staff, and we did our best to encourage terror in every battalion. When the unfortunate students arrived they hardly knew what had hit them, running everywhere from morning till night, often carrying huge loads, live ammunition whistling round their ears, instructors yelling at them to do the most frightful things, such as to jump into deep water, run through a house on fire or lie on top of a barbed wire obstacle so that a dozen men could run over their backs. But gradually physical fitness and a sort of dogged bloody-mindedness won through; they took a masochistic delight in enduring every form of torture to which they were subjected. In particular, everyone took great pleasure in the inadequacy and discomfiture of others.

The main test of endurance was the long exercise. This would start before dawn on Day One and continue through two or even three days, with two nights spent in the open with no cover and very little food. Perhaps the most enjoyable part of the whole battle school business lay in the construction of this exercise. Michael and I were the keenest tacticians and we would seek out escarpments for lines of defence, dead ground for cover, defiles for ambush and steadily build up a master plan to fill every moment of the three days with colourful incidents and surprises. Thus, just as the great assault on Muckle Roe had succeeded and the worn-out troops were consolidating and getting their fingers round a cup of tea, they would be subjected to a sudden enfilade of MG fire from a boat on the voe below, or from the rocks above, or a stampede of sheep and cattle would set off mines in their midst.

The chief instructor's contributions to the design of exercises were more to do with the physical than the tactical aspects of the exercises.

'We could make No. 2 platoon advance through the rocks until they reach the harbour and then attack up the road to the lighthouse,' Michael said.

Menday considered this. 'Make them swim across from the other side first. Make their clothes heavier. Then advance along the shingle, not the rocks. Get gravel in their boots. Then climb the cliff face before the harbour and put a minefield at the top so they have to climb down again. Time it so when they get to the bottom the tide is up to the harbour wall and they have to wade. Put barbed wire just below the surface. Get hung up on it. Chuck grenades in when they are struggling.' And so on.

The exercises were dangerous, but we never lost a man. One moonless night we were conducting a combined op with the navy. An assault force embarked at Lerwick and would have assaulted the air base there, had not our destroyer struck a rock and begun to sink, an episode which confirmed our contempt for the senior service. What would we do in a real war situation, we asked ourselves – as always slaves to reality. Why, go ashore in the destroyer's long boat, we thought. This was launched, but landed on the water upside down. What next? Why, have a man swim over to the shore with a rope and then the assault party haul themselves through the breakers and go about their business. This happened, but it was a dicey business. As I watched each man dangle from the rope, being dashed against the rocks and stumbling about to get a foothold, I was sure we were bound to lose a few. At the critical moment when there were four men hanging on the line, I was startled by a burst of fire over my left shoulder. Two of the four dropped into the sea immediately. I turned to see a sergeant instructor firing bren gun tracers over the men on the rope.

'You bloody fool,' I shouted. 'Stop it.'

But he didn't hear me. He was seized by the sort of frenzy I was later to recognise in battle in the heat of an assault. I took hold of the gun and wrenched it out of his hands, hitting him on the face as he lunged at me to get it back. It was over in an instant: the men got ashore, none was drowned, the destroyer was refloated and two days later I had a phone call from the GSO II at Brigade.

'Been hearing strange stories about your nautical expedition,' he said.

'Oh,' said I.

'A fracas aboard ship. An officer struck an NCO. Court martial offence.'

'Who told you this?' I asked. I thought he was kidding.

'Naval HQ been in touch. Got it from an officer aboard the destroyer.'

I had been aware of a disdainful presence of naval officers during the episode. Perhaps he wasn't kidding. Bleeding silent service, I thought, gossiping like fishwives.

'Shall I tell you what happened?' I asked.

'Irregular if there are going to be charges,' he said.

'Piss off, Jimmie,' I said, 'LISTEN.' And I told him.

There was a long silence. 'No charges,' he said.

Another sea landing exercise led to my first encounter with film-making. I pointed out to John Pateman that if we made a film of one particularly good exercise it would teach nearly all the lessons in forty minutes rather than ten hours; it would save an enormous amount of ammunition (which was rationed) and could be used widely beyond the limits of our battle school. John immediately set me to work with a colleague to write a script. Everyone was delighted with it, especially the brigadier, and although no film was ever made it might have been the prospect of such an exciting event that led to a visit from General Thorne, the GOC Scottish Command who decided as a result of his visit to set up battle schools in all the relevant units under his command.

We became discontented with the site of our battle school. The Shetland Isles were not ideal for training men to fight on the continent of Europe, or indeed for any theatre except perhaps the Faroes or the Falkland Islands, both of which seemed unlikely options. I wrote to Lionel for advice. I enlisted John Pateman's help and we pestered OSDEF HQ to move us to the Scottish mainland. Just before Christmas I heard that we were to move to Invershin, near Bonar Bridge, as soon as we could pack up and get there.

Michael and I decided to celebrate our prospective release by taking four days' leave. We would travel to our home in the Borders for Christmas. Accordingly, in the small hours of Christmas Eve we drove down the Shetland mainland in a truck and boarded an RAF Shackleton. We landed at Thurso and were picked up by an army truck travelling to Inverness. I never quite got to the bottom of the arrangement concerning this truck, which had been made by Michael through his KOSB connections and had overtones of hanky-panky. It was certainly irregular for two officers on leave to be conveyed over a hundred miles in WD transport. I held my peace.

Late that afternoon the truck broke down. At the start its average speed might have been twenty miles an hour, but this declined to fifteen and then ten; indeed, I suggested to Michael that we might get to Inverness sooner if we got out and ran. Now it had stopped. I sat in the cabin while Michael and the driver lay on their backs in the road and grappled with some item in its reproductive organs. Eventually it started, then stopped again, and started and stopped, each move forward getting shorter and shorter until at last it packed up on the outskirts of Inverness itself.

By now the night train had gone, but we boarded the fish train and were lucky enough to find an empty van, where Michael sat in one corner, I in another and my Shetland collie Robin disdainfully pacing the space between, sneezing and coughing through the overpowering smell of fish. After an eternity of shunting, crawling up gradients, stopping, starting and shunting again, we reached Perth. It was daylight on Christmas Day, and as we emerged from our van we saw a passenger train about to depart. It was pointing south and we made a dash for it. Robin, whom I had released so that he might relieve himself before the next leg, still half-crazed by his ordeal by fish, turned and bit a small girl in the leg. She sent up a great squawk, but there was no time for niceties so, grabbing the dog by the neck, we sprinted for the train and jumped aboard. Again our progress was slow, but comfortable, for, although the train was packed with troops on leave, we smelled so strongly of fish that we were accorded a decent amount of space. It was not possible to discover whether or not our train stopped at Beattock, our home station, but it did, and we jumped off and arrived home in good time for Christmas dinner. The trip would have formed a good initiative exercise for our students, we told each other.

The new battle school was situated in Altnagar, a capacious shooting lodge built to serve the sporting needs of the great Andrew Carnegie, and in an adjacent farm, Achinduich. There were some changes in the cast: Menday had gone off to the commandos and his place was taken by Raymond Henderson, an elegant young executive in Coutts Bank with prematurely grey hair, the profile of Disraeli and the manner and bearing of a diplomat. He was both intelligent and enthusiastic and an enormous source of strength. We lost Cardigan but retained Hay and Dick and recruited several more young officers because I felt we had asked too much of our small team at Voxter.

Now we had forests, arable land, rivers, villages and towns as the raw material for our exercises. The shooting lodge was sited on the lip of a gorge through which the river Shin hurtled down in a series of cataracts. The assault course now started by our front door, went down the precipice on the west side of the river, crossed the road, ascended the cliffs on the far side, recrossed the river by means of two ropes – one for the feet, one for the hands – some thirty feet above the swirling waters, and ended with an upward scramble through barbed-wire entanglements and a cannonade of thunderflashes.

The assault course led to my only serious brush with authority. The OSDEF GSO I, now another Dumfriesshire friend, Jim Melville, sent me a sharp note saying that COs were complaining that we were injuring too many of their men. Thirty had been sent back to their units with broken ribs, strained backs and sprained ankles, and our MO had reported over a hundred serious injuries among those who completed the course. He raised the ghost of an old complaint that in Shetland the battle school had caused seven officers and NCOs to spend some weeks in hospital by forcing them to stay inside a burning house filled with acrid smoke from smoke canisters. I was ashamed of the Shetland episode. Two of my friends in the Argylls, Mike Kenneth, my first company commander, and Hamish Fraser Campbell, had been in serious danger. Pat had insisted I come down to the battalion and listen to a grand remonstrance from my fellow officers.

But I knew that our safety standards were above those of any other battle school. Overall many students had been killed and there was at least one school (Leyburn) where it was rumoured that a quota of deaths was set for each course. Better to kill a few in training, the argument went, than to lose large numbers in battle. Compared with the more reckless schools, our .303 bullet through the fleshy part of Captain Sword's backside, Sapper Fleming's hand blown off and the odd sprinkling of two-inch mortar shrapnel seemed mild.

I thought the best thing to do was to ask the general commanding OSDEF and his staff to come to see for themselves, meanwhile making only one concession by reducing the downward leap on the assault course from fourteen feet to twelve. The general and his retinue duly arrived and, as the visit progressed, their attitude of cold scepticism thawed and they were finally converted by a vivid sand-table exercise which we laid on after dinner.

These were a combination of *son et lumière*, music-hall sketches and battle experiences. Michael and I scripted these events with the utmost care and played the two leading roles. They would start conventionally enough with the class seated comfortably around the sand-table listening to some comic dialogue between members of the high command. The first surprise involved the sound of real, though distant, artillery fire. As this was called down, little puffs of smoke rose from the sand-table (activated by Jack Hay crawling beneath the table and puffing cigarette smoke through a network of rubber tubes) and by sharp little exploding caps detonated from outside, which sent spurts of sand into the laps of the front row. As the exercise developed more reality began to break in: 'As you are proceeding down the wood the advance guard shows itself,' Michael said, 'and –' his voice was drowned by a sustained burst of fire from three bren guns placed just outside the windows, supported by a cacophony of thunderflashes, gun-cotton and mortar bombs. So the exercise developed towards its climax, when the company O group was trapped in a farmhouse. The demonstration platoon broke in through windows and doors, threatening the audience with fixed bayonets and hand grenades. Whether or not these antics equipped the students to perform better in battle is an open question, but without doubt they won over the OSDEF high command who from that day on were our loyal supporters.

All exercises were not so happy. There was one major battle exercise which took place on the west bank of the Shin and involved live artillery fire. On the day of the exercise all roads leading into the battle area were sealed off with a sentry on each road. Red flags were hoisted on poles on the surrounding high ground. On a clear and frosty morning, I was standing with my batman on a knoll observing the course of events. Half a mile behind me the attacking infantry were forming up. In front of them a troop of twenty-five-pounders were ranging on the target which lay astride a road perhaps a mile directly in front of me. Suddenly, to my horror, I saw the local school bus appear over the horizon followed, bizarrely, by an ambulance. I looked at my watch. It was three minutes to zero: the bus would reach the target area just as the artillery barrage was due to begin. The gunner observation post was six hundred yards on my left.

'Run like hell to Captain Sword,' I yelled at my batman, 'and tell him to cancel the barrage.' Meanwhile I sprinted towards the OP. Six hundred yards on the track would take me about two minutes forty-five seconds, over heather and bog three minutes. Even if the OP officer couldn't see the bus I might be able to stop the fire in time.

As I ran, the shells began to fall. The compulsion to watch was too great. I stopped and looked. The bus wended its way in stately fashion through shell bursts, some of them very close. I waited until it was clear, then ran on to the OP. It was unmanned. I ran back to try to find Sword, who was re-forming the attacking company. I couldn't find him, or my batman. The 18 set (the portable infantry wireless) was not working. The telephone line to the battery commander from the command post had gone dead. Nothing was right.

The school bus arrived and the driver jumped out.

'That was great,' he said, 'they were going off all round me.' The bus was empty. My vision of dead children faded. I could see no shrapnel holes, but I thought it best to allow him to continue to believe, at least for the time being, that they had been dummy shells.

The ambulance driver, however, was a shaken man. Again there were no marks except that a stone had broken one of the side windows.

I was overwhelmed with shame. This was my battle school. There had been a series of ghastly errors. It was a miracle that no one had been killed. How dared we laugh at the old army régime. They were at least meticulous in ensuring the safety of civilians.

I drove back to the school with Jack Hay to set up an immediate enquiry.

'What conclusions do you draw from this day's work, Jack?' I asked in deep misery.

'Thae twenty-five-pounder shells couldnie make a hole in a paper bag,' he replied.

About this time I felt I could not go on teaching in a battle school until I had seen some active service. After Dunkirk and during the desert campaign there was no real opportunity to gain battle experience for a war in Europe. But now we were in North Africa and would shortly be invading Sicily and Italy. I wrote to

Lionel and he wrote back saying he felt much the same. It was time to go, but we had to ensure that the battle-school movement did not lose its impetus. Would I succeed him at Barnard Castle? He would come back to relieve me in six months' time. I wrote again that my time as an instructor was at an end. I was beginning to feel a bit of a phoney.

6

EMBARKATION LEAVE WENT IN A FLASH: four days with Polly at her West Highland retreat near Poolewe; three days at Dumcrieff; three days in London; and then back to duty for a period in limbo at a transit camp in Ulverston in Barrow-in-Furness where fellow embarkees gathered to await the next convoy out of Liverpool. The mood of the dozen or so officers in the transit mess was uncertain; some of them sat like prisoners in a condemned cell writing long letters to their nearest and dearest, others – I was one of them – relieved of all responsibility, seized the opportunity to have a rollicking time. It might be the last chance. We behaved like schoolboys let loose, commandeering civilian cars to career through the Lake District, arranging steamroller races with the ack-ack battalion protecting the Barrow shipyard, setting up impromptu dances and playing poker through the night.

There was an extraordinarily attractive company sergeant major of some sixteen stone, a young woman who appeared to be in charge of the administration arrangements at the depot. Juno-esque, overflowing with fun and affection, but also a firm disciplinarian, there was a convention that she had to give every officer a goodnight kiss before she retired, but no one got much further than this except one very small officer in the Signal Corps, a mere wisp of a man, who seemed to enjoy most-favoured-nation status. As he appeared at breakfast blearily wiping his eyes, we would crowd around him solicitously to make sure that he had suffered no bodily damage, such as a cracked rib or collapsed lung, as a result of his dalliance with this amazon CSM. On one occasion, when it was deduced from a chance remark that he had been overlaid, we insisted on an X-ray and a certificate from the doctor before he went on parade. He did not much enjoy this interest in his welfare, but the object of his affections thought the whole thing hilarious and began to send him back to the mess with messages written on his forearm in lipstick. He became known as 'the walking telegram'.

After two weeks the convoy sailed from Liverpool and was at sea for another two weeks. There was wide and fanciful speculation about our destination; the odds clearly had to be on North Africa, but Norway and Spain could not be ruled out and there was some wild idea that we might be a task force on our way to fight alongside the Russians. The theory was given some support by the fact that we were hanging about off Greenland.

The conditions aboard ship were disgusting. Men were penned up between bulkheads, living and sleeping cheek by jowl. They messed by relays and there was no time between 6 a.m. and 10 p.m. when there was not a queue outside the galley. Even so, some unfortunates only managed to get one instead of two hot meals a day – if they wanted it. The demand for latrines greatly outstripped the supply on what was a converted passenger liner, and in rough weather the makeshift lavatories of buckets and canvas screens were neither comfortable nor continent. Sewage, urine and vomit swilled down companionways and the stench on stepping out of the salty breeze on deck into one of the low caverns between bulkheads crowded with sick, sweaty men was overpowering. I was in charge of a vertical section of the ship and demanded to see the CO, which took two days, and the captain, which took another three, and was told patiently in each case that there was a war on. However, by mustering tradesmen in my section and by stealing stores, I did manage to increase the number of lavatories by nearly half and to furnish a rope on each side of lavatory seats to steady the client in rough seas.

At last the weather changed, the sea flattened and someone said that the previous night he had recognised the outline of the Rock in the moonlight. We were in the Mediterranean. Soon we were lying off Philippeville and remained there for two days – final aggravation – while the other ships discharged. By now the only food and drink available to the troops on our boat were water, tea, bully beef and ship's biscuit. The sight of tenders passing by our ship loaded with oranges induced near mutiny.

The North African coast from Tangier to Bizerta consisted of what were known in the military trade as Rear Areas. The last Germans had just been corralled on Cap Bon and the Sicilian campaign was under way. Around Philippeville regimental signs clustered around every telegraph pole: Signals Base Depot, REME

63

Heavy Repair Shop, Catering Corps Training School, Naval Ordnance Supply Point, Town Major. Everywhere there were huge supply dumps (many of them no doubt in the wrong place) and everywhere there were Transit Camps. It was in one of these that I learnt the facts of North African life.

I found myself in one of a hundred bell tents in an orange grove with two other officers. One of them was Pat Spens, a fellow Argyll aiming, like mysef, for the 8th battalion. The other was Major Herbert Pointer. Pat told me he had heard from a wounded officer of the 8th Argylls that Lionel Wigram had been posted to their brigade (the 36th) as an observer. As I unpacked my kit bag and valise Major Pointer's eye lighted on a plain pint flask of aluminium which Polly had given me. It had been knocked about a bit and the screw top had been lost and replaced by a common cork: nevertheless, it was to become the cynosure of Major Pointer's eye. He would pick it up and fondle it, gazing at it as if it were some exquisite object of art. After a day or two he plucked up courage.

'I would like to buy this flask, Forman,' he said.

'Not for sale, Pointer,' I said.

'Five pounds.' He looked at me with the triumphant air of a man who has pre-empted all opposition.

'Not for sale,' I said.

He was astounded, for he was a trader from the East End and believed that everything was, in the end, a matter of price.

'Five pounds and twenty Players,' said Pointer.

'Not for sale,' said I.

At ten pounds and a hundred Players he gave up and decided on a waiting game. The flask could not have been worth more than five shillings, and Players were a rarity, fetching up to a pound for twenty. It was beyond his comprehension that, given time, I would not succumb. He thought that in respect of the flask I was an admirable negotiator, no more.

'The Players are fresh – two tins of fifty,' he said as he flashed them in front of my eyes, then he gazed at me like a wounded deer as he slowly stowed them back in his kit bag.

'I never really knew what the word "covet" meant,' said Pat one night when we were alone in the tent, 'until I saw Pointer looking at that bloody flask of yours.' Pointer had not given up.

Life in a transit camp was dreary, the day spent inspecting

drafts, organising training for men who did not care about anything much except the next meal, where their impending posting would take them and how to wangle a twenty-four-hour pass to get to the brothels of Constantine. The day began with the Green Howards Reveille, the most beautiful bugle call of all, and ended with the 'Last Post', sounding above the faint cries of the Fuck-Off men in the adjacent orange grove.

The Fuck-Off men were one of the Algerians' deterrents against the presence of the invader. It was impossible to surround all the orange groves with barbed wire, so the proprietor paid Arab boys to sit in the trees and whenever a marauding British soldier stretched out his hand to pluck an orange a menacing voice would utter the words 'You Fuck Off You', and if the invader did not fuck off, he would be subjected to a bombardment of well-aimed small stones. Other, more aggressive, aspects of the Algerian war effort were to tunnel under the wire guarding MT posts and drain all the petrol tanks down a hose, which ended at a point some distance outside the perimeter fence. Here a queue of clients took their share in an assortment of jars, amphorae and goatskins. They also tunnelled into a luggage compound and turned the officers' trunks upside down, cut out the bottoms with a tin-opener, removed the contents and replaced them with sand exactly equal in weight. The bottoms were then soldered in key places and the joins sealed with chewing gum. I witnessed the dismay of several fellow-officers who, reunited with their trunks after the long voyage, opened them to find a pile of sand. Sometimes a bit of paper broke the surface which bore the message, universally applicable to all unwelcome visitors, 'You Fuck Off You', or 'Allies Fuck Off'.

Occasionally an officer would have to make the fifty-mile journey to Constantine to pick up prisoners. These were men who the Military Police had dragged out of the brothels which were out of bounds. One afternoon, while I was waiting for my consignment, an obliging brothel owner put on a floor show for the Military Police and me: it was a bizarre act concerning two girls and an extremely amorous snake. The girls were about ten years old and were stripped naked to reveal body make-up which was the most elaborate essay in eroticism I was ever to see. Their owner kept offering further delights involving goats, dogs, a donkey and in one case a cast of one girl and six men.

'It will be simultaneous, I swear,' he said. 'All six boys will

65

be simultaneous. It will be half-hour but by god at the end all at once. It will be simultaneous, I promise you, if not simultaneous money back.'

We refused his kind offer, but the sergeant who was with me said 'Bit different from a ten-bob poke against a pub wall in Leeds, sir. You can see why they come here.' Indeed I could. As we loaded some twenty men on to our fifteen-hundredweight truck I reflected on the restricted view the army took on this matter. The Army Education Corps could learn a great deal in Constantine.

At last the order to move came through. I was to be in charge of a detachment of reinforcements travelling by train from Philippeville to Bizerta, a distance of about two hundred miles.

'You report to the RTO at Bizerta on arrival,' said the adjutant.

'When will that be?' I asked. 'How long is the trip?'

'Anything between two and six days is the usual,' he said.

'Why so long?'

'Engine shortage,' he said. 'Very few engines work and you need three or four to get you over the steepest inclines. Also power failure. Also track repairs. It's all open now, I think, but you never know. The last lot had to march fifteen miles between rail heads.'

'Rations?' I said.

'Q on train,' he said. 'Q knows ropes.'

'Discipline?' I said.

'Problem,' he said. 'You've got three subalterns and four sergeants between fourteen coaches. One for every two coaches.'

'Not enough,' I said.

'Never enough,' he said. 'There is a war on. You will lose a few dozen for sure. Go past Constantine as fast as you can and by daylight. And remember to hand in your casualty list in Bizerta.'

'Casualty list?' I asked.

'Last lot five dead, twenty wounded,' he said, 'Lot of them drunk. Fall out. Lie on top of the coaches. Get swept off at bridges.'

'Thank you very much,' I said.

That night I entrained eight hundred men into fourteen carriages in a siding outside Philippeville. They came from every

66

known branch of the services, from Catering Corps to the Brigade of Guards; there were RAF mechanics, naval ratings, some Americans, many Canadians and a few Goums. Each officer and NCO was responsible for one hundred and twenty men. There were to be three roll-calls a day, four feeding and watering points and lying on the roof was forbidden. Any girls picked up were to be ejected at once. Each commander was to have a small guard unit with one up the spout to prevent pilfering and fire-raising.

But it was no good. The nightmare began with a twenty-four-hour delay. We lost over a hundred men that night, but most drifted back before we departed. The train often went at from four to six miles an hour and as it passed through a station an army of Algerians selling eggs, arak, wine, chickens and pornography would close in on the train and trot beside it for several miles until they had exhausted their stock. The troops would brew up inside their coaches and set them on fire, or on the track during a stop and get left behind. Girls would get aboard and be hidden from sight and then cause fights between rivals seeking an equal share of their favours. There were never less than a hundred men drunk, and two rooftop sunbathers were killed by bridges on the first day. The officers and NCOs were in a state of nervous exhaustion. There were no corridors, so they had no access to the troops. Rifle shots went off from time to time and no one could spot the offenders or discover what they were shooting at – except that a number of sheep were being chopped up at impromptu wayside butchers' shops. I could only survey the scene with despair. Subsequently I made a good story of it, but then it was not funny.

The harbour at Bizerta was full of sunk ships. I was detailed to go aboard an American tank-landing craft. There were no tanks, only a handful of men and six officers to make the crossing to Italy. As we chugged past the outer breakwater, someone suggested a game of poker. When we arrived at Taranto, thirty-six hours later, the game was still in full swing. The three American officers who ran the ship had joined early and, except when we seemed to veer about too much and the skipper sent one of his mates to supervise the steering of the ship, they never left, despite their lack of success. First of all we won their money, which was a lot. Most of us carried ten or twenty pounds of local currency in our back battle-dress pocket, no more. The Americans had hundreds of dollars' worth of lire, issued in advance, and huge rolls of greenbacks to boot. These were transferred to their European allies within the first few hours. Then the Americans began writing cheques. We were not quite clear how we were going to cash them, but accepted them with good grace. But then their bank credit began to run out and when I found myself playing for a ship in a bottle owned by the young lieutenant from Kansas City, we decided that enough was enough, and the Americans had to withdraw from the school. This they were loath to do, having visions of winning back at least some of the loot they could see lying in piles in front of the British. Words were about to lead to blows when a crew member appeared and said we had struck the mast of a submerged ship. We rushed on deck to discover that we were in Taranto harbour, which was full of sunk ships, so full that there was scarcely room for our clumsy carrier to find its way to the one dock which appeared to be operational.

In Taranto, there were long lines of bedraggled Italian soldiers queueing outside police stations to be demobilised. Some were in uniform, some carried small arms, some German weapons, some, in sharp city suits, looked as if they were demobilised already. I went into one police station where a bulky sergeant major sat behind the desk, neck open, salami sandwich and glass of wine in front of him, in voluble conversation with a group of would-be civilians. Behind him there was a six-foot poster of a gigantic and quite horrible fly about to alight on a piece of meat. It was a hangover from one of Mussolini's campaigns and had across the bottom LA GUERRA CONTRA IL MOSCO. I turned to the sergeant major.

'How did you get on in that war?' I asked.

'We lost,' he replied, and shrugged.

Once again I was posted to a transit camp, this time near Bari, and once again I found myself in a three-officer bell tent with a captain in the Buffs and – surprisingly – once again with the covetous Major Pointer. I had a quick meal in the mess, and when I returned I found Major Pointer standing with his back to the opening of the tent, holding my flask tenderly in both hands as if it were a Stradivarius.

'Put that down,' I shouted sternly. He jumped around in an agony of guilt, inanely holding the flask behind his back.

'You took that flask out of my kitbag,' I said. 'You stole it.'

'Not stole, not stole,' cried the wretched Pointer. 'I admire it. I admire it so much.'

'Too much,' I said. 'I've a good mind to report you.'

'Please, please,' said Pointer, 'my wife, my wife, my family,' and he broke down into uncontrollable sobs, whether because of his guilt, the fear of exposure or a more general fear of going into action, or simply because he was overcome by the memory of his family, I do not know. I found myself in the ridiculous position of holding his arm, patting his back and offering him whisky out of the flask.

'Never mind, Pointer,' I said, like a nanny. 'Never mind. There, there.'

Pointer began to howl as if he were at the wailing wall. 'I am so bad,' he yelled. 'I am shitty. I am so shitty.'

'Not shitty at all,' I said. 'You are a major in the –' I looked at his regimental badge but couldn't recognise it, 'in the – what the hell regiment are you in?'

'Norfolks,' he gulped. 'Transferred from REME,' and once again he was convulsed with sobs.

'Let's forget the whole thing,' I said. 'You can have the bloody flask. Forget it.'

At this Major Pointer let out a yell guaranteed to alarm the whole transit camp.

'O God,' he sobbed, 'you are so good. You are a SAINT.' He said the word with an upward shout that embarrassed me. 'I am shitty, shitty, shitty and you are a SAINT.'

'Look, Pointer,' I said, 'I think you had better lie down,' and I took him by the hand and gently laid him, still shaking with sobs, on his palliasse.

When I woke the next morning, Major Pointer had gone. I later heard that he had become town major of Brindisi and had got into some terrible scrape. I just hoped it didn't make him cry too much.

Then began a slow and frustrating progress up the Adriatic coast. The 5th Army was advancing from Salerno on the left through Naples towards Rome, the 8th Army on the right up the Adriatic, with 13 Corps on the left and 5 Corps on the coast; 78th Division was on the right of 5 Corps and within the 78th Division was 36 Brigade made up of a battalion of Argylls, of Royal West Kents and of Buffs. This was my target, and as we passed Foggia and San Severo, I watched the myriad of directional signs closely. I passed 78 Divisional HQ, to which I should have reported, passed 36 Brigade HQ and made a beeline for the 8th Argylls. I found their mess in a farmhouse near Termoli, and as news of my arrival spread old friends began to drop in. James Campbell greeted me.

'Bloody awful news, old man. You're not coming to us, you're going to the West Kents – frightful dougs.'

'Oh God,' I said, 'I've struggled halfway across the world to get to the 8th Argylls and now I'm not wanted.'

'We have too many field officers and they have too few,' James explained. 'No use arguing. The COs will have done a deal with Swifty.'

'Swifty?'

'Swifty Howlett – brigade commander.'

'Are the West Kents really so terrible?'

'Common as dirt. But they've got a good man as CO and two or three decent company commanders. They ran like bloody rabbits outside Termoli when the Boche made a tank attack. But they are better than the Buffs – frightful shits.'

I gradually established that the 6 RWK were, after the Argylls, the least bad battalion in the division, and felt a lot better.

That night was a convivial evening in the Argyll mess, with a pibroch, highland dancing and recitations from The Book. But as I went to bed, I heard the distant crump and crash of artillery from the Trigno front, some ten miles to the north, and I felt fear in the pit of my stomach. No use pretending to yourself, I thought, it's going to be nasty.

Next day I left the Argylls HQ in a jeep, passed the brickworks outside Termoli where Jack Anderson, much loved hero of the Argylls and a VC, had been killed earlier in the week, and up a twisty road past deserted farms and uncut crops, to Guglionesi. As I sat in the CO's office waiting for him, I saw a photograph on his desk of a woman, probably his wife. I thought I knew the face. Late in the afternoon I saw a jeep draw up in the yard, and a fresh-faced blond young man jumped out and came towards HQ. He was telling a story to a companion in a powerful baritone voice which carried up the stairwell and from time to time exploded with peals of bright laughter. He came into the room, saw me, and said 'Major Forman? I'm Paul Bryan. I've just been to see a friend of yours who has just joined the battalion.'

'Who's that?' I asked.

'Lionel Wigram,' said Paul.

Map 1

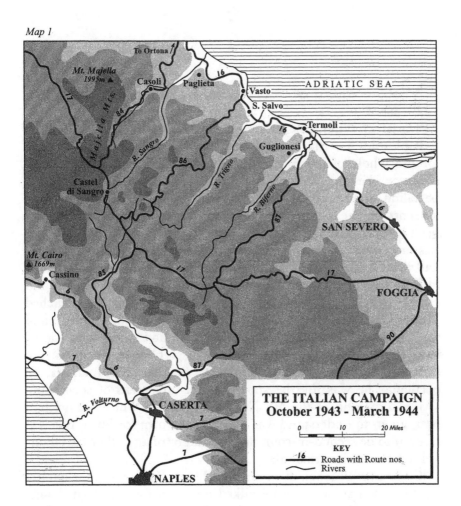

THE ITALIAN CAMPAIGN
October 1943 - March 1944

KEY
Roads with Route nos.
Rivers

7

'YOU'VE HEARD OF COURSE ABOUT LIONEL'S DISASTER?' Paul
asked.

'Disaster? What disaster?'

Paul told me that Lionel had been attached to 36 Brigade
for the whole of the Sicilian campaign. Although ostensibly an
observer, he had commanded every unit from a section to a
battalion ending up in charge of the 5th Buffs. He had written
a report on the campaign. Paul hadn't seen it, but it must have
been critical of the High Command and of the strategy and tactics employed. A copy had been sent to the War Office. Lionel
had been given a few days in the UK to pass on his experiences
to Barnard Castle (now accepted by the army establishment and
called the School of Infantry). News of Lionel's report had reached
Monty's ears (he was then still commanding the 8th Army), and
what he heard had made him furious. He had summoned Lionel
to Bari and given him a violent wigging. He had demoted him
from acting battalion commander to company commander, in
particular he was told he should forget any ideas of succeeding
to the command of the 5th Northants (a post which Lionel had
been given to understand was being kept warm for him), nor was
he even to be second-in-command of that or of any other battalion.

I sat stunned at this tale.

'Good Lord! Lionel, of all people!' I said. 'How has he taken it?'

'When I first saw him he talked non-stop for nearly an hour,'
said Paul. 'He's very sorry for himself. After he'd got things off his
chest I tried to convince him that there was nothing surprising in
Monty's attitude. He probably hadn't read the report, just heard
that some unknown novice called Wigram had conducted a post-
mortem on his successful Sicilian campaign which was full of
criticisms. There was no point in arguing that his analysis of
the campaign was correct – Monty would have none of it. But
I failed to make any impression. I told him his only chance of

rehabilitation was by commanding his company so well that I could give really good reports of his progress to Brigade. I said I would do this. But he didn't seem to respond. Lionel will be round here to see you later tonight.'

Paul introduced me to other members of the HQ mess and continued on his rounds. I sat bemused: Lionel in disgrace. That meant the battle-school movement in disgrace. All the work of the past two years would be under threat. And Lionel himself? He was proud, he was passionate, he was much more than a lieutenant colonel in charge of a training school, he was a leader whose word was law to many hundreds of disciples, some of them the best officers in the infantry. It was almost as if the Almighty had deposed Moses as he was leading the Israelites out of Egypt.

The mess was in the mayor's house in the centre of the unsalubrious village of Guglionesi. The anteroom, such as it was, was over some pigsties and the smell and the noise of the pigs below contributed to the slight feeling of nightmare that was creeping over me. I had a large whisky and waited for Lionel. When he came round the door many hours later he looked a different man from the cheerful, ebullient instructor I had last seen at Barnard Castle. His shoulders were bowed, the way he threw off his greatcoat was listless and unmilitary, the corners of his mouth were down and his eyes were dull. He seized my arm not so much with the grip of an old friend as of a man clutching for help.

'You've heard then?' he said.

'Yes,' I said. 'Monty is a turd.'

He sat silent, then: 'I don't know what to do, I simply don't know what to do. It's totally unfair. It's wrong. Never happened to me in my life before. It's unjust. And I can't appeal. There is absolutely no machinery for appeal.'

'You'll have to lump it,' I said. 'Monty is such a prima donna. Until someone can persuade him that you have repented of your wickedness and have worked your passage to become a good, loyal officer again, you will just have to soldier on. Tell me all.'

So Lionel told me all. He had been in at the start of the Sicilian campaign. He saw every important action on the east side of the island. Although starting as an observer, he became so trusted by battalion commanders that they allowed him to take command of

73

platoons, sections and companies and finally at Rivoglia he had been appointed to command a battalion in action. It had been an exciting experience and an absolute eye-opener. Some of what we had taught at the battle school had been absolutely right but a great deal was hopelessly wrong. He made notes throughout the campaign. He had discussed them with a wide cross-section of officers from brigade staff to ex-Barnard Castle students commanding companies. He had taken immense pains to ensure that his views were endorsed by the majority of officers in the field, he had written his report carefully, had been sent back to Barnard Castle to deliver it and to adjust the syllabus and methods of training in accordance with his experience in battle.

What was in the report to get up Monty's pipe? I asked. Lionel didn't know. Honestly he couldn't think what had so upset Monty. His report was forthright, it was true, but there was nothing in it with which the soldiers fighting in Sicily would disagree. Monty had been there, had seen the same scenes as he had. He simply could not explain it. He had no copy of the report with him but he pretty well had it by heart.

So we went through it together. It began by stating that the Germans had scored a success in Sicily. They had withdrawn painlessly with few casualties; we had suffered heavy casualties. The reason why we had suffered so badly was because we employed the wrong minor tactics. Advance by infiltration with very small groups penetrating and getting behind the enemy posts would have been more effective than the traditional frontal attack with a barrage and lines of advancing infantry. The Japs used the infiltration technique successfully, so could we if we stratified our men into those who were 'gutful' and capable of solo operations and those who weren't. Battle drill as taught at Barnard Castle should be entirely revised to take account of the realities of morale in the field. About five men in every twenty would run away if offered the chance. Lionel had checked the figures carefully. Each battalion had court-martialled a number of men for running away. This had to be taken account of in training. There should be more battle inoculation in training (firing all types of weapons at and over students so they could learn to distinguish degrees of danger by sound): the brigade support group was no good: 4.2-inch mortars should be scrapped: many and various improvements in tactics and weapon usage should be adopted.

When we had started to talk the half-a-dozen or so RWK officers sitting around drinking *vino* and passing the time of day had been surprised to see two newcomers to their domestic circle embark on intense and apparently intimate conversation. As they melted away one by one I realised that Lionel and I were not exactly making friends in our new environment, and indeed, later on, we were to pay a penalty for this; but meanwhile Lionel's acute distress made any form of politeness impossible. Soon we were alone, even the pigs ceased to rumble and grunt, although their smell did not diminish, and all we could hear of the world outside was the crump and crash of the artillery fire on the nearby Trigno front.

Lionel was indignant, crestfallen and demoralised. He felt he had made an honest report, had checked it carefully and had presented it as his personal view. Monty had heard about it from the commander of the 78th Division, who had been given a garbled and wholly inaccurate account of what Lionel had said at Barnard Castle, and had exploded with fury. Lionel had been marched in front of Monty like a prisoner in an orderly room, and had been told that his report was written out of ignorance of military affairs and would undermine morale. Monty had simply torn him off a strip and dismissed him. He had no chance to say a word in his own defence and no one to put his side of the case. If it had been a court martial at least he would have had a Prisoner's Friend. He had been treated like a criminal; demoted and forfeited any chance of a command, although Monty had said that he could in due course appeal to him for the ban on his promotion to be lifted.

I told Lionel what I thought had caused Monty to fly off the handle. He was unpopular both with the troops and with many of the officers in the 1st Army. They felt that he had won the desert war on the backs of Wavell and Auchinleck and had become a tiresome and vain martinet who knew nothing about the kind of warfare experienced in North Africa and now being practised in the Adriatic. It is true that the casualties in the Sicilian campaign had been excessive and that he was not doing well in Italy, while at the same time he was making a desperate bid to be in charge of the Second Front. In addition to the allegation of German success and British failure, Lionel had touched the most sensitive nerve in any general – he had said his troops ran away in the face of the enemy, he had used words like 'panic' and 'hysteria'. This sort of language broke the most sacred of military taboos. Monty would see him as a disloyal 1st Army man, an amateur who had never seen any action before Sicily, a schoolmaster, a jumped-up and self-appointed military critic – and a Jew. We debated this last point for some time and reached the conclusion that Monty, along with most of the military establishment, almost certainly didn't like Jews. Because normally they had to suppress this prejudice, when it did surface it could drive them to be intemperate and irrational. We compared notes on the several mini-Dreyfus cases we had encountered. Just before dawn Lionel said he had to go, took two aspirins (his hands were shaking) and left me to doss down just as the pigs were greeting a new day.

I reflected on the traumatic effect on Lionel of the interview with Monty. Everything he had lived and worked for over the past years had been snatched away and, in a way, desecrated. I could think of no more shattering experience for a person with his passionate dedication to the cause of winning the war than to be told he was disloyal, disgraced and unwanted. I wondered how he would weather the storm, but as events turned out I worried too much. His letters home show the most astonishing degree of composure. Not only do they make no mention of any setback but they continue the even and cheerful tone of earlier letters. After the evening I have described he wrote to his wife:

6 RWK.
Please note my change of address; it doesn't signify anything – only that I am very busy just now.

I am getting my leisure somewhat better organised now. I have got a set of pocket chessmen and a pack of cards and the CO has produced a roulette wheel . . .

This Bn is very sociable and whenever possible we have a bn mess – usually about once per fortnight. This goes very well. Another luxury is ENSA. They came up and gave us quite a decent concert in a local hall. No girls unfortunately. Yet a new officer from a battle school has joined us – Denis Forman who is an old friend of mine. We have a wonderful collection of officers now – all keen fit and intelligent so we ought to do well I think . . .

I didn't see Lionel for two days. He had taken over 'B' company which was stationed at Montecilfone some six miles away. I had 'C' company which was on the other side of Guglionesi. Morale was low, especially in Lionel's company, which had suffered most in the débâcle of Termoli. In this battle 36 Brigade had crossed the Biferno and formed a bridgehead on the high plateau of land on the north side with the RWK in front. Allied tanks could not cross the Biferno until a Bailey bridge had been built. It was a nasty exposed position, and Paul had asked Swifty Howlett, the brigade commander, what he should do if German tanks were sent in against them.

'Get out,' said Swifty.

Sure enough, the German tanks came and opened fire, the 6th RWK did get out and there was not much decorum in the way they did it. Men had raced across the open ground chucking away their weapons and making for the cover of a nearby wood. It was the battalion's first retreat in action and the indignity of such an unmilitary scramble affected everyone. One of Lionel's first assignments on arrival had been to give a conducted tour of the Termoli battlefield to fellow RWK officers from the 5th battalion who had just become our neighbours on the left. Later a major who had been one of the party told me how impressed they had been by Lionel's performance that day, and since he must have been hot from his ordeal with Monty, I marvelled at his professionalism.

When next I met him he was standing in the middle of a flock of sheep with the CQMS, talking in sign language and dog-Italian with a group of ferocious-looking farmers. When the negotations were finished, we sat down under an olive tree.

'I'm trying to get our chaps to behave decently,' said Lionel. 'It's fair enough to take abandoned animals, but if there's an owner he should be paid.'

'Some hope,' I said; the practice of 'winning' animals for the cookhouse, especially pigs, was widespread.

'It's disgraceful,' said Lionel. 'We're not at war with these people, they should get a proper price. Anyone in my company who takes an animal without paying a fair price is on a charge.'

'Fair price?' I said, 'What is a fair price? The allied military lira has devalued the old lira by 400 per cent and these people don't even know that.'

'I've taken that into account,' said Lionel, pulling a notebook out of his pocket and opening it at a page covered in calculations. 'Also that the war means there is no true market. So I base the value of a sheep on one week's civilian wage as recommended by the Allied Military Government, a pig on two and a cow on eight.' He continued to refine these calculations with various additional factors such as the size and condition of the animal, the value of objects introduced as barter, such as bully beef, petrol and cigarettes and many others until I had quite lost him.

'Lionel,' I said, 'there is a war on.'

'We are fighting this war for the principle of a decent life,' he replied. 'If we don't behave decently to these people we are no better than the Boche.' He was still sitting there figuring earnestly in his notebook when I drove away in my jeep.

For the weeks ahead, when not actually under fire, and even then if the fire was not too intense, Lionel was often to be seen standing in the centre of a knot of animals, usually goats or sheep, negotiating between the owner and some representative of the allied forces. His fame as a fair broker had spread like lightning across the countryside and if any soldier in my company laid unlawful hands on a pig or a bullock he was likely to be greeted by shouts of 'Veegum, Veegum' – an appeal to the British sense of fair play in the shape of the only arbiter trusted by the Italian peasant, Major Wigram of 'B' company 6 RWK.

His letters home at this time show how he revelled in the unusual experience of Italian peasant life:

I remember reading one of C. E. Montague's books about the last war in which he said that the whole outlook on life could be altered by whether the farmer's wife asked you into the kitchen or left you outside in the cold. We have found out how true that is but fortunately we can walk in if we feel like it and don't have to wait to be invited. This leads to some situations which are very amusing – afterwards. A short time ago we moved into a farm. Italian farms consist always of only two large rooms with an intercommunicating door. All the family live, wash, eat and sleep in one room and the farm animals all do the same in the other. If they get a bit mixed up (the humans and the animals) nobody worries very much about it. So at one time when I woke up I found we had 2 horses, 1 pig, 1 dog, 2 cats, some chickens, 6 officers, 4 batmen and 5 assorted Italians all sleeping quite comfortably in various corners. Their attempts to eat breakfast, wash etcetera in the morning without getting into each other's way were too funny to describe. In the next building they had a very unfortunate night. In order to make more room, they moved a large horse from a far corner and parked it with two other small ones in the other corner.

The old Italian gesticulated a bit but they took no notice of *him*. Well it turned out that the big horse was a stallion and the two little ones were mares so there was no little restlessness.

Please tell the children I am writing this in the farmhouse kitchen. There is a little boy here called Angelo aged eight who sends them all his love. I have just given him a large piece of chocolate and a very nice Italian tommy gun with which he shoots me every five minutes. I only wish I could give the children as much happiness but don't see any chance of getting a gun home.

And again:

I am very very well in spite of the tough life we are leading now (or perhaps because of it). It is a very simple life in which things like food and comfort assume ridiculous proportions. For instance 'scrounging' means the ability to nose around and supplement the ration. We have done extremely well in this respect – bread, chickens, sheep, a pig, even geese and a few eggs. All this makes life well worth living and there is a tremendous sense of satisfaction to be gained out of seeing the men eat with gusto.

It is a weird life in many ways. We keep driving the Germans before us and often catch them up. The result is that we find ourselves billeted in farms which they have just hurriedly vacated. Imagine the situation: for two or three weeks about thirty Germans have been lording in a farm. They have turned out the family (twenty-eight, including many little children) and made them live in a cow barn. Every day they eat all they want – kill chickens, cows and pigs without paying a sou – and drink all the farmer's *vino*. They even fill lorries with food and drive them off to the rear. If there is any protest from the farmer or his family out come the revolvers.

Then one never to be forgotten night. The German sentry on duty at the gate comes running up about midnight 'The English! The English!' There is a hasty gathering of kit, shots ring out in the darkness, the family cower down low in their stable, the children yelling and screaming at all the strange noises. Then at last off go the Germans up into the hills, on foot, running for dear life. Quite a lot of them don't get away. Out come the family – and what a welcome we receive! All the women are crying for joy and the entire population turns out cheering and screaming.

For a week we hung around waiting apprehensively for the next battle – the crossing of the Trigno, another in the series of short rivers running in deep defiles from the central mass of the Apennines into the sea, and providing the Germans with exactly

79

the sort of obstacle a retreating army prays for. During this time I saw little of Lionel but had the pleasure of getting acquainted with Paul.

Paul Bryan was the seventh of nine children. His father had been a university lecturer in Japan – where Paul was born – who made an income from writing short stories for American magazines and books about Japan. He was also in holy orders and had for a time been Tokyo correspondent for the *Economist*. Paul spent much of his childhood with relatives in England and had been to Cambridge just before me. At the age of twenty-nine he found himself commanding the 6 RWK in the North African campaign. He had won an MC and a DSO and had the reputation of the most outstanding commanding officer in the First Army. He had the build of a rugby forward, was exceedingly (almost excessively) blond, eyelashes and all, had the memory of an elephant, a laugh that could be heard (and frequently was) half a mile away and could sing all the verses of most of the hymns ancient and modern. We sat in an olive grove for hours on end passing the time of day. Sometimes I would quiz him about the North African war: Djebel Abiod, Longstop, or Centuripe in Sicily, the meeting with the 8th Army, the incompetence of the Americans. Sometimes we would talk of England and his wife Betty, who as a girl in Yorkshire, Betty Hoyle, I had met at dances and parties before the war. Although clouded by the undercurrent of fear of the coming battle, these were among the happiest hours of the war and laid the foundation for a friendship which flourishes today.

The days before a major battle are long and fidgety. Every man is suffering in his own way from fear constantly kept alive by the big guns rumbling on by day and by night. There is a great deal of forced activity – inspections, competitions, lectures on the coming encounter – and a lot of forced cheerfulness. All units are in a state of readiness, of perhaps one hour or even less. As the days drag on, confused reports of action seep back, usually alarmist.

It was, therefore, a relief when, on the first day of November, Paul sent for his O group. I left my company billet in the small village of Petacciato, and drove and then walked to the appointed spot, a farmhouse just below the lip of a ridge of high ground on the south bank of the Trigno. The farm smelt of pigs, fennel, which grew wild in great quantities and which had been crushed

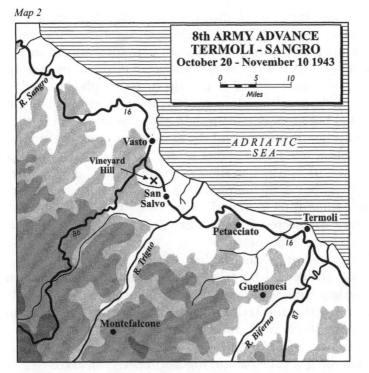

Map 2

**8th ARMY ADVANCE
TERMOLI - SANGRO
October 20 - November 10 1943**

0   5   10
Miles

R. Sangro

16

Vasto

Vineyard
Hill

ADRIATIC
SEA

San
Salvo

Termoli

86

Petacciato

16

R. Trigno

Guglionesi

Montefalcone

R. Biferno

87

and bruised by our military activity – and of death, for corpses of decomposing Germans were still being dragged from the farm outbuildings. Throughout my time in Italy (and even today) a whiff from a pigsty or from a sprig of fennel aroused the memory of my first encounter with the stench of death.

Paul was alert and full of optimism. We were to cross the river by midnight into an already formed bridgehead. At dawn there would be a heavy artillery barrage and the Buffs would lead an attack on San Salvo, a small town among rolling hills some three miles beyond the Trigno. We would be in reserve and would later pass through the Buffs and capture a more distant objective, Vineyard Hill. We sent back for our company O groups in turn, and then waited for the statutory hot meal which was the prelude to any attack.

At dusk it began to rain. By midnight it was a steady downpour and the Trigno was thigh-deep as we crossed it. The Germans knew what was afoot and as we halted on the north bank we came under sporadic shellfire. I became familiar with the woodpecker cycle: as each bout of shelling began every man would start digging frantically with his entrenching tool, and all

81

around and far into the distance one would hear a cacophony of striking and hacking. As the shelling ended, the noises diminished in volume until one heard only one or two determined soloists still at work. I had a piece of shrapnel tear through my gascape but no one was hurt much. A private in No. 1 platoon had an ear shorn off but, as the platoon sergeant pointed out, his ears had been too big anyway. Communications, as always in battle, were pretty well non-existent and the most usual way of getting reliable information was from another officer, often the IO, who had been sent forward by the battalion commander. So, as we waited and waited in our half-completed foxholes, I went across to visit Lionel, some three hundred yards away on my left. He was in a superbly engineered foxhole, very deep and with a place for his map-case and binoculars.

'Pretty boring,' I said. 'When will the show start?'

Lionel showed me his map-case covered with chinagraph arrows and dashes. 'Judging from the sound of the barrage ten minutes ago and the fact that the MG posts here and here have been eliminated, I judge the Buffs to be about here.'

I was sure he was right.

'Can you get your men to dig in properly?' I asked.

'No,' he said. 'They never do until someone gets killed.' I went back and waited.

Sometime after midday the firing in front slackened and we moved forward. The Buffs had taken San Salvo. We were to move up parallel with them. As we set off towards the front we met little groups of men in sixes and sevens travelling the other way. They had had enough of fighting. When challenged, they said they were lost and looking for their platoon. I made all the deserters we met fall in between two of my platoons, who then escorted them back where they had come from. Soon the company had almost doubled in size. We found a German tank with the turret blown off and two of the crew lying on the tracks with their scalps turned back and hanging from their necks. I was horrified: it was the nastiest sight I had ever seen. If it shocked me, I reflected, it might well daunt others, for the route we were on was sure to become the main axis for the whole brigade. I told two private soldiers to move the corpses, but they wouldn't touch them. So the CSM and I pulled them off the tracks and turned them over, and I got a further shock when I realised the bodies were still warm. (When I later recounted this episode to Lionel he remarked, 'Quite wrong. Waste of time. No place for queasiness in battle.' I felt mortified.)

So the long day wore on. Sometimes we were under fire and flopped down, sometimes the fire stopped and we moved forward a few hundred yards. A few men were hit and either walked back or were left with a companion until a stretcher-bearer came. The deserters deserted again, disappearing goodness knows how. Four of my company went with them. Late in the afternoon we were told to stop and dig in.

Then, to quote from notes I made subsequently for the battle school:

By about 1700 hours the whole of the first objective was reported to be securely held, and the CO [Paul], on receiving orders to carry out a night attack on Vineyard Hill, sent Lionel Wigram and myself forward to make a plan for the battalion attack, while he obeyed a summons to the brigade commander.

We reached the edge of the San Salvo feature with some difficulty, and there, in the fading light, we evolved a hasty plan for what appeared to be an extremely difficult night attack. The country was close and scattered with infantry obstacles and wood. No time to reconnoitre or mark any routes or FUPs. Just as we were receiving the Bn O Group, a tank battle, which had been fluctuating about half a mile away, began to approach very much nearer. The troops on the San Salvo feature had no anti-tank guns and a general withdrawal was taking place. Lionel, however, was completely oblivious of this, and it was not until a German tank was within 150 yards and firing over his head that I could persuade him to withdraw to safety. Even then he had some idea of finding a better OP from which to point out the route to the company commanders.

Subsequently we realised that we were in fact the last members of the British army to leave the San Salvo feature, and as we approached the town, through the confusion of the tank battle, we saw the infantry had fallen back on its perimeter. Lionel could not bear to see such an advantageous piece of ground lost. Two British tanks were withdrawing into the town along with the infantry, the troop commander, whose tank had received a direct hit, walking behind them. Nothing would satisfy Lionel but that we should tackle him and two company commanders of the battalion which had left the ridge, and exhort them to attempt a counterattack. But it was obvious that a counterattack was not going to be staged, and again with great difficulty we persuaded Lionel to return to the town. To the last he was

83

very loath to leave this depressing situation, and for two pins would have stayed and organised a counterattack himself.

Back in San Salvo, as darkness fell, and as sergeant majors collected and counted their men and quartermasters attempted a hot meal, Paul collected his O group in a convenient stable. Lionel and I told them of the difficulties, and tried to make the map come alive with vivid descriptions of steep slopes covered with vines, deep ditches, wire fences and thickets. Paul formulated a plan. We were to set out from San Salvo at 2200 with my company in the van. It would take about two hours to reach the FUP.

I could not absolutely swear to it, but my recollection is that the first two soldiers in the advance up the main road from San Salvo to the next major town, Vasto, were Paul and me. I believe we might have been singing, certainly we were chatting to each other and laughing in a most uninhibited way. It had, after all, been a long day, we had been told that the Germans had withdrawn to Vineyard Hill and it is just possible that we had taken a glass of *vino* in San Salvo. It is not easy to rationalise the fluctuation of morale when suffering from excessive fatigue – despair often gave way to euphoria in an instant, sometimes for a good reason – the end of an attack, the breaking of dawn, a shot of rum, sometimes for no reason at all. The whole battalion was cheery that night and followed Paul and me in what was euphemistically called 'snake formation' but which was in fact the string of platoons walking in single file, sometimes overlapping each other, sometimes not.

It was a pleasant night, warm with a gentle breeze and a little moonlight. Suddenly, as we approached a complex of farm buildings, all hell broke loose. Red and green tracer zipped past us, pinging off the road and slicing through the olive trees on either side. In a trice every man was in the ditch. Paul went back to battalion HQ and I found everyone else was going back too. Yelling and shouting, I got a sergeant and a lance corporal to stay with me and open fire with a bren gun on the farm buildings. Now we could hear tanks revving up their engines (dreaded sound) and see the outline of individual tanks shunting and pushing to get a better field of fire. One of their moves revealed a surprising sight, a dozen or so Germans sitting around an open fire drinking tea. Our bren gun scattered them, causing casualties. But now our fire had given the German tanks a better indication of our position and we were showered with continuous bursts of green tracer. There was a little sporadic fire from the rest of the battalion, but it seemed a long way farther back and I found that my desire to get out was increasing all the time.

'Back to the telegraph pole at the corner,' I yelled, and we all three half-crawled half-ran away from the German fire. At the corner there were a few hardy souls behind a wall, among them Lionel.

'The CO says your company is to fall back on San Salvo,' said Lionel. 'Most of them are there already.'

We retreated, circumspectly at first, but as we got out of range of the tanks we began to walk, first like anthropoid apes and then to run, erect like homo sapiens.

'What happened?' asked Lionel.

'Paul and I were leading the battalion into battle and we bumped into a tank laager,' I said.

'Good God!' he said, 'No patrol in front?'

'No patrol,' I said.

'No advance guard of any kind?'

'Not of any kind.'

'No scouts?'

'None.'

'You mean to say that the two senior officers in the battalion were the spearhead of the battalion when it walked into a German tank laager?'

'Paul and I were the spearhead.'

Lionel was at first puzzled, then vexed and then exceedingly angry. He abused me all the way back to San Salvo. I was so mortified that in a mad moment I almost turned around and walked back towards the German tanks, thinking green tracer preferable to being beaten about the head by Lionel.

Lionel never forgot the episode, and again I quote from my campaign notes:

Of all the incidents in the Italian Campaign this one worried Lionel most. The idea that a whole bn had chanced upon a tank laager at night and had withdrawn without capturing any tanks, (although we did in fact inflict casualties) would continually prey upon his mind. He had a hundred and one solutions as to the correct action which should have been taken, and every one ended with the RWKs leading a triumphant procession of captured tanks back into San Salvo.

In San Salvo all was confusion. Morale, so high half an hour earlier, had slumped, and all over the place men were lying down or going to sleep where they stood. At battalion HQ, again in some animal shed, I witnessed an example of Paul's extraordinary powers of persuasion. He was in dialogue on the phone with Swifty Howlett, the brigadier. Swifty was irritated by the little contretemps which had delayed the night attack and wanted the battalion to set out again, now, immediately, by-pass the tanks and find a way through to Vineyard Hill, and carry out the attack, late but still under cover of darkness. Owing to army protocol, Paul could not say that the battalion was totally demoralised, simply would not move, much less obey an order to get after the Boche. They had to have some sleep and some food. I listened to him with growing admiration as he explained the innumerable reasons for postponing the attack: excessive fatigue of the troops, the likelihood of tanks not only on the road but spread widely across the country, the danger of encountering mines at night and the near impossibility of forcing a way through furze thickets (of whose density he had received authentic and alarming reports) in complete darkness. He reminded Swifty that the moon had just set. After half an hour he wore Swifty down and we settled down thankfully to a few hours' sleep and a hot meal before the attack at dawn the next day.

Again from my notes:

The next day was perhaps the high spot of Lionel's career with the bn. By 0900 hours we were 1200 yards from Vineyard Hill and Lionel and I evolved the plan of attack. We tossed for which company should make the assault first and he won. The approach to the Hill was made in bounds, with one company being always on the ground. At a farm at the base of the Hill, where we were rapturously received by a farmer, his wife and family, we were told that there were Germans in the neighbourhood and in all probability on the Hill. Vineyard Hill is about 600 feet high, the slopes are steep and covered with olive groves, orchards and vineyards, which cut down the visibility often to 100 or 200 yards. The Hill is in the shape of a sausage with a saddle in the middle and a peak about 50 feet above the saddle on either end, with a farm perched on each.

Lionel reached his FUP to attack the first farm without drawing fire. Germans were observed as he was forming up. A large number of British tanks appeared providentially from nowhere and, making a troop of tanks his fire unit, he carried out a battle drill right flanking attack with complete success. The company saw the Germans running before he reached the farm, and this put them in great heart. No sooner was he in the first farm then he was fired at from the second at about 800 yards range. At this point a troop of tanks went forward but one of them was knocked out. Lionel immediately arranged a second flanking attack similar to the first with the same result. He was now firmly established in the second farm, and he suffered only one or two casualties, when very heavy mortar fire and shellfire came down on the whole ridge. It was during this that a sgt major of Lionel's company noticed the wounded crew trying to get clear of the blazing tank, in which the ammunition was now exploding. Lionel and one of his platoon commanders immediately ran up to the tank and managed to pull clear two of the crew before they were burnt to death. (The subaltern was recommended for gallantry and awarded the MC, but we did not find out that Lionel had played the leading part in this action until some months later.)

Looking towards the enemy from the second farm, Lionel could see a large villa about 1400 yards away situated on a spur of the hill. Between his position and the villa ran the main road. German activity was spotted in the farms and outbuildings round the villa. For the third time Lionel arranged his fire plan, and led another flanking attack. For the third time the Germans ran and Lionel's company consolidated round the villa dominating the main road, whilst A and D companies moved into the first and second farms. During this day Lionel had planned the bn attack and carried out three company flanking attacks, leading the assault in person in each case.

That night I was reserve company, and after dinner at the bn headquarters I walked up to see Lionel in his villa. I had some difficulty in finding his company headquarters. When I reached it I saw a figure in a German greatcoat with a Luger in each pocket, supervising the unloading of the company's mules. It was Lionel, absolutely jubilant. He was full of the day's exploits and refought each attack with me with tremendous energy and interest. The tired dispirited company which he had taken over one month earlier had now carried out three successful attacks in one day. They had wounded and killed some Germans, and they had seen them run.

After everyone, except one hoped the sentries, had gone to sleep, Lionel and I sat talking over the embers of an open fire. He was once again his old self, but more so. What would he have done if the tanks had not appeared? Why was there no German counter-attack? Could he have withstood it had it come from there, from here, from behind? Why did tanks not carry effective fire-fighting equipment? There should be a nozzle on top and when the tank commander pressed a button the whole vehicle should be covered in foam.

At last Lionel rose to his feet, yawned and said (he was a man who had never used a four-letter word in my hearing before): 'Fuck Monty'.

The next day Lionel's company was permitted, most unreasonably I thought, to lead the advance up the road to Vasto. In a letter to his wife Lionel described the scene:

On the next day we had an experience I shall never forget. The news came early that the Germans were thought to be really on the run – so we were on the move bright and early again – again the mobile column. We pushed on a long way on our feet but finally entered quite a big town just as the Boche were trying to get out the other end. There was actually a little fighting before he finally cleared out, and there we were in possession. Now it turned out to be a high-class city about the size and style of Guildford. So we next had the thrill of marching down the main street as the very first British troops to enter the city. Well I can't describe it to you – every car and vehicle was buried in masses of flowers feet deep – every man was kissed and kissed and kissed again; bottles of wine, bread, apples, oranges showered on us. As we reached the main square the crowd became vast and uncontrollable and the cheering and clapping deafening. Dozens of women fell to the ground on their knees crying their eyes out. There was no mistaking the genuineness of the welcome.

But the euphoria was not to last long. My report takes up the story:

Several buildings had just been blown up by the retreating Boche, so that they formed an effective block across the main road. The Germans had given no warning to the families who were asleep inside, and consequently the ruined masonry was full of dead and wounded. As Lionel cleared this obstacle his company came under fire from snipers; in a flash the streets cleared and the bn moved into the houses on each side of the street. When the snipers withdrew the CO decided that Lionel had had enough, and my company passed through his.' Lionel never quite forgave me for this. He thought I had been working on the CO all along the line of march, and he could see no reason why he should not have been allowed to carry on in front.

About two o'clock that afternoon, when we had been fighting against stiffening competition, I decided to launch a company attack upon a German position which lay astride the axis. Our field regiments were all out of range and only one gun of the medium regiment could reach the target area. Of my own three-inch mortars one was hopelessly bogged a mile back, the other, with its carrier also bogged, was being manhandled along with my company headquarters with a very small supply of bombs.

In despair for some HE support, I got bn headquarters on the 18 set. Lionel was at the other end. I told him my dilemma and we agreed that the medium gun was too inaccurate, but he promised some HE support within fifteen minutes. Sure enough, ten minutes later he rang up to say he had some mortars ready to range. They could not see the target, and so, as we had practised at Barnard Castle dozens of times, I directed the fire and Lionel gave the corrections. He said afterwards that when the ranging was in progress and he heard my 'reference last shot – one hundred yards north' and he gave the correction at the base plate end, he could almost have wept for joy. The mortar shoot was accurate and the attack successful. At the time I could not understand how he managed to reach the target, since my mortar was firing at maximum range (1600 yards) and I knew him to be at least half a mile behind me. Later I learnt that he had commandeered two mortars from the recce regiment which he had noticed nearby, and with the newly issued base plate they could just reach my target.

The following three or four days were a joy. Our advance to the Sangro was only mildly contested, but Paul allowed our two companies to work together in the minor skirmishes and company attacks which cleared the northward route for the 8th Army. Lionel made friends with the commander of the tank regiment which had helped him on Vineyard Hill, and they became part of his private army. I won a rather beautiful horse. I rode him at all times and called him Mussolini. Lionel thought riding a horse was pure swank (he didn't ride himself) and that Mussolini was a silly name, until I reminded him about the Always In Action in Italy. By the time we got to Torino di Sangro we were exhausted, dirty, short of reinforcements and up to our knees in mud, but we were happy. We had tested our battle-school tactics together for a week and more, and they had worked. And it is hard for any victorious army to be glum.

Then Lionel fell ill with malaria and I was appointed second-in-command of the 6 RWK. I had a special assignment, to be in charge of all divisional patrolling on the Sangro front. It was to be quite a change.

CHAPTER

8

Map 3

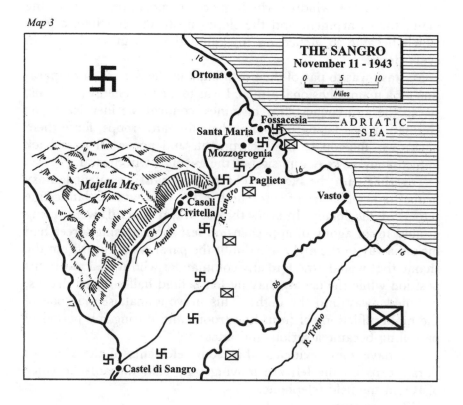

IN ITS LAST STAGES THE RIVER SANGRO runs from the massive
mountain-cliff of Monte Majella eastwards into the Adriatic.
In summer it is a mild affair, no larger than the Tweed at
Peebles, and one could find one's way across from stone to
stone virtually dryshod. In winter and spring it becomes a surly
fast-flowing flood, impossible to cross on foot and a test for the
ablest swimmer. On the penultimate stretch to the sea there are
two road bridges, three miles apart: to the north of the river a flat
plain one mile in depth, bounded by an escarpment one hundred

91

feet high. Beyond that there is a gently rising slope to a crestline broken by the outline of the villages of Mozzagrognia, Fossacesia and Santa Maria. On the south bank of the river there is a steep wooded slope some 250 feet in height, and on the crest of this, in the attic of a farmhouse half-concealed by trees, I made my OP and headquarters. The room was open to the beams and had no furniture, only a number of sacks of dried figs, but its chief glory was a wide, low window which gave a commanding view of the plain, the escarpment and the slopes up to the crestline, a view which became so etched on my mind that I can see it still in every detail.

My task was to patrol the north bank of the Sangro in preparation for a major divisional attack. I was to identify enemy positions, sweep the approaches clear of mines, confirm the identity of the German troops facing us, harry their forward troops, force them back over the top of the escarpment, and above all pass back immediately news of any sign of the enemy's withdrawal.

Together with the bayonet charge, the most prevalent fantasy in the higher reaches of command in the field was of clandestine retreat by the enemy. In every theatre of war generals were sitting around in an agony of apprehension lest the opposing forces had melted away in the night. No doubt the paranoia derived from the shame that would attach to any commander who stayed put in his position while the enemy, having left behind half-a-dozen decoys, trundled away into the night. This nervous malaise was one of the main afflictions of front-line troops and during my period of patrolling became a serious nuisance.

'We have some evidence that some elements of the German Para Corps on the left are moving out,' said the ant-like voice of IO on the field telephone.

'What evidence?' I asked.

'Significant evidence.'

'Precisely what?' I asked again.

'Small parties moving up the road with horse transport.'

'It's market day in Lanciano. I have been watching that road. Those were Italian families and farm carts.'

'The general would like a reconnaissance,' he said.

'Not possible, it would upset the whole pattern of today's patrolling.'

And so the argument proceeded until one side or the other

gave way. I often wondered how many lives were' lost in World War Two because of paranoia about phantom withdrawals.

There was never any real sign of the Germans withdrawing from the north bank of the Sangro. On my first day in the farmhouse attic, when I was considering my plan of action, Lionel came to visit me. He had been released from medical care, but was not well and had to report back to the field hospital in Vasto the next day. His spirits were low and he was brooding once again on the Monty affair; all the gaiety and swagger of the Vineyard Hill episode had disappeared. He gave me a draft of a seven-page letter to Monty.

'You can't possibly send a letter like that,' I said.

'Why not?'

'For one thing, it's too long. No letters in the army are more than a front and a back. Generals can't read more than that at a sitting. If there's more material than will go on one page it's put into annexes and the staff read them and tell the general as much as they think he needs to know, or as much as they think he can absorb or understand. For another thing, your letter is abject. You apologise for something you should be proud of. You seek to ingratiate yourself, you whine. Tear it up. It isn't you at all.'

Lionel sat on a sack moodily eating a fig.

'The problem is that it *is* like me, now. I've never been like this before. I've always fought and always won. I know how to win at law. I persuaded the top brass to back the battle school. But now I have no recourse, no appeal, nothing. When I approached Eveleigh (the divisional general) he refused to see me. I could write to the Army Council, but I know that would put me even further into the doghouse. So if the only way is to crawl – I will crawl.'

We argued for a long time. Lionel got more and more depressed and I became more and more impatient.

'It's a racial characteristic,' said he. 'If Jews lose out they suck up to the winning side. I know that's what you're thinking.'

'Not thinking that at all,' I said. 'You've had a shock, you are ill and you can't seem to accept the inevitable. You just have to shrug your shoulders. If you send that letter you will come to despise yourself, even if it is effective. Anyway you should send it through the appropriate channels – to Swifty Howlett who will pass it up the chain with a recommendation. Paul has already

93

given him a good report of you.'

In the end he agreed to redraft the letter on two sides of a sheet of paper and not to send it until we had talked again. (See appendix, p.213.)

I asked him for his advice on the patrolling operation and he perked up immediately. We ran over the ground, lying together with our binoculars resting on sacks of figs. We discussed primary objectives, secondary objectives and ways and means.

'Whatever you do,' said Lionel, who was steadily eating his way through his sack of figs, 'let the NCO who is leading the patrol choose his men from his own unit.'

'I had thought of picking, say, a hundred men from the battalion and bringing them up here to train and operate as a special patrol force,' I said. 'And, by the way, I would go easy on the figs if I were you.'

'Hopeless,' said Lionel. 'Never let officers choose men for someone else's task force.'

'Recce corps?' I asked (it was well known that when commanding officers had been asked to name candidates for the newly formed Reconnaissance Corps, they had dumped on it all their misfits and incompetents).

'A bit of that,' said Lionel. 'But none of the people who nominate are likely to *lead* a patrol. If your life depends on the people you pick, you pick carefully. And the NCO has seen his men in battle. He knows them intimately. He knows who has real guts, who is a phoney, who is a sheep and who is a coward.' (Lionel was right and I subsequently followed his advice.)

When he packed up to go he went outside for a pee and on returning reported that his urine had been the colour of army rum.

'Jaundice,' I said and he ruefully agreed, for there was a lot of it about. Taking with him the uneaten portion of the sack of figs, he set off sadly for the hospital in Termoli. I feared for him: he was already seriously depressed by the Monty affair, without the added bouts of black despair which are the consequence of jaundice. Within a few hours, however, I had forgotten Lionel and his problems, for all my faculties were engrossed in the job on hand.

Swifty Howlett and Paul Bryan treated me like a patient about

94

to go in for an operation, probably terminal. Nothing was too good for the patrolling force. I was to have an adjutant, a briefing officer, a sergeant and three men from intelligence, permanent staff to run the OP, signallers, cooks, batmen, one regiment of twenty-five pounders and one medium regiment on call, and first-class accommodation for Mussolini. Nothing, however, could alleviate the weight I carried in the pit of my stomach, which was the weight of fear: fear not of the Germans but of my failing to do what everyone expected me to do.

When the operation got under way, however, fear gave way to tension. As each patrol slipped over the brow of the hill, I wondered – would it reach its objective? Would it find out if the Red Farm [see p.104] was occupied? How many casualties? Would it come back on time? Would it come back at all? For ten days from the ninth of November I sent out from four to seven patrols each night – in all usually between fifty and a hundred men. At first the reconnaissance of enemy positions ranked in equal priority with a search for crossing places for tanks (both the Sangro bridges had been blown) and mine-searching and mine-sweeping on the approach routes for the coming attack. But then another hazard threatened the whole operation. It rained continuously on the fourteenth and fifteenth of November, and the Sangro began to rise and began to cause casualties. The report of Sergeant Knight's patrol ('Hope') is a record of extraordinary achievement whose conclusion was marred by the malevolent power of the Sangro itself. I quote from the patrolling log verbatim:

Patrol 'HOPE'
Composition: Sgt Knight
            L/Cpl Lingham, R.
Date: 14 Nov 43
Task: To answer question 'Do the Germans use MT on the Santa Maria – Paglieta rd to supply outpost line on the escarpment?'
Briefed: 0900 hrs 14 Nov 43
Time out: 1900 hrs 14 Nov 43
Time in: 0730 hrs 16 Nov 43
The patrol was sent out in company with two other small patrols. Each was then to carry out a separate task.

The river was crossed without incident, but, just as the patrols reached the point at which they were to disperse they were fired on by a hitherto unlocated gun from the top of the escarpment, immediately

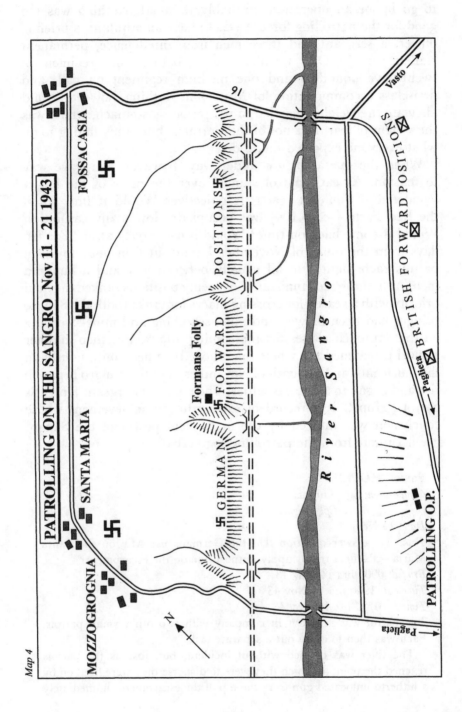

PATROLLING ON THE SANGRO Nov 11 - 21 1943

Map 4

FOSSACASIA

SANTA MARIA

MOZZOGROGNIA

Formans Folly

GERMAN FORWARD POSITIONS

River Sangro

Vasto

BRITISH FORWARD POSITIONS

Paglieta

PATROLLING O.P.

Paglieta

N

91

96

opposite them. All patrols withdrew some 200 yds, and after 20 mins wait the other two patrols proceeded on their routes.

Sgt Knight struck the escarpment about 150 yds to the left of the posn from which the gun had fired. He scrambled to the top of the bank, and, as he poked his head over the crest, he saw a German sentry a few yards away. The sentry heard him and lay down. No action was taken by either side. After a few minutes Sgt Knight slipped down the escarpment and tried again between the sentry and the gun posn. This time he succeeded in penetrating up the stream without being observed.

He followed the line of the stream, and then struck SOUTH WEST, towards the Santa Maria rd. At one point on the route on scrambling up a wooded bank Sgt Knight found himself looking into a German MG pit, which was manned by a sentry. The sentry raised the alarm and grenades were thrown down the bank, not near enough however to wound Sgt Knight or L/Cpl Lingham. When the alarm had died down he continued until he reached the gully running parallel with the Santa Maria rd.

In his search for a good OP Sgt Knight again found himself looking into a German MG posn, in which the gunner was asleep. He proceeded NW up the rd for some 400 yds and lay up until dawn. He then went to a lying up area which had been previously selected, and throughout the hours of daylight he and L/Cpl Lingham lay in a bank of brambles. No enemy movement was heard during the day.

At nightfall the patrol again moved to within ear-shot of the rd and listened for some five hours. Nothing was heard.

On the return journey, which followed approximately the same route, a German MG posn was being relieved, and the patrol watched the relief march in and take over, and the party relieved march out towards a fm hs. The remainder of the journey to the bank of the Sangro was without incident.

During the patrol there had been a heavy fall of rain and the river had risen about two feet. Sgt Knight and L/Cpl Lingham attempted to cross in two places and failed. On the third attempt, when they had nearly reached the home bank, L/Cpl Lingham was swept off his feet, and, as the current was too strong to make swimming possible, he was drowned. Sgt Knight was swept off his feet also, but was luckily cast upon the home bank, where he lay for some time in a state of exhaustion.

He reached patrol headquarters at about 0730 hrs on 16 Nov 43, having achieved his object and gained certain information that the Santa Maria rd was not used by German MT, and was therefore almost certainly demolished and mined.

Throughout this patrol there had been continuous rain, and although the NCOs had taken some food with them they had been too cold to eat anything except one or two biscuits.

Sgt Knight carried a revolver only, and L/Cpl Lingham a tommy gun. Both men wore gym shoes although the distance covered was between six and seven miles. They carried greatcoats and wore them when lying up. These they discarded before attempting to cross the river on the return journey.

After this astonishing display of stamina, Sergeant Knight was unable to give coherent identification of the positions he had encountered on his first day back. During his debriefing his eyes turned dull and after a time he could no longer answer questions, rolling his head slowly from side to side and crying out for Corporal Lingham. He was placed ceremoniously in a shed a few hundred yards from my OP, where medical orderlies ministered to his needs. He went to sleep about noon and the MO insisted I should not wake him up for twenty-four hours. When at last he was in a fit state to be questioned, it took us three days, debriefing him in short spells of two hours at a time, in order fully to identify his route on the map and on the ground with any certainty. This is one of the hazards of patrol life: the information about the MG positions was desperately needed to brief patrols which were going out that night.

But no patrols were to go further than the river Sangro, which had become quite unmanageable. We tried a human chain, one man linking arms with the next, but the smaller men got washed away and, but for lifelines, would have drowned. We thought of a line across the river, and by dawn one sturdy swimmer had taken a light line across and hauled over ropes of increasing thickness until we had two reliable and secure ropes for the next night's work. But at nightfall the Germans cut the ropes and placed Schu mines all over the north bank at any point where we could have tried again. So for two nights the log reads 'Unable to cross the river'. But on the third night there was a chance that some patrols might get over.

I personally briefed a young second lieutenant who was reported to be a strong swimmer to select two men in order to attempt a crossing just below the upper bridge. During the afternoon I was woken by a sergeant who told me his officer had asked him to tell me that he felt he couldn't go out that night. I went over to the lying up area and found the young officer in a desolate state

– pale, shivering, vomiting from time to time into à jerrycan. He was, however, quite composed and able to explain his predicament to me. He knew if he failed to go out he would be court-martialled. He would rather be killed than face that shame and humiliation. but he knew he would be physically and mentally unable to lead a patrol. He was paralysed with fear. I looked at him for a minute or two and made my decision, which was a harsh one. I would come and pick him up twenty minutes before start time. I would conduct him to the start-line where there would be two military policemen waiting. If he led his patrol out, well and good. If not, he would be taken straight back to the battalion orderly room on a charge of cowardice and disobeying an order in action. As the start time approached I was probably almost as nervous as he. But he appeared, white as a ghost, with his patrol behind him. He said nothing to me, but handed me a letter to his mother. About an hour later we heard some firing in the area of his patrol and an hour or so after that one of his patrol returned to report that they had run into a German fighting patrol and his officer had been shot dead with a bullet through his head. As I wrote to his mother that night, I reflected on the nature of courage and felt able to say to her that her son had shown himself to be a very brave man.

At one of our debriefings Paul told me of a mass meeting with Monty at Vasto, which he had attended together with other senior officers of the 8th Army. It was noticeable that those officers who had met Monty had a much higher opinion of him than those who, like me, had not. Paul was full of his praises: he had used bulldozers to turn a natural dip in the landscape into a perfectly calculated arena for his rally (waste of scarce resources, I thought), his description of his plans for the attack across the Sangro were meticulous and convincing (wait and see), he had produced out of the bag double the number of bombers anyone thought possible (hot line to Churchill?), he had given a wonderfully effective lecturette on the duties of a field officer (always had the gift of the gab) and he knew every detail about my patrolling activities. This last item rather impressed me and I felt slightly more warmly towards him. 'I went there,' concluded Paul, 'wondering how on earth we could win the battle and I left feeling rather sorry for the Germans.'

At the patrol HQ there was constant activity over the whole

twenty-four hours. From two o'clock in the afternoon until five-thirty I slept. At dusk the briefing officer and I would begin to see the patrols off, one or other of us often accompanying the more important patrols as far as the river. During the night we lay with our elbows on the fig bags watching and waiting, calling down fire on prearranged signals, usually to divert the enemy's attention from our activities. Sometimes the gunner officer would leave his OP and join us, and towards the end of the first week we had established such rapport that we could call down artillery fire in seconds on any one of over a hundred squares on an imaginary grid we had laid across our front. The Boche had not yet twigged where our patrol HQ was sited and we suffered only an occasional routine bout of shelling, probably because I had laid it down that there was to be no small-arm fire directed at the enemy from any position within six hundred yards of the OP and that staff officers with red hat bands were to be kept well below the crest.

In the small hours the patrols began to return. There were wounded men, men missing, exhausted men and every single man was, of course, wet to the skin. Everyone was served with a hot rum toddy and later with a hot meal. There was a short debriefing session with each patrol commander and a report of the night's work would be sent to battalion HQ for distribution onwards and upwards.

Paul arrived at first light, and we took stock and then decided on the patrolling plan for that night. Patrol commanders were called up (most had been forewarned of the likelihood of a patrol) and the briefing officer and I discussed with each one the tactics he should employ. Apart from the objective of the patrol, which was always fixed and clearly stated, we allowed the patrol commanders to make most of the decisions. In a conversational way we discussed which men should be selected for the patrol and how many, what arms were best suited to the job, what was the best form of dress, the route, the timings, signals, the supporting fire plan and other matters, right down to how much rum should be served and when. This might take up to an hour for each patrol but by noon the adjutant would have a complete schedule of all timings, routes, fire plans and signals for onward transmission to all concerned. During the afternoon the patrol commander briefed his men, studied the route with them and rehearsed any tactical moves which could be planned in advance.

As the light began to fade each patrol commander got his final orders, now in a crisp and imperative mode, a confirmation of what had been agreed by the earlier discussion. Then began the period of waiting, the worst moments of the twenty-four hours. Some patrols could leave as soon as darkness fell, some had to wait for the moon to go in or come out, and occasionally a second patrol would have to stand by for information brought back by an earlier one. When the wait was long, we had no effective way of easing the agony of men who had to sit for four, five or six hours awaiting the start signal. Some slept, some talked in low voices, most just lay still and thought. A few had a physical reaction – diarrhoea was frequent, vomiting less so, occasionally a man would plead migraine and dizziness and ask to be taken off, but never were my worst fears realised: no man ever melted away into the darkness; all patrols went out at full strength and no one ever deserted en route. When all the patrols had gone out, our own vigil began, which in its way was just as taxing.

After just over a week of patrolling it was clear that we were on top. The official account was:

> In spite of all difficulties, at the end of nine days all the mines had been lifted; tank crossings and routes had been reconnoitred; the enemy had numerous casualties and had withdrawn from his forward positions to the escarpment; and above all the Germans had been reduced to a state of nervous tension. It was, however, a great strain on the battalion, which, in those nine days, lost more casualties than any unit which took part in the subsequent attack.

But it was not quite like that. There was one German position in a gully in the centre of the escarpment, known as the Red Farm, which was obstinately held. I decided that to complete our task we had to eliminate it. On 16 November I crossed the river with a subaltern and three NCOs. We went forward to carry out a full reconnaissance. We observed a German platoon digging in and located three weapon pits which were likely to hold MGs. We saw two sentries against the skyline three hundred yards away. I decided it would need a strong fighting patrol to capture this position and that I should lead it myself. Paul reluctantly agreed.

On the sixteenth (the night after Sergeant Knight's return) we had crossed the Sangro with great difficulty. It was chest-high and we had no ropes. Two of the smaller men were unable to make it and I sent them back. We planned our attack for the next night, but at four o'clock in the afternoon I went down to look at the river. It had risen a further foot and I judged it to be impassable. Again, on the eighteenth, although down a little, it was still too high. So it was not until the night of the nineteenth that I set out through the dusk with a force of eighty-one men. They crossed the river holding with one hand their weapons and ammunition wrapped in a gascape on the tops of their heads, and in the other hand a stout staff for use as a wading stick.

Seventy-nine got across: two were swept back on to our own bank. The man carrying the 18 set on his head toppled over and the set was immersed. Otherwise, the force was intact and made its way safely to the patrol base, about two-thirds of the way across the plain bang in front of the Red Farm, which was now some six hundred yards away. We stopped and issued rum, about an eighth of a pint to each man. Some did not take it and it was one of the hazards of patrolling life that an individual might collect and consume as much as a pint of rum, with the risk (which actually happened on one occasion) of bursting into song within earshot of the enemy and then passing out happily (to be collected later by stretcher-bearers who took him back to face the orderly room the next day).

I had allowed any man who wanted to do so to take a dry shirt inside his gascape, and several had done this. Although the temperature was just above freezing and every man was soaked to the skin, nobody wanted to change his shirt.

So now the force split up. Three bren gunners worked their way towards the Red Farm. One platoon moved out to the left and one to the right. Each one was to get astride the escarpment about three hundred yards on either side of the Red Farm. I was to lead an assault force of thirty-eight men in a wide sweep right round the farm position and take it from the rear. There was to be no firing, if possible, until the assault began. At this point the time was eight-forty.

I waited for ten minutes. Everything was quiet. We started across the fields which were bordered by deep ditches full of water. We reached the escarpment and clambered up through thorny scrub. I remember thinking that the pervasive smell of wild thyme seemed out of key with our enterprise. When I reached the

102

top of the escarpment I was totally disoriented. Although for ten days I had gazed at this strip of land and memorised every feature, I was now at a loss. That tree should not be there. The rows of vines were 180 degrees out of their correct alignment. There was a thing which looked like a haystack. The nearest haystack was half a mile away. The moon had not yet risen. The wind had changed. I simply could not construe what my compass was telling me. I left the patrol with the NCOs and walked a few hundred yards towards the haystack on the skyline, where I would get a better view. I'd had no rum, so I sat down and indulged in a refreshing draught of Johnnie Walker. As I lowered my flask everything clicked into place. It wasn't *that* tree, of course, it was *that* tree. The vines were in dead ground from my OP. The haystack had a black tarpaulin over it and did not reveal its identity as a haystack to us at the OP, being known only as Blackspot. The wind had not changed. I felt deeply grateful to Johnnie Walker (still going strong) and for many years afterwards, out of sheer loyalty, preferred it to all other brands. We were almost exactly in the right place. I went back to the patrol to await moonrise at eleven o'clock, when suddenly two shots rang out from the most distant platoon.

'Bugger that,' I thought. 'Bound to stir up a hornets' nest.' But nothing happened. (Later I learnt that the left-hand platoon had been challenged by two sentries and had no option but to shoot them.) We waited. I called together the NCOs with whom I had rehearsed the operation. They were all experienced soldiers, much more experienced than I; they were on their toes, but calm, sensible and easy. My God, I thought, how lucky I am to have this lot.

The moon rose and we silently approached a pile of ruins just on the lip of the escarpment on my side of the gully where the Red Farm stood. We split up – B group going up the gully to our right, A group (my assault force) closing on the ruins which were some one hundred and fifty yards from the German position. Suddenly we heard firing from B group behind us. I sprinted back to find that they had stumbled on a working party of Germans, had killed two, taken two prisoner. I raced back to A group, who were lying behind the ruins. As I reached them they were fired on from the direction of B group by members of the German working party who had moved back to higher ground. My group immediately ran for cover around the ruins and returned the fire. But then the forward German position opened up with two machine guns

Map 5

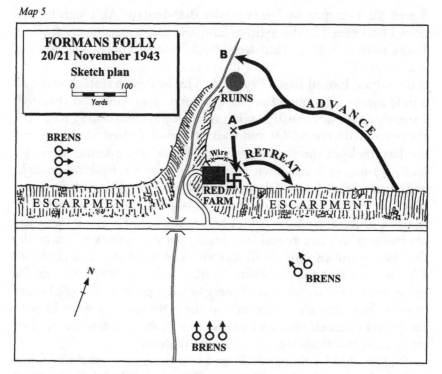

FORMANS FOLLY
20/21 November 1943
Sketch plan

0   100
Yards

BRENS

RUINS
A
ADVANCE
Wire
RETREAT
RED
FARM
ESCARPMENT   ESCARPMENT

N

BRENS

BRENS

on the back of my group. We were now between two fires, but happily all my forces, right, left and front, opened fire (eight bren guns in all) on the Red Farm position. There was red and green tracer everywhere, but, thank God, it began to move away from us and return the fire from the three other sides. I shouted for B group to join us, I shouted for the A group sergeant to get the men to form up for the assault. He was dead. I shouted for the B group sergeant to take his place. He was lying on his back with blood pouring from his side. I shouted for the A group corporal. He was doubled up in pain and unable to move. I stumbled over the body of the B group corporal. He was dead. There were no NCOs left. I shouted 'Form up behind me! Form up behind me!' but nobody formed up, nobody seemed to hear me. The men were lying in twos and threes all around the ruins. I ran from one to another ordering them, begging them, threatening them. Soon I had nine men ready to assault and off we went, shouting, firing our stens, stumbling towards the edge of the escarpment. I was a few yards in front when suddenly I was tripped up. 'Christ,' I thought. 'Wire.'

Wire it was, and a complete surprise. I yelled, 'Lie Down! Lie Down! Grenades! Grenades!' Each man had six grenades and we flung them as far as we could. Some of them reached the German trench, and firing stopped. We had no wire-cutters. I stood in the middle holding the top strand down, shouting 'Here! Here!' and the assault force flailed their way through. An alsatian dog rushed at me but stopped with a scream as he was shot by one of the German MGs.

Once over the wire, we lay down. My hands were cut. I could hear the Germans shouting hysterically. They were very near, perhaps thirty yards away. Their MG right opposite us was now firing continuously away from us at one of our central brens and this was a mistake, for he could have wiped us out in a couple of bursts. I shouted for another volley of grenades and as soon as they exploded I yelled 'Up and On for Father Christmas!' I have never been able to decide why I should have involved Santa Claus at this critical moment, but it worked, or perhaps anything would have worked, for five men ran forward with me to the German trench. The Germans were now evacuating fast. Six were killed at point-blank range, mostly shot through the back, and the rest scarpered into the gully, but the solitary machine gunner on the left flank kept at his post until, after some ten minutes, he was silenced by one of the assault group advancing up his own trench and shooting him from below. The German position was now clear.

Firing stopped and figures from A and B groups began to appear out of the darkness. We had two prisoners. The first two we had taken had been killed. In addition to our two dead NCOs and two wounded NCOs there were two more wounded who couldn't move, and several walking wounded. I decided to try to evacuate the wounded and man the position against counterattack.

One of the prisoners was a Pole and one of the men in B group – strange things happen in war – was bilingual English/Polish. The Pole told us that all the German positions had been abandoned, that the fatigue party had been setting up another wire barricade in the rear and had now escaped in a truck, and that the Germans would form up in the gully to counterattack.

He was right. I could hear orders being given below and rallying noises. I wondered, could we hold out against them? I checked for ammunition – the first bren gunner had only half a magazine left and his gun fixed in the single-shot mode. The second had none. The third's gun had jammed and he had chucked away his ammunition. Some had no grenades left, some had one or two. We hadn't a hope. I decided to stick there only as long as it took to get the wounded to the edge of the escarpment. But we failed to do that, for moving the wounded men was slow work, a few yards and then rest, and their pain was such that they tended to fight off any helping hands, just wishing to be left alone to die. The counterattack was halfway up the hill, heralded by yells and shouts and the firing of Schmeissers. Our number was up. 'Leave them and run for it!' I shouted, and we all sprinted for the cover of the escarpment. When we were only halfway there streaks of green tracer began to whizz past our knees. The man on my left fell, the tracer ricocheted, hummed and whistled round my ears. I simply could not believe that I was not hit, but I wasn't, and made the remaining hundred yards in record time.

Under cover of the escarpment we tried to re-form and count our losses, but among the thick scrub it was impossible. I waited five minutes and called down the artillery concentration on the whole of the Red Farm area, which thundered and crashed as we made our way back to the patrol base. Here, as the other platoons joined us, we began to count our losses. Of the thirty-eight men who had gone forward in assault groups A and B with me, eighteen had returned, twenty had not. The other groups had suffered no casualties. We waited forty minutes for stragglers, then went back to face our final hazard, the return crossing of the Sangro, but here we were lucky: the river had dropped over a foot since we had crossed it some eight hours earlier.

As soon as the patrol was safely in base I went out again with five fresh men and four stretcher-bearers to search for stragglers and wounded men. We found none.

Just after first light Paul came to debrief me. I told the story step by step, minute by minute. I told him about the wire. We had faced no wire anywhere on the whole front – it was a surprise, and we had no wire-cutters. I told him that if we had been able to reconnoitre the position on the previous night all would have been well. I told him of my feeling of total frustration when I was at first unable to rally an assault group for the final attack. I didn't know the names of the private soldiers. Once their NCOs, whom I did know, had been killed or wounded, I was powerless. This had to be wrong.

Paul went through the logic of the matter carefully. Men from my old company had not been available because they were in reserve to form a bridgehead over the Sangro on the following night. For the last ten days I had had hundreds of men, picked by their leaders, passing through my hands. There was no way I could have picked a group of soldiers whom I knew. It was one of those things which happen in war – wrong, but inevitable.

I told him how my spirits rose when nine men had eventually volunteered to come with me in the assault.

'I know,' said Paul. 'You could kiss them.'

I told him that during the assault I was gripped by a sort of frenzy, yelling and laying about me in a manic desire to kill. Then I told him of the moment when I had to decide whether to try to evacuate the wounded or abandon them.

'Of course I should have left them,' I said, and now my upper lip was not as stiff as I would have wished. 'It was a fatal misjudgement – but I just couldn't do it. They had been the ones out in front, they were screaming "Don't leave us", they relied on us to get them out, they deserved to be got out. But if we had buggered off as soon as we had chased the Germans out, we would have lost no more men, come back with several prisoners and done everything we set out to do. By trying to save four wounded men, I must have killed twice as many and allowed the attack to end up in a rout.'

'It happens,' said Paul. 'Sometimes a friend won't leave a wounded friend and gets killed, or you try to save life in a battle by doing something quite against the book and then things go wrong and it's a terrible cock-up. But it would be pretty awful if no one gave a thought to saving life.'

But I was inconsolable. I tried to rationalise my feelings of shame and failure. First, there was the heavy burden of having caused unnecessarily the death and capture of so many men. I would have to write to their wives and mothers and what could I say? The usual stuff about John being a gallant member of the battalion, and on his final patrol showing extraordinary bravery with total disregard for his own safety? What I would like to write was 'Please forgive me. It was my fault. I took a wrong decision. If I had taken the right decision, John would still be alive today. Please, please forgive me.' The second cause for shame was my sheer military incompetence. Here I was, critic

107

of the old army, ex-battle school commandant, specialist in the art of decision-taking under duress, and what had I done? Cocked it up.

I went to bed but, despite a shot of something in my tea, I could not sleep. In my desolation I got up and began to write a full account of the affair for Lionel, but a welcome whiff of common sense made me realise that ten days of strain in charge of the patrolling, culminating in this final disaster, was about as much as my nervous system could stand. I got a shot of morphine from a friendly medical orderly and slept for eight hours.

When I woke up I was surprised to discover that I was a hero. The patrol had been a success. There were congratulations from Swifty and from Division, not only on the whole patrolling exercise but on my gallantry and determination (or words to that effect) in leading the final assault. This struck me at the time as a fine example of army mendacity, comparable to 'withdrew in the face of stiff opposition' (ran away as they came under fire) or 'conducting a phased retreat to previously planned positions' (getting the hell out of it helter-skelter) and other gems of military PR doublespeak. Since then, too, I have read with incredulity the accounts of the patrol in the regimental and military histories of the Italian campaign. They are all couched in laudatory terms, the casualties are quoted at between five and nine and in general they report a successful little enterprise, a model of what a major fighting patrol should be.

But you can't fool the soldiers in the field. From that day on the gully in the escarpment with the Red Farm at its base was known throughout the division as Forman's Folly.

CHAPTER

9

Later that day, the twentieth of November, 'C' company of the Royal West Kents crossed the river and took up a position on the top of the escarpment: the start line for the divisional attack. It was some small consolation to learn that the Germans had evacuated Forman's Folly and indeed that the whole start line – from bridge to bridge, some three miles in all – was clear of the enemy.

Just after midnight the 'C' company commander arrived dripping wet at the OP where Paul and I were watching for signs of German resistance. He said he had come back (a little irregularly, I thought, for his place was with his men) to report the situation and to seek further orders. While we were talking, a signal came through from Division. The attack had been postponed for at least twenty-four hours because the tanks were unable to make the approach through the flooded ground to the river where the pontoons were being assembled. We discussed the prospect and after telephoning Brigade Paul decided (much to the relief of the 'C' company commander) to take the rest of the battalion across next day to reinforce 'B' company and to make the start line secure.

The following night I stayed behind in my OP with the battalion LOBs (left out of battle) all around me, moodily chewing inferior figs, for by now all the best had gone. On the twenty-third the Buffs crossed the river and relieved the RWKs who straggled back wet, muddy, hungry and mightily relieved to be out of the battle at last. The battalion collected itself in the dreary village of Paglieta and set about becoming a recognisable military unit once again: ablution centres provided hot showers, clean dry clothes were issued, old wet clothes were deloused and dried, incipient beards were shaved off, there were three hot meals a day, and six itinerant Italian barbers and a New Zealand dentist, whom I kicked in the chest when he tried to administer gas I thought unnecessary. He reported me to Corps HQ, but it was a long way away and nothing ever happened. But the chief activity was sleep. Men slept all night, slept by day in billets, slept in trucks and fell sleeping off the benches in the extempore canteen which had been rigged up in a church hall.

On 28 November I was woken by the distant thunder of big guns, our big guns, and I crept back to my old OP and watched with satisfaction the 4th Indian Division pass through the Buffs, over the escarpment and up the slopes I knew so well, and capture, one by one, Fossacesia, Santa Maria and Mozzagrognia. As I threw the last figs at the rats, which had become very numerous, I felt for the first time since my disaster a little cheerfulness breaking in. Patrolling had played its part.

I wrote a longish report of my patrolling activities to Lionel, who was still in hospital and reported to be very sick. All in all he was absent from the battalion for over a month. He described some of his experiences in Termoli in letters home, which once again valiantly conceal the effects of post-jaundice depression:

Dearest Cipolla,
You will notice that I have dug up your *real* name today. This is for a very peculiar reason. I was looking idly through my Italian dictionary when I discovered that *cipolla* is an Italian word meaning 'little onion' and really this seemed so appropriate that I thought I must start to use it again because that's just what you are – a little onion – my little onion . . . I am still at our rest flat and beginning at last to feel very much better. I have now gone completely yellow all over – but *completely*: even quite unmentionable parts of my anatomy – it is very remarkable. The treatment is still diet – no fats at all but plenty of fruit and sugar. I have been very lucky having got hold of six whole packets of American boiled sweets and I am munching these very contentedly all day long. I've lost an awful lot of weight again owing to the diet but that's all to the good really: I think those chins and that stomach have gone for good this time . . .

This is a very large block of flats – very like Bickenhall Mansions. It was occupied by German officers until a few days ago. The old lady who owns it has just come back lamenting (though there is very little damage) and has actually got a carpenter at work – just as if it were peacetime. I have had a long talk to her. Her chief personal grievance is that a German soldier pinched her spectacles because they were gold, so she can't see a yard. This is a pity as she is a really marvellous pianist even without her glasses. I am trying to get our doctor to give her some glasses.

110

By the way one of the Germans left his overcoat behind which I find very useful as a dressing gown. In one of the pockets is a letter from his sister talking about the Xmas parcels they are all excitedly preparing for him – and I have beside me an identical remark from you. Isn't it a funny business!

And later:

You will gather from the above remarks that I am now out and about. I am very much better, nearly all my yellowness has gone and I can just manage to toddle round. But I feel terribly weak – just as if I'm going to fall over every minute. I can't climb stairs at all. My old 'landlady' is a dear. The delicacies now pour in thick and fast and she comes in to see me about every hour. I've managed to do her a good turn though in getting her two new pairs of glasses out of the army authorities so she fairly beams at me now (She's like Auntie Maud, always putting on the wrong pair or losing one pair or pretending she can manage without them). I only told her once about you and the children and showed her the photographs but she has got all the names off pat and gets very excited whenever I get a letter from home. She has already invited you all to come out and stay here as soon as the war is over.

Paglietta was no more than a staging post. The division had been in battle continuously since the landing at Termoli in October. The RWK in particular had had a hard time – in the van all the way and losing more men on the Sangro than any other battalion. There were a thousand rumours: we were to be seconded to the 1st Army, now approaching Cassino, we were to be part of a seaborne landing in Yugoslavia, we were going back to base in North Africa for a rest and refit and (this one was a hardy annual) we were to be part of an army group going to reinforce the Russian front. When the news broke it was less exciting: we were to be in reserve at Campobasso, a provincial town in the Apennines some seventy miles away.

Paul sent me ahead in the advance party, some twenty in number led by the quartermaster, a short enigmatic figure whom I always suspected of villainy – as it turned out correctly, because in civilian life he fetched up behind bars. We had, however, the glorious opportunity of awarding ourselves the best billets and earmarking the second best for our friends and assigning some really disgusting accommodation to those we did not favour, such as the company commander of 'D' company, a greedy grasping fellow who always commandeered the best quarters and outwitted his peers in matters of comfort and high living. To him we allocated what could loosely have been described as a pigsty.

On the day of the battalion move the rain turned to sleet. As the vehicles churned their way up the mountain roads, some got stuck in the mud, two overturned and many had to be dragged up the steeper slopes by carriers, where bridges had been blown. The average speed was ten miles an hour, but at last they arrived, cheerful and eager to settle into our designated area: the small, trim Apennine hill village of Baranello.

The QM and I sat in the mayor's parlour answering questions, assuaging anger and dispensing information. Yes, there were four waterpoints for 'B' company; yes there was a hundred tons of firewood in a barn two miles away, but you had to provide your own transport; no, it was not possible tonight to change the billets of 14 platoon, they would have to put up with the goats, and so on.

The next morning dawned bright and frosty. There had been a light powdering of snow. As second-in-command, I had seen the battalion into its billets and had no immediate responsibilities. Nobody was stirring. I told the clerk at battalion HQ that I was going on a trip to Campobasso to secure provisions for the HQ mess, jumped into a jeep which the owner had carelessly left unattended, and drove to the top of the highest hill I could see.

I sat for half an hour boxing the compass with binoculars and map. There on the skyline to the north stood Campobasso, its outer ring of ten-storey tenements fringing it like a massive rampart; to the west were the mountains of the central Apennines; and all around were the steep pincushion foothills with black patches of woodland spatchcocked on their slopes, deeply serrated by the valleys of a dozen streams, receding in an unending chain of snowy summits as far as the eye could reach. The air was crystal: I could see ant-like peasant movements five miles away. The clarity of vision was matched by the clarity of sound: I heard two distant dogs barking as they hunted in a copse, the clamour of far-off schoolchildren let out to play, and the chip-chop of a couple of woodmen as they swung their axes alternately, felling in a clearing below. I was puzzled because the sound seemed not to be delayed by distance but synchronised with their blows, until they stopped

112

– and then I realised the chops reaching me were precisely one blow behind, for the last came winging its way to my ears while both men were resting on their axes, as in a film five frames out of synch.

I looked at the sun, at the snow and at my map and decided I would purge myself of the Sangro mud, clear my mind of the blood and death at the Red Farm and shake off the sense of shame and guilt which still hung around me like a bad smell. I would do it by walking. So I walked all day, and only once met another human being. Our conversation was sparse.

'*Tedesco?*' he said.

'*Scozzesi,*' I replied, and he nodded his head. It didn't seem to make much difference to him.

At dusk I drove back to battalion HQ, situated in a handsome house next to the mayor's. It was a scene of intense activity. Paul had called a company commanders' conference and the courtyard was full of jeeps and drivers, including one driver who was happy to be reunited with the jeep in which I was sitting. I put him on a charge for idleness and left him wondering how he would account for the low level of petrol in his tank.

Paul's O group was like a family reunion. Officers in an infantry battalion see little of each other in battle, except when one company commander visits another, or sometimes an O group gathers in an unsociably prone position behind a crestline, to receive orders. This military assembly soon became an entirely social event. There was no enemy within miles, there was no danger and no urgent need for anyone to do anything. As time went on roast pork was served and *vino* drunk in quantity, and this led to song. On the midst of a rousing rendering of 'For Those in Peril on the Sea', led, as ever, by Paul, I looked up to see Lionel standing in the doorway. His face was a ghastly greyish-green, he had lost a stone in weight and his ears, always protuberant, seemed to reach to each side of the door frame.

Singing stopped: Lionel was warmly greeted and carried shoulder-high to a stool. Drink was proffered from all sides, but he requested only a glass of fresh goats' milk. He had been told he would be released from hospital in a week's time, but had jumped ship that morning in a borrowed jeep. He felt he had to join the battalion at once, in case he was posted to non-combatant duties in the rear areas. Monty's staff would post him to ignominy if they

113

could. He required two bottles of whisky immediately to pay off his debt to the owner of the jeep, and these were promptly forthcoming from the braggart 'D' company commander (who in twenty-four hours had moved two farms up the social ladder and now had the best billet of all).

The battalion settled contentedly into a period of rest and recuperation, a little square-bashing, foraging parties for food and fuel, a few gentle field exercises, lectures on current affairs and twelve-hour passes to Campobasso where there was an army cinema, two brothels and a good deal of private enterprise.

For some reason Lionel and I were deemed to be responsible for officers' and other ranks' entertainment and I decided that the main feature for officers should be a grand ball to be held in Campobasso. To this end I recruited a small organising group: a company commander, one Ian Roper; the villainous quartermaster; my batman and a defrocked corporal who had been a band-leader in civilian life. Lionel preferred to pursue other projects. We soon identified the grandest family in the grandest house in the town, but met with some difficulty in that the *barone* and his wife had scarpered to safer territory near Venice, where they had an estate. Thus the senior member of the family was a pale but attractive young lady of eighteen who lived for art in all its forms and for art alone. Roper and I were the best the battalion could do in the field of the arts, but we were soon floundering. Even in English our ability to discuss Proust was limited, and in running over the finer parts of *Swann's Way* in Italian we were soon hopelessly adrift. I had high hopes of proving a match for her in music but, alas, she considered music had reached its zenith in the fifteenth century and was all downhill after that and not worth discussing. The reverse was true of painting: all painting before Mussolini's time was a religious hoax, or, if not that, an attempt to invent the camera before it was ready to be born, but there was a young group of abstract artists working somewhere near the Pontine Marshes who knew what real art was. Despite these strange enthusiasms, she had no zest for life: she was always listless and bored and affected a deep sadness which seemed to engulf her entire life. '*Sono sempre triste, Forman*,' she would say, drawing me aside and looking soulfully into my eyes while delicately holding my wrist, as would a doctor taking a pulse. '*Sempre triste.*' She repeated this act when alone with Roper and when I would ask him 'How was it today?' he would reply '*Sempre triste*'. And so the lady came to be known as Sempre Triste and we both courted her assiduously until she agreed to a ball in the baronial house at which she, as the leading aristocrat in the territory, would be the hostess.

The ball was a total disaster. The run up to it was bad enough. Sempre Triste revealed a malevolent streak behind her sadness and, whereas we had no difficulty in recruiting fifty officers from the division as the male guests, she found it hard to get much above thirty or so eligible young women who were fit to consort with such an aristocratic host. In despair, we went to her with women supplied by outside agents, but she was hard to please, screaming out '*schifosa*' or '*brutta*' at each name put forward. She treated the QM as a house servant and yelled at him like a harridan when he was unable to produce smoked quail breasts or a Neapolitan water-ice made with fresh seaweed.

On the night itself the first surprise was that each young woman was accompanied by her mother or a duenna. This increased the number by thirty per cent and we hastily sent out for more food. Then the execrable town band got drunk sooner than we had anticipated and, when the piper we had borrowed from the Argylls began to play, instead of setting about the business of learning how to dance reels and country dances, the guests formed a circle around him and gazed at him with eyes like saucers.

But worse was to come. I had noticed that every mother and every duenna was equipped with a singularly large handbag, some almost the size of a small sack. Roper and I had exchanged uneasy glances when we first saw them and feared what was to come. Sure enough, when supper was announced there was a stampede through the double doors into the supper room and a violent struggle broke out as each woman fought to fill her bag. Some worked a double act, the mother holding the bag open while the daughter scooped up the swag; some of the frailer old women were crushed underfoot; some of the more active leapt over the tables to reach the food on the far side. In two minutes it was over – there was not a morsel of food to be seen and no one had eaten a mouthful; not one chicken drumstick or sausage roll had enjoyed the dignity of even being put on a plate. As the female guests put

115

on their coats and ran for home, Sempre Triste surveyed the scene of devastation and with tears of rage shouted after them '*animali . . . brutte . . . cattive*'.

I was sharing a billet with Lionel. He had stood aloof from the ball and was drinking a glass of warm goats' milk. He was surprised to see me back so soon.

'How did it go?' he asked.

'Disaster,' I said and told him.

A slow smile spread across Lionel's face and he relapsed into what was rare for him – a fit of uncontrollable laughter.

'Not so funny really,' I said. 'Those people are near starvation and we never thought of it.'

But he continued to laugh until he at last gasped, '*Dio mio*. What a cock-up.' Our ball continued to amuse him over the next few days and undoubtedly helped to cure his post-jaundice depression. Indeed he was now becoming his old self again, moving around the several company areas energising every group he contacted and throwing himself into his new role with his usual energy. He wrote to his wife:

I am almost quite better now and am roaming around pretty cheerfully. As I am supposed to be convalescent, still I have been given a variety of odd jobs to keep me out of mischief. The first one is getting all the Xmas fare for the battalion. The Italians keep quite a lot of so called turkeys – miserable things (about the size of a large chicken at home) – but still turkeys. I calculate we will need about one hundred for one meal – Xmas dinner – so I have got two men who are chicken experts and have opened a turkey farm! I have got hold of a lot of children who run all round the local farms (this means climbing mountains) to advertise – and all day peasants come in from miles around in their queer peasant dress bringing turkeys, pigs, young cows, chickens and goodness knows what. I wish I had you here to manage the show for me because with your expert knowledge we should be really well off.

As it is I make all kinds of mistakes and birds die! Still it is going to be a wonderful sight to see our hundred turkeys all being fattened up for Xmas. In addition we are able to buy lots of oranges, and in the 'High Street' of the little town here we are fixing up two shops, one as a country pub and the other as a fish and chip shop – all looking very homely. I have even got hold of three fairly attentive women to act as barmaids – motherly types of course. We have got a large room fixed as a dance hall and cinema so Xmas is going to be Xmas after all.

Four Forman brothers Christmas 1942
Left to right Sholto, Lieutenant Royal Army Medical Corps: Michael, Captain, Kings Own Scottish
Borderers: Dennis, Major, Argyl and Sutherland Highlanders: Patrick, officer cadet.

Sangro Patrolling: Santa Maria as seen from 78 Division Patrolling O.P.

Sangro Patrolling: approaching to a forward O.P.

Civitella from the north: Majella out of picture right

The Majella massif from the fort, Civitella.

Nick Williams

Myself as a major in the Argylls

Lional Wigram, newly commissioned into the Royal Fusiliers

Guerilla volunteers outside the recruiting station, Casoli.
Damaged film taken from Lionel Wigram's camera some
weeks later.

Wigforce country: Fallo from Quadri

Wigforce Country – near Pizzoferrato

Pizzoferrato: the chapel and the First House.

QUESTO CROCIFISSO
MIRACOLOSAMENTE INCOLUME
DALLA FURIA NEMICA
CI RENDA INCOLUMI
NELLE LOTTE DELLA VITA
3 FEBB. 1944

The crucifix in the chapel as it is today.

My second rest job is not so amusing. I am having to run a school again for a lot of NCOs. I'm afraid I shall never get rid of my scholastic associations; they follow me around everywhere and it is going to be a lot of hard work for which I am not really in the mood; still I suppose the old enthusiasm will return once the plunge has been taken.

The third job is really amusing. When we occupy a town all sorts of problems arise. The civilians come pouring back from the hills to find their homes ruined or damaged, no water or light and no food. Somehow we have got to get things back to normal as quickly as possible and of course there is a big organisation for doing this, but in the smaller towns we have to do the job when we aren't fighting as they simply can't afford a special officer everywhere. So I am looking after this too just for a few days. It is tremendously interesting. Some of the people here are refugees who have got out of concentration camps after being imprisoned for more than two years. They include Russians, Poles, Yugoslavs and Czechs and their experiences would melt a heart of stone.

If Lionel was indeed reluctant to return to instruction, he certainly fooled me, for he tackled the job of improving the battle performance of our NCOs with apparent relish. We spent hours discussing the syllabus. It was not the enemy but fear of the enemy that was the greatest hazard in battle. The prime purpose of training should therefore be to cope with the manifestations of fear, such as running away, refusing to obey an order and shamming illness. But this was never mentioned in normal training. There were manuals for weapons training, drill, field engineering, map-reading, but no guidance at all on the matter of how to make soldiers fight rather than run away. The few references there were to morale concerned things like the importance of hot meals, acting in a smart and soldierlike manner, the prompt delivery of letters from home, and how drill was the basis for all discipline in battle, which we both agreed it wasn't. It was true that square bashing did induce an immediate reflex action to obey a sharply barked command, but even a modest degree of fear could nullify this. Nevertheless, in a fit of perversity, we decided to begin the course with a burst of high-powered square bashing, just to give everyone a surprise. We raked over the analyses of fear which Tom Main had propounded at Barnard Castle. We rated individually the strength of the will to fight in all the NCOs we knew. We also

117

debated the factors which augmented fear – lack of sleep, thirst, loud explosions, cold, the sight of blood, isolation – as well as those which diminished it – rum, hot food, a sense of community and occasionally anger.

It was against this background that Lionel set up his cadre. We scripted a score on more situations and selected half a dozen actors. We rehearsed them secretly in their roles and, when we were satisfied, the course began.

From the first day it went well. Lionel was delighted, as this letter shows:

> I am very very much better and as my course is going extremely well I am beginning to feel better and better every day. It is a very big problem having to handle a lot of men who have just come straight out of a battle and who therefore think they know all the answers. It is a tremendous relief to be able to say 'my experience was . . .' I was determined that the only course to be taken was to get hold of them right at the start and take the wind out of their sails, so just to surprise them we opened up with some 100 per cent guardee drill and plenty of it. They were so terrified at the end of the morning that one squad marched all the way home in threes at the slope up a very steep flight of stairs (which is what they have here sometimes instead of streets).
>
> As you know I am always happy as a schoolmaster.

Lionel would then set up some standard minor tactical exercise: A platoon attacking a farm, and all would go smoothly until the platoon commander leapt up to lead the assault and dashed forward, only to find that half the assault force refused to move. This surprised him greatly because such things did not happen in training. He would go back and urge them to obey, then perhaps put them on a charge, at which point they would run away, and if he tried to prevent them they sometimes got abusive and hit him. When the victim was thoroughly nonplussed, Lionel would stop the show and invite the audience to give their views. Since everyone recognised the reality of such scenes, discussion became animated and intense. Lionel ruled out the commonest school solution – to shoot, or to threaten to shoot the deserter – simply on the grounds that experience showed it didn't happen. The average junior officer or NCO in the British army was incapable of shooting a comrade in cold blood however efficacious it might be *pour encourager les autres*. If he *was* capable of doing so, perhaps he was not the right sort of man to be an officer or an NCO. Instead, he preached the importance of stratifying each platoon into men who would fight, men who would follow and men who would run away, and of deploying them in appropriate groups, each with its own sub-leader; of keeping in constant touch with each group even under fire; and of discussing the problem of fear openly and frequently.

We both enjoyed the course enormously and when it finished Lionel wrote to his wife in a very different mood from that of two weeks earlier: 'I am winding up the school tomorrow. It has been a very great success and I have really had a lot of fun with it.'

As with the battle-school movement itself, the fame of Lionel's activities spread by word of mouth and visitors from other units in the division dropped in to see for themselves what was afoot. Many who came as sceptics were converted, but some were not, and Lionel began to worry again that disturbing tales might reach Monty's ears.

Quite early during our stay at Baranello, I became aware that it was some six months since I had been in the company of a female. I decided to put that right. My first essay was with Amelia, a girl from Naples, whom I had met at the baker's. Lionel and I were both determined to master the Italian language and although we spent half an hour every evening coaching each other, we decided also to arrange Italian lessons with native speakers. Lionel, ever methodical, spent ninety minutes a day with the village school-master, whereas I found it both more instructive and pleasant to have my tutorials from Amelia. She had two equally beautiful sisters, younger than she, a mother of immense girth but modest height, and a father, Ettore: a small wiry man, the best pistol shot in Naples and president of the Naples pistol shooting club. Although the family had brought few of their possessions from Naples, he had pistols stowed away by the dozen all over the house.

The family had only one living room and Amelia and I sat at a table against the wall while family life went on around us. I would bring a couple of tins of bully beef or a compo-ration stew, and after the lesson we would sit down to mounds of pasta reinforced by my speciality and chatter and gossip far into the night. When

I crept into the billet in the small hours, Lionel would take me to task. He was critical of my socialising and correctly suspected that I had impure motives. He felt he had achieved more in a stiff ninety minutes with his schoolmaster than I could possibly have done in chattering with girls. I told him that it was terribly important to pick up the idiom of Italian youth.

As our lessons progressed, Amelia and I grew friendly. '*Amelia molta bella*,' I would write in the exercise book.

'*Forman: bella figura*,' she would reply.

I would reply, '*Per me Amelia è probabilmente la più bella ragazza di tutta Napoli, forse anche Sorrento e le isole.*'

Soon our lessons took place on two planes; sound, for we would continue to rehearse irregular verbs and the like for the benefit of the family; and vision, as we wrote what came to be longer and longer love letters to each other. Our knees came to touch quite a lot, and unobtrusively our hands, but further than this we could not go, for father Ettore watched us like a hawk, and with a pistol in nearly every pocket. I did, however, become more or less a member of the family and felt that their affection for me did not derive solely from my ability to slip them the odd gallon of petrol or packet of cigarettes.

One night some German planes flew over and dropped several sticks of bombs on the village. Instantly the four women dived under the table and started to scream. Ettore was disgusted. '*Corraggio!*' he shouted '*Siete femmine italiane.*' But nothing would shift them, even though the mother's vast bulk could scarcely be accommodated under what was a pretty large table. With her stomach on the floor, her back touched the underside of the tabletop, so every time she screamed the tabletop wobbled as in a spiritualist's séance. To make matters worse, there was not quite room enough for all four and whenever the mother felt some part of her anatomy threatened with exposure, she would fling out one of the girls, who would then desperately force her way back into the mêlée. Meanwhile Ettore stood by urging them to be brave, to remember that they were Italian women, until a bomb dropped very close, when his stream of imprecations ceased. '*Mia Mamma*,' he said, going white, and then, as a second crashed into the house next door, '*Dio*,' and with that he jumped into the chimney.

Another night soon afterwards a blizzard blew up, and by the time we had eaten dinner the snow was deep and drifting.

My billet was some distance off and Ettore invited me to spend the night on the kitchen couch. I accepted and in a final short lesson with Amelia I wrote 'May I come to see you tonight?' to which she replied 'Be careful.'

I knew she slept in a small box-like area between the bedrooms of her parents and the two younger girls. When the house was quiet I crept along the passage and opened the door. The room was larger than I thought it should be, and suddenly there was a noise as if a large cat had been disturbed in its lair and someone was standing in front of me. The light went on and I found I was looking down the barrel of a pistol, held in the best Neapolitan style by Ettore in a long grey nightdress, whilst behind him his wife's massive bulk pitched and tossed on the *letto matrimoniale*.

'*Mi scusi*,' I said. '*Non è il gabinetto?*'

But he wasn't fooled and when I went for my lesson the following night Amelia had gone to stay with an aunt in Capua.

My next adventure was in Campobasso after a performance by an ENSA concert party. I and two or three other RWK officers took the cast off to supper. I found myself attracted to identical twins billed as Smeralda and Smerilda who, together with a huge blond young man named Leo, made up a juggling act. As the evening went on and the party dwindled, the twins, who addressed each other as Dot and Dottie, apparently indiscriminately, became affectionate and I found myself with one leaning against each shoulder with an identical degree of intimacy. By now the party was reduced to us three and Leo, who I imagined had some *droit de seigneur* over the twins, but, no, he yawned, flexed his huge biceps two or three times and said he was off to 'it the 'igh. In a trice we were in the girls' bedroom upstairs where they set about stripping off in a matter-of-fact way just as if they were changing for the 800 metres. In a very short time they were lying stark naked on each side of the *letto matrimoniale*. The large expanse in the middle was evidently meant for me and, after undressing more deliberately and with greater modesty than they had done, I cautiously filled the empty space. I put my right arm round Dot and left arm round Dottie (or vice versa), receiving from each an identical response. But as matters progressed I encountered a difficulty. If I favoured Dot at the expense of Dottie even to the slightest extent, the less favoured twin immediately took reprisals, pushing and shoving and using her elbows to assert her equal rights. I was perplexed.

121

The conventional script for a man in bed with two girls assumed co-operation: all manner of high jinks could take place so long as all three were going at the thing in a harmonious spirit. But here we had rivalry. There was no sign of any give and take, much less co-operation. For perhaps ten minutes I indulged in subterfuges and elaborate tactical schemes to lull one into the belief that she was the primary target while slipping into secret intimacy with the other. It was no good. I decided to make a dash for it, and thrusting Dot (or Dottie) aside, I seized Dottie (or Dot) in a violent embrace and began to make love to her. It was a good try, but Dot (or Dottie) seized her sister's hair with one hand and tried to twist off one of my ears with the other. Passion could not be sustained in the face of such excruciating pain and we all fell back on the pillows panting. The girls were now moody. I tried reasoning with them. We would toss. The winner and I would have a little time together while the other went back to the bar. Then a change of partners.

'I'm not leaving her alone with you,' said Dot to me.

'And I'm not leaving him alone with you,' said Dottie to Dot.

It seemed hopeless. 'Why don't we all go to sleep?' I said.

They lay down and soon I heard identical snores. Stealthily I crept up on the right-hand twin and touched her gently on the shoulder. She responded and soon, with the minimum of movement, it seemed that things might go all right when, alas, Dot or Dottie with whom I was engaged let out the faintest of sexual cries. This was enough to make the other Dot or Dottie spring on us like a tigress, scratching, biting, swearing and hitting us over the head with the bedside lamp.

I got out of the bed and as I slowly put on my trousers I heard the gentle identical breathing of both twins, sleeping like babies. Slinking downstairs, I spent the night on a settee in the bar, wondering whether the extraordinary twins had put on their act simply to tease, whether they were subconsciously protecting each other's virginity (if any), or whether identical jealousies genuinely raged in their identical breasts.

My third and final attempt to bring some romance into my life at Baranello was the shortest and most painful. Paul and I had secured a twenty-four-hour leave in Naples, and after an evening of convivial drinking with several friends of Paul's who were stationed, it seemed, at points very far apart, we all fetched up at what appeared to be an officers' mess party of some significance. There was dancing, and I found myself partnered by a tall red-haired girl with snow-white skin and a substantial but elegant bust. In no time at all we were good friends. She was a VAD, she came from Perth, she adored the Argylls and she had a flat gill bottle of Johnnie Walker strapped to her leg. We sat down, unstrapped the Johnnie Walker and demolished it. It was, I remember, warm to the point of being hot. We danced again and then I revealed that I had a half bottle of Haig inside my battle-dress blouse (which I had been planning to take back as a peace offering to Ettore). We sat down and drank that. It was warm, but not so warm as the Johnnie Walker. We then danced again, with abandon. We made a slightly confused plan. She had a room to herself in a nurses' hostel and there was a fire escape. Before leaving we withdrew into an alcove for an urgently desired embrace. In the course of the embrace she suddenly went limp in my arms and slumped to the floor. Christ, I thought, she's passed out. I laid her across three chairs and went to get a glass of water. I prised her upright and held it to her lips, upon which she seized my arm and sank her teeth deep into the side of my hand. I jumped back and fell over a table. A knot of concerned young officers gathered round. One bound my hand, now streaming with blood, another went to get his jeep. We delivered the lady to the hospital inert – all handling her carefully in case she should snap again. I then went to Casualty where I got a dressing for my hand. I thought of an anti-rabies injection, but rejected the idea. We all drove back to the mess, where I joined up with Paul.

'What happened to you?' he asked looking at my hand.

'Bitten by a nurse,' I replied.

Back at Baranello, before we went to bed Lionel and I sat most nights on either side of the wood stove in our greatcoats. Outside the zone of the stove's heat it was bitterly cold. As we thawed out, we opened the front of our coats to let in the warmth, revealing, in Lionel's case, two pairs of long johns, one on top of the other, tartan golfing stockings up to his knees and a school scarf around his neck. More conventionally, I slept in my battle dress.

The talk was almost exclusively of training, of tactics, or of the possibilities of Lionel's redeeming his status vis-à-vis Monty, but occasionally it became personal.

I discovered that Lionel had been the *enfant terrible* of the solicitors' trade, defying convention, pulling off well-nigh impossible deals and introducing the unfamiliar notions of speed, aggression and accuracy into the work he did for his clients. He was immensely successful and had been entrusted with one of the biggest deals of the decade: the sale of Lord Bute's estates in Wales. By the time he was thirty he was earning £30,000 a year – a staggering sum in days when a middle-aged man might think £5000 a year a good income.

'How do you keep in touch?' I asked.

'I don't,' he replied.

'But all those millionaire clients. Who's looking after them? Won't some slip away?'

'Most will stick with the firm until I return. Or if they don't they'll come back when I do.'

'But all that money milling around,' I said. 'Who watches the investments?'

'My colleagues,' said Lionel. 'I've handed over everything. I've put a lot of my clients' interests in trusts. The day I joined up I had to sign hundreds of documents. It took about twelve hours.'

'Do you get reports as to how things are going?'

'I don't get reports. An occasional letter.'

'What do you do if you read of some financial disaster in the press?'

'I don't read the financial pages.'

'If a client writes to you? Lord Bute?'

'I would send it back.'

'So you have cut out completely?'

'I have opted out of my business life. No time for it. When we've won the war I'll get back to it – and I'll see what I feel.'

He'll probably come out all right, I thought. People who have faith on that scale are usually winners.

I asked him about his family. Did he think of them a lot?

'In time, not a lot,' said Lionel. 'But when I do it is intense and sometimes painful.'

'When do you do it?' I asked.

'I make occasions,' said Lionel. 'Every night before I go to sleep and on route marches.'

'Route marches?'

'A route march is good. The movement helps your mind to

124

drift. There are no interruptions. Pleasant nostalgia can come drifting over you on a route march. The best kind of nostalgia. Short reminders can be painful. Pangs. The sadness of being parted. Fear, the fear of the unknown.'

'The unknown?'

'I love and trust my wife. I can't believe for a moment that she could be unfaithful. But you can't kill the fear of the other man. Everyone has it. Anyone who says he doesn't is a liar.'

'Any other fears?'

'Illness, accidents – nothing to match the other one.'

Lionel was less communicative when we talked about religion. He was interested in my robust atheism and often quizzed me about my Scottish upbringing.

'And what about you?' I asked. 'As an atheist yourself and with a mind like yours, you can't possibly believe all the rubbish that hangs around the Jewish religion.'

'What rubbish?' he asked sharply.

'Well, the dietary laws for one thing,' I said. 'Clear practical instruction for good food hygiene in a hot climate. But now we have refrigerators, outdated.'

'Not entirely,' said he. 'They have a symbolic meaning.'

'Symbolic? Symbolic?' I said, 'Symbolic of what?'

'Only pure food should enter the body, only pure thoughts should enter the mind.'

'But the beef and mutton you get at a good butcher *is* pure. So is the pork. So what is so wrong in eating a hygienic pig?'

'Jews see the pig as a dirty feeder. Also shellfish.'

'Dirty feeder? What about all those red mullet hanging around the sewage pipes in Taranto harbour? The filthy *rouget* is not proscribed because the dietary laws pre-dated sewage pipes. It doesn't make sense. And what about that ridiculous Jehovah, the God of Wrath, mean, cruel, vindictive . . .'

But by now Lionel was in a huff. He turned his back on me and hunched his shoulders over a detailed study of the Cassino front.

When we discussed politics, I found that Lionel tended to be liberal in intention but authoritarian in devising structures to execute his liberal policies. He had a romantic notion that something like the battle-school movement could be founded in civilian life to clean up politics and to promote rational social policies.

'Not a good idea,' I said. 'Oswald Mosley had it and look how that turned out.'

'But people like you and I could never turn into fascists.'

'Maybe not you and I, but a political party must get votes. Either from the left or the right. Policies must be identified with personal interest as well as ideals. Enlightened liberalism will not get enough votes.'

'But look what we've done in the army. We've changed attitudes. We've changed policy. Why should we be afraid to try the same thing in civilian life?'

So the argument would go on. I thought Lionel's defence of the Jewish religion unworthy of him and his political views naive, but the closer we became the more conscious I grew of the drive and honesty of his intellect and his almost superhuman powers of application. He had by now examined in detail the whole allied front and decided to which theatre we were most likely to be posted.

He turned out to be nearly right. Suddenly one night an O group was called and Paul told us the battalion was going to move into the line near Castel di Sangro. This had been Lionel's first choice, and he pulled out the relevant map for all of us to see. We travelled for hours in two trucks and did a dawn reconnaissance of the new position. But it came to nothing. The order to move was cancelled and we settled back for a few more relaxing days at Baranello.

I knew that the time could be put to good use. Neither Lionel nor I had command of a company (I because I was second-in-command, Lionel because his old company had been taken over by another when he went sick). The four companies of the battalion were therefore all commanded by veterans of the North African campaign (De Freitas, Miskin, Roper, Wakefield) and two of them at least made no secret of the fact that they felt they and not I should have become second-in-command. Although they respected Lionel, they saw him as something of a visiting academic and the pair of us as an intrusion into their happy family. They were a close-knit group and vied for the good opinion of Paul, whom they admired just this side of idolatry. I had no North African experience, I was younger than they, and I had been a close friend of Paul and took up time which might have been spent with them. All this was bad news and I knew that there were bridges to be built and bonds to be formed, for it was now known that after Christmas Paul was to take a long trip round the hospitals of Algeria visiting the battalion wounded and that I would be in command of the battalion.

So, with Paul, and sometimes alone, I assiduously visited, dining at company headquarters, watching exercises, judging competitions, listening to personal problems, until I felt that I was coming to be regarded as part of the management and not just a bastard from out of town. The culmination of our visiting régime came on Christmas Day, when Paul, Lionel and I were faced with the daunting prospect of eating five festive dinners between noon and 7 p.m. Paul, whose appetite was immense, fared better than I, but for all of us it was easier to dodge the food than the drink. Heel-tapping was thought unmanly in regimental messes and as the afternoon wore on I thought nostalgically of Grey McKelvie, an ancient Argyll major, the relic of an earlier age, who had a small tank built into his sporran for the double purpose of receiving unwanted whisky when he was forced to drink with the boys beyond his capacity, and also (for he had a weak bladder) to act as a reservoir for micturition on official occasions when a dash to the loo was not on the cards.

Our final dinner was with 'D' company, for which the braggadocio company commander had ravaged the surrounding countryside and, I suspect, the larders of some private citizens. There was turtle soup, followed by a strange mashed-up fish dish with curry, followed by roast sucking pig, black pudding, guinea fowl or turkey, plum pudding, mince pies and then bananas and custard and four different wines. Finally the dreaded host presented Paul and me with tumblers holding at least half a pint of choice old brandy. Paul, amazingly enough, stood up to make his usual perfectly considered speech and, in giving the toast of 'D' company, drained the glass to the bottom. Meanwhile, I cautiously poured the bulk of my brandy into my boots, which retained its bouquet mingled with normal foot smell to the last.

Later that night the officers of the battalion plus a few guests, in all thirty-two souls, sat down to their own Christmas dinner which none could eat since it was the second for everyone and for our trio the fifth. Only the egregious 'D' company commander, who shared with the ruminant kind a capacity for continuous intake of food, put on a show of conspicuous consumption. Singing broke out

127

early, Paul and I alternating with Hymns Ancient and Modern and scatological ditties enshrined in The Book. After dinner we played 'News of the World', described here by Lionel:

I have invented a new party game which is sweeping Italy – quite by accident. I'm sure it will be a big success at home. It is called 'News of the World', and we play it here whenever there are enough of us together. It all happened like this. We were rather bored one evening so started to play 'The Game' – you remember? It went fairly well but we soon got tired of it and I happened to pick up a copy of the 'News of the World' which someone had received from home. It occurred to me that some of the incredible stories which appear in that paper, if acted in the same way as The Game but with a running commentary by a live commentator, would be incredibly funny. They are usually about a man who commits bigamy seven or eight times, which gives everyone a part. The game is acted just as if it were a film with the commentator reading the script from the newspaper. Our officers now take it very seriously – they dress up for their parts and rehearse and produce new twiddly bits every time. We have a book with all the cuttings in it which gives us a very varied repertoire. You ought to try it with some of your girls. It is the funniest game in the world.

I must confess that I was somewhat nettled when I read of Lionel's claim to have invented 'News of the World'. I thought I had. Certainly we acted as joint producers and, as he says, built a wonderful repertory of striking cases, among which were such favourites as The Romford Lad (sexually assaulted in a train by a vicar); the Rottingdean Dentist (whom we introduced with a jingle containing the immortal couplet: In a fit of depravity/He filled the wrong cavity); the Plumber's Mate (after intimacy in the bedroom walked off with the housewife's loose cash and watch, of which seventy-two were found in his lodgings). This production culminated with the chorus:

> He offered his services free
> And was plumbing his third after tea
> When she cried 'Stop your plumbing
> There's somebody coming'
> Said the plumber, still plumbing, 'that's me'.

How Lionel thought that such a game even in bowdlerised form could be suitable for his family I do not know, but in the mess it certainly went with a swing. Lionel's zest for life was now fully restored: he was not only accepted by his fellow members in the mess but had become a central figure, often the life and soul of the party. As he steered me to bed that night, I was vaguely aware that Lionel was showing me a map and pointing to the upper Sangro valley in a meaningful way.

The following morning Paul told me our next destination was Casoli, where we had been assigned a ten-mile sector on the upper Sangro valley at the western end of the central front. He was leaving on his African trip the next day. I went to Brigade to get my briefing, wondering what the next few weeks held in store.

10

O N NEW YEAR'S DAY 1944 I stood at the topmost point of the church tower in the hill village of Casoli. Next to me the outgoing commander pointed out in the crystal air relevant features in the landscape. He towered above me, for not only was he standing one step up, but he was six foot six in height and dressed extravagantly in the tradition of the desert, but now for cold weather. He wore a white beret, Monty-style, an old fur coat, and around his neck he had draped what could only be described as an Astrakhan boa. All of this, plus the fact that he affected a monocle and a huge moustache, helped to explain his nickname, which was Willie Boy. In conversation he affected several strange conceits, one of which was to refer to the enemy as Mr Smith.

'Mr Smith had the cheek to try to cross the bridge down there last night,' he said. 'But we gave him a dusting and he went boo-hoo and ran away. Vairy vairy fast.' As he went on to chatter about the suitability of the Abruzzi woods for pheasant shooting I surveyed the scene.

The strategic picture was clear. Twenty miles away to the east the Adriatic shone in the sun. The Germans had been pushed north some fifteen miles up the low coastal strip nearly to Pescara, the eastern anchor for their winter line. To the west the huge wall of the Majella massif sprang almost vertically from the plain. The Sangro ran straight as a die from the centre of the Majella through my old patrolling ground to the sea, but about five miles from where I was standing it dived to the south and ran up a deep valley to Castel di Sangro in the very heart of the Apennines. The Allied line ran along this valley, holding both sides for the first ten or twelve miles and then ceding the west bank to the Germans. Between the upper Sangro valley and the great mountains lay an extensive no-man's-land, twelve miles wide at its broadest and coming to an apex where I was standing in Casoli, with the Sangro in front and the mountain wall behind. It was lumpy, broken territory: steep

Map 6

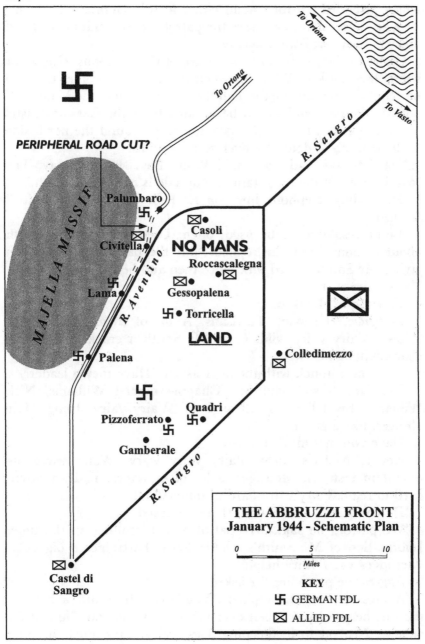

PERIPHERAL ROAD CUT?

MAJELLA MASSIF

Palumbaro

Civitella

Casoli

NO MANS

Roccascalegna

Lama

Gessopalena

Torricella

LAND

Palena

Colledimezzo

Quadri

Pizzoferrato

Gamberale

R. Sangro

R. Aventino

To Ortona

To Ortona

To Vasto

R. Sangro

Castel di
Sangro

THE ABBRUZZI FRONT
January 1944 - Schematic Plan

0   5   10
              Miles

KEY

卐 GERMAN FDL

⊠ ALLIED FDL

sharp foothills up to 3000 feet high, only just agricultural, dotted with hill villages perched on high points and pinnacles, each one of which provided a strong point either for the Germans or for us. Around these island fortresses the patrols of both sides ebbed and flowed. There was snow everywhere.

Castel di Sangro was at the centre of the Germans' Gustav or winter line. I asked Willie Boy whether the two ends of the German line could communicate through the road in front of the Majella? If not, the Pescara end would be isolated from the Cassino–Castel di Sangro end. They would have to travel around the north side of the massif – a detour of over seventy miles.

'Hard to say, old boy,' said Willie Boy. 'Hard to say. The road in front of the mountain on our side is out of our reach.'

'Have they telephone lines on it? Is it used by Mr Smith?' I asked.

'Lines yes, used to be used, often. Used a lot by Mr Smith about a month ago,' he replied. 'But the partridges have been giving Mr Smith a hard time since then and he is now very wary. Vairy vairy wary.'

'Partridges?' I asked.

'*Partigiani*,' he said. 'Partisans. A lot of them about. Wild fellows. Vairy vairy wild. Gave Mr Smith a crack up the arse near Civitella last week.'

'Are you in touch with them?' I asked. 'Have they a leader?'

'Very much so,' said he. 'Chappie named Williams, Nick Williams. Big fellow as tall as I am. Vairy vairy strong. Hair all over, like a gorilla.'

'Have you met him?' I asked.

'Not I. Nick is wary. Vairy vairy wary. Won't leave his mountain fastness. Messages, a lot of messages. Badly written, hard to read. Vairy vairy hard to understand.'

'Do you patrol actively out there?' I asked.

'We patrol,' he said. 'We patrol, yes. Patrolling all the time. Information of Mr Smith's whereabouts. Partridges a big help. Partridges vairy vairy helpful.'

'Aggressive patrolling?' I asked.

'Aggressive, no,' he replied. 'You give Mr Smith a belt on the ear, he gives you a belt over the arse. Tit for tat. No rest for anyone. No end to it. Sleeping dogs, vairy vairy much sleeping dogs. Specially in this bloody snow. Mr Smith – Alpine troops.

Alpine Mr Smith has snow clothes, skis, very mobile. Sleeping dogs best.'

I went on quizzing Willie Boy about his dispositions and those of Mr Smith until the light began to fade and, at the third time of asking, I accepted his invitation to join him for a 'refresher' in the HQ mess in what was once the albergo at the foot of Casoli's central pinnacle.

Next day I started at first light and visited all the troop dispositions in the battalion area. There was a company in Roccascalegnia up a road which ran deep into the foothills from the point where the Sangro made its dive to the south – a Walt Disney village with a buttress of rock two hundred feet high in the middle, surmounted by a chapel. Then to Gessopalena, a mile and a half from Roccascalegnia as the crow flies, but twelve miles by jeep along snow-blocked roads. Everywhere I saw men in foxholes, their fingers numb, their eyebrows festooned with hoar frost, stamping their feet to keep their circulation going, or more often curled up in a deep hibernative sleep from which, I thought, if they were left alone, they might never wake.

Gessopalena was a ghastly sight. Half the village, which was perched on a high rocky spine, had been demolished by the Germans. They had blown up over fifty houses at three in the morning while the inmates slept. Only a few of the bodies had been extricated and the stench of death was everywhere. Three miles away, on a still higher perch, stood the village of Toricella. Was it occupied by Mr Smith? I asked Willie Boy.

'Off and on, yes certainly, vairy vairy occupied.'

'By patrols? Or is it permanently manned? A strongpoint?' I asked.

'Hard to say,' said Willie Boy. 'Firing sporadic. Mr Smith uses the tower as an OP. May be there all hours, may not. Vairy vairy hard to say.'

'No information from partridges?' I asked.

'No partridges here,' he said. 'All partridges near Majella. This too far for Nick.'

Again I looked at the shivering semi-conscious men in their open foxholes and wondered what would happen if Mr Smith did make a sudden determined daylight raid.

Back at the mess, Willie Boy sat down in front of a roaring fire, called for whisky and set his batman the task of extricating him from a pair of highly polished hunting boots.

'So what do you make of toy town, old boy?' he asked.

'A lot of snow and an awful lot of territory,' I replied. 'Tell me, what were your orders when you were posted here? What were you told to do?'

'Do? Do? Occupy. Be here. Buffer between our line and Mr Smith.'

'You weren't given a brief to cut the line between east and west? To be aggressive?' I asked.

'Nothing like that, old boy,' he said. 'Nothing at all. Be prepared against attack. Vairy vairy prepared. Not aggressive. Never aggravate Mr Smith or he will aggravate you. That's my motto.' And with that he played, for the fifth time since my arrival, the dwarfs' marching song from *Snow White* on the mess gramophone, urging all present to join in. I had taken a great liking to Willie Boy and was sad when next day he departed on some mysterious mission to Bizerta. 'Vairy vairy hush-hush, old boy,' he said.

On the third of January the battalion moved out of Baranello as the snow began to fall. It snowed all day, and the wind blew and formed drifts up to six feet deep. Progress was slow and they did not arrive until late on the fifth, having had to overnight en route. We had rum, hot food and roaring fires awaiting them in Casoli, but after only three hours they had to move out to relieve the sitting tenants, already twenty-four hours behind schedule.

I took a firm initial decision. I would put everyone, so far as possible, inside buildings. Men in slit trenches became so cold as to be ineffective within a few hours. I would put one company in Roccascalegnia and one in Gessopalena and eliminate all the outposts and platoon positions Willie Boy had spread across the access routes. I would keep two companies under my hand in Casoli. By the end of the next day ninety per cent of the battalion had fire positions inside buildings and those men who were in slit trenches were relieved every two hours.

When I got back at dusk from a complete round of the battalion positions, I found Lionel waiting in the mess. He had fought his way back from Naples (where he had been on a short leave) through the snow. It had taken him five days and he described his adventures in a letter home:

134

I had a very exciting time getting back off leave. The place where I spent my holiday was very warm and sunny but you haven't left there very long when you find yourself right up in the mountains and in the snow. We went on and on as I had to get back but finally ran into a full scale blizzard. I haven't been in a blizzard before and didn't know how frightful they are. The snow is driven at you by a very high wind and it hits your face at such a speed that every little piece seems to cut like a red hot needle. Visibility was down to about three yds – a sort of impenetrable fog wall of snow in which it was quite impossible to drive on. The only thing for it was to get out and try to find shelter – it was beginning to get dark. When we got out we found after some time that it was only possible to walk forward backwards (Irish) taking an occasional painful peep in order to avoid falling. We found a whole row of lorries ahead of us but the drivers were Indians and couldn't understand a word we said. I cursed them – and then found I had been speaking Italian! I tried English but they couldn't understand that either, so we just left them to it.

We finally came to one of those typical Italian farms – 3 rooms 6 children 6 grown ups and the usual pigs donkeys pigeons dogs and chickens. They were even poorer than usual but made us welcome for the night. The way they lived was amazing. All the food they needed for the whole winter was stored inside the house – mostly under the beds and tables, and they reckon to stay indoors throughout the snowy season. The children's clothes were all rags: no gloves or stockings and their food consisted of two meals per day, mostly cabbage. The whole family sat in the evening round a tiny charcoal fire and ate in turn out of one bowl of cabbage broth. Fortunately I had a large box of food with me including sweets, meat and cigarettes so we gave them a party the like of which they had never before seen. I wish you could have seen the children's faces as they sucked the sweets, taking them out of their mouths every few minutes to feel them and make sure they were really there.

Lionel was highly excited.

'Have you heard about the partisans?' he asked.

I told him I had.

'There are enormous possibilities,' he said. 'I've been talking to three of them for the last two hours. Come and meet them – they're in the café.'

But I thought not. We sent a message for them to come to see us in half an hour in the battalion office. I made Lionel put on his best battle dress and a tie, and I did the same. We got the RSM and two orderlies to smarten up and the little charade opened with the RSM ushering in the three peasants with 'Partisans to see the commanding officer, sah'. They were marched in and sat down, duly impressed, and after appropriate formalities (I offered them thanks for their good work on behalf of King George VI), we started to talk, they in the strong Abruzzi *patois* and Lionel and myself in our still-halting Italian.

There were many of them. Perhaps a hundred. Nick Williams was their leader. He had learnt English during ten years in Chicago, where he had been employed by Al Capone. There were many other men of Civitella who had been to Chicago. Most of them had worked for Al Capone. They had killed seven Germans. They fired on any Germans using the road around the foot of the mountain. The Germans were brutal: they had taken reprisals on the families of two of the partisans, first raped the women and then shot every one. The German battalion HQ was in Palena, some six miles south down the mountain road to Castel di Sangro. Their forward permanent position was in Lama, just two miles away on the same road. The Germans pillaged farms and if anyone remonstrated they shot. And so on. Their main message was that they needed arms and ammunition. Without these, their capacity to fight would diminish.

Lionel and I asked them to leave us alone for a moment. We decided to send a formal message in Italian from the Allied Forces in Italy to Nick Williams, summoning him to a meeting in Casoli the next day. While this was being typed, we invited the three partisans into the mess where toasts were drunk to the Allied cause, to Nick Williams, to freedom, Italy, England, Scotland, and death to the hated Tedeschi.

When the partisans had gone, singing cheerfully, we considered the next item on the agenda, an invitation to dinner from the baron who resided in a large quasi-palace occupying one whole block in the centre of Casoli. Lionel thought we should not accept. There were rumours that he was a fifth columnist, certainly he was not loved by his tenants, as we had learnt from our three partisans. I thought we should go: if he were a fifth columnist, he would hear nothing from us and we might learn something from him. It would be folly to miss a chance of gaining local intelligence, and a good meal and a bath were included in the invitation. We went.

The gates of the baron's palace were on the scale of an Oxford college, but there was no man-size aperture for human beings, so the whole vast structure had to be opened by two manservants who wore peasant trousers and boots from the waist down but whose upper parts were adorned by velvet jackets which had once been part of a livery, piping and all.

The baron received us in the great hall, in front of a blazing log fire. I thought someone had played a practical joke on me, for in front of my eyes stood Donald Wolfit. Not only did he look like the famous actor–manager, he spoke and moved like him. His deep port-wine voice and huge mobile face made his simple greeting – '*Cari amici inglesi, vi saluto e vi do il benvenuto a casa mia. Mi fa un gran piacere di vedervi*' – into an operatic recitative. He ushered us into the library, which was lined with books from floor to ceiling, and his three daughters rose to their feet as one. It was immediately clear who ran the household: the eldest girl, Francesca. She greeted us in perfect English and with an air of great authority told us of the arrangements, the colonel to have his bath first (I was a major), then dinner and the major (Lionel) to have his bath after the main course. Coffee and dessert would await his descent from the bathroom. She introduced, perfunctorily, her younger sisters who simpered and bobbed, and set us at ease by showing us a short history of the town of Casoli, written by an uncle. She kept up an amusing commentary in a silvery voice, occasionally interrupted by the deep diapason of her father interjecting '*è vero, è giusto*' or '*esattamente*'. After a few minutes she laid down the book and said 'And now, colonel, it is time for you to have your bath.'

When I came down the conversation had turned to law. She had discovered that Lionel was a solicitor. At the age of twenty-four, she had just qualified as an advocate in Rome. They debated the reasons why Roman law had taken root in some parts of Europe and not in others, the different concepts of law which influenced the Normans, the Moors and others. Occasionally the baron, a devoted classicist, walked to the bookshelves and plucked out from a volume a quotation from Virgil, Cicero or Thucydides which contained some ancient bromide about the law. Francesca could barely conceal her impatience at these paternal interruptions.

Dinner was ample and excellent, with French wine and white port. The four immediate family and the two guests dined at the high table. A little distance away at a much larger table in the recesses of the dining room sat assorted relatives, the factor, his wife and a priest. Among these I noticed a woman of striking beauty, with deep black eyes and a sensuous mouth. She was introduced as Cousin Elena.

The conversation was mainly about literature, why some authors were internationally known and others not. When we got round to Shakespeare the baron favoured us with several passages in Italian from *Hamlet*. But it was not until Lionel returned from his ablutions that he performed his *pièce de résistance* – the fables of Phaedrus declaimed with immense gusto from a standing position behind his chair. I felt some response was needed, so gave a rendering of two of the odes of Horace, using the pronunciation current at Loretto and Cambridge in the 1930s. This was evidently a great shock to everyone and the baron asked me to read them again. As he listened he gestured in pantomime with his huge hands; thus when I reached the line '*cras donaberis haedo*', he was leading a goat to its death, and when I read '*praecipe lugubres cantus, Melpomene*', he was playing the lyre with an expression of utter gloom. We demolished the white port, Francesca taking only a ladylike sip but her sisters guzzling it down like puppies.

As we walked home through the snow Lionel said, 'Probably is a fifth columnist.' I responded: 'Let's not put him in prison until we've had a few more dinners like that.'

Next morning before dawn we had a message from Nick Williams. He could not come to Casoli. It was too dangerous for him to leave Civitella. We were to come to Civitella. He had sent a bodyguard; there would be guides along the way; we were to follow the road he had constructed across the river below Casoli; all would be well.

I discussed this proposition with Lionel. Our route lay straight up the Aventino valley (a tributary of the Sangro) right to the base of the Majella. Here it joined the mountain peripheral road, which the Germans had been using to connect the two extremities of their line. They might be using it still despite the partisans' claim. But a few days before an AMGOT (Allied Military Government Overseas Territories) officer, poor innocent fool, had driven right round nearly to Civitella, not knowing where he was, to check the state of an electricity generating station. He had come to no harm. We decided to go in two bren gun carriers. The round trip would be about fifteen miles.

The first surprise was Nick Williams's road. It was about a mile long and crossed the river where the Germans had blown a long viaduct. Despite the snow, it had been well made and as we travelled towards the great overhanging cliff of the Majella we passed a dozen working parties making passable the gulleys and ravines where the bridges had been destroyed. In all we thought we had seen about two hundred men working on the road. When we reached the peripheral road we paused. There was no sign of the enemy. Round the first corner we came to the village of Fara lying at the bottom of a ravine at the base of the mountain. It had been completely demolished by the Germans and we could never have picked our way through the rubble without our partisan guides. As we ground our way up the side of the ravine towards Civitella, which stood crowning the ridge ahead, partisans leapt out from behind rocks and buildings and climbed aboard our carriers. By the time we reached the centre of Civitella we looked as if we were the advance guard of a victory parade.

We drew up at the base of a massive rectangular fort and were greeted by emissaries from Nick Williams. The outer walls of the fort were about thirty feet high. Inside there were buildings twenty feet wide all around with a sizeable courtyard in the middle. This was full of men, mules, sacks of grain and piles of snow-clearing tools. Next we entered the armoury, a collection of amazingly heterogeneous weapons, ranging from sawn-off shot guns and a tommy gun smuggled back from Chicago to Czech automatic weapons used in the Spanish Civil War, automatic rifles from Austria, sporting guns and a number of captured German weapons including an MG 34. We were led through the communal kitchen, where the partisans' women were poking and prodding steaming vats of boiling pork, to an upper room where, not to be outdone in matters of protocol, Nick Williams sat, flanked by his adjutant on one side and his second-in-command on the other.

Contrary to Willie Boy's information, he was not a tall man, perhaps five foot eight, but his girth was enormous. He wore his best blue suit with a white shirt, collar and tie, and was clean shaven – apparently just, for his face was patched with sticking plaster and cotton wool. He greeted us impetuously, with open arms, saying 'Hey, you guys, you come good time', upon which there was a brief orgy of hand-shaking and embracing.

'Comeonasee,' said Nick and we moved out on to the ramparts, from which we had a superb view of the battalion front. Nick went over the terrain methodically from left to right. 'No Teds thatta one', he would say. 'Fired, bruta bastards, all a-bust out', or 'Thatta one still visit, not much', and so on as we identified each farm and hamlet on the map. After an hour we went inside to a meal of pork, macaroni, cake and wine, and after lunch settled down to a long discussion.

Nick was clearly in command of his forces and well briefed on the tactical situation. He wanted British troops in Civitella to safeguard the women and children from a reprisal raid which he felt sure the Germans would mount if they could. He wanted arms and ammunition which matched each other. Half his present weapons (which he called 'gats') were useless because there was no ammunition for them and half his ammunition was useless because he did not have the right weapons to fire it. He wanted boots, binoculars, warm clothing and above all he wanted the priest to be shot. At this point Achille Gattone, the schoolmaster, and his wife (who had grown up in Chicago and was standing by as an interpreter) rushed into the fray with violent philippics against the priest, the mayor and other civic notables, all of whom were collaborators, traitors and fifth columnists. 'If Nick shoots the *padre* it will be strife in Civitella,' cried the woman. 'Many people church people, many black and still fascists. If British shoot, then OK no strife.'

Lionel and I withdrew. 'Better shoot at least one,' said the sergeant who accompanied us. 'We need the help of these people.'

'Buggered if we'll shoot anyone,' said Lionel. I agreed.

'We'll take all chief suspects as prisoners to Casoli and hold an enquiry to see what evidence there is. Then we'll decide,' I said.

'But will they wear it?' asked Lionel.

We went back. I explained that we took the most serious view of fifth columnists but we had to have evidence against the traitors in Civitella and this would entail interrogating the leading suspects at our HQ in Casoli. This was accepted (but it was the beginning of internal bickering among the partisans and their fellow citizens which was to become a threat to the whole enterprise).

We then settled down to a serious debate on tactics. We

140

decided that we would make an advance patrol base for a mixed force of British–partisan troops at Calazzotto, a hamlet about one mile away on a spur below Civitella, about half a mile short of the nearest occupied German position. We pointed out that there was no bridge over the river Aventino which ran at the foot of the valley between Casoli and Calazzotto and this would slow down the supply of ammunition and stores. Nick said he would have one constructed within twenty-four hours and have a partisan garrison in place in Calazzotto by first light. He also undertook to lay a telephone line and once again requested arms, ammunition and boots for the partisans and a 'mucha forces' with 'plenny guts' to garrison Civitella. We told Nick we would be back the next day for further reconnaissance. He said we should come direct across country by mule. He would arrange everything. As we road home, Lionel yelled at me above the roar of the carrier and I yelled back, and by the time we had reached Casoli we had a plan.

I would pass the responsibility for garrisoning Roccascalegnia to the battalion on our left. It was too far back to play any part in our scheme of things. Nothing was going to happen there. We would put a company into Civitella and mine the peripheral road at both ends as far east and west as we could. We would keep a standing patrol of partisans opposite each minefield, and cut all signal and telephone lines. We would get a troop of anti-tank guns if we could, in case of an attack by an armoured column. We would then have sealed off the mountain peripheral once and for all. Lionel would take command of a combined force of fifty to eighty men at Calazzotto, and immediately start pushing and probing the enemy outposts; if this went well, we would run another company into Calazzotto. We would set up a formal partisan force with its headquarters at Casoli. We were euphoric. Once back in the mess, I persuaded Lionel to have a rare dash of whisky in his goats' milk and we went off down to the baron's for dinner in high feather.

The dinner was as long and as jolly as before and we stayed later than we would have wished for a Chopin recital which Francesca had prepared for our benefit. She played enchantingly well, with bold delivery and power, the only negative factor being the baron, who turned the pages. He displayed the appropriate emotion for each piece, sometimes clutching his heart with his spare hand, sometimes using the mobility of his huge face to indicate the tension of a climax or allowing two massive tears to roll down his cheeks when sadness was the order of the day. Again I noticed Elena, and when she gave me a flashing glance something inside me jumped.

But as the evening wore on doubts began to arise in my mind about the day's exploits and as we walked back through driving snow I began to shout them out to Lionel.

'Nick won't leave Civitella, not because of the Germans but because he's afraid of losing command of the situation,' I said. 'Must be so. Maybe he has a rival for the leadership. Maybe it's fear of the fascists. He wanted us to shoot them. They are just as likely to shoot him.'

'But they've now got the main suspects locked up,' said Lionel. 'We told them to do it.'

'Might make it all the more likely they'll liquidate Nick and his friends in order to release the prisoners before we get there,' I said. 'And another thing, do the people on high want us to get all aggressive like this? It's second nature to you and me, but remember Willie Boy. Contain. Sit on your arse, don't stir it up. Maybe Brigade and Division won't support us if we have a bash, partisans and all.'

'You've turned chicken,' said Lionel as we entered the mess. 'It must be all that Chopin. We have a wonderful chance of doing exactly what the Japs did in Burma. With the help of the partisans we can get behind the German strongpoints one by one and wipe them out. We can push them back to Castel di Sangro.'

'Suppose we could,' I said, 'how would that really advance the cause? They will have to evacuate anyway as the line pushes north on the west side.'

This was too much for Lionel. His eyes blazed; he thumped the table. War was about morale, he said. If you weren't on the attack you were on the defensive. We had to be on the attack day and night; harry, scare, push, shove the German line; we had to cow them; force them back. Before long he was back at the maps, drawing circles and squares, regardless of the consequences, to show the stages by which we could demoralise and undermine the whole system of German strongpoints in the mountain area.

'All right,' I said. 'Tomorrow we will know whether or not

142

Nick can deliver the bridge and the garrison for Calazzotto. And I should at least inform Brigade that I have a madman on my hands who with a handful of Italian peasants intends to tear a hole in the centre of the Gustav line.'

11

BEFORE GOING TO BED I sent a signal to Brigade asking for a full discussion on patrolling policy and mentioning the possibility of working with the partisans; at first light I had a reply. Brigadier Spencer would visit Casoli that afternoon. Lionel and I figured we had time to get to Civitella and back, and set out to the rendezvous, where four villainous-looking partisans and two mules awaited us. We were to split into two parties of three, each party taking a different route. The journey would take about two hours each way.

Lionel wore the purple homburg he had cherished since Vineyard Hill and a black cloak. I wore a scarf around my head and a poncho. We had discussed the etiquette of dress at length. I held that so long as one wore battle dress underneath, any outer additions were permissible, and quoted the Americans in Algeria who wore all manner of fantasy clothing in action. Lionel doggedly held to the view that any attempt to conceal military uniform laid the wearer open to being shot, quite properly, as a spy. Nevertheless, we dressed as peasants, knowing that if we looked like soldiers we would be almost certain to be spotted by the vigilant Mr Smith.

As we moved out of Casoli in dead ground, it was clear that our progress was not going to be entirely smooth. Lionel had never ridden any form of quadruped in his life and the mule unsettled him. He tended to treat animals as if they were mechanical objects and there was a clear lack of empathy between the beast and its master. When we encountered a steep bank and the mule's back moved into an angle of some sixty degrees from the level, Lionel began to slip backwards. Panting heavily, he seized the mule's ears, which caused the creature to rear up and deposit him on the snow, where it made as if to roll on him. It was clear that progress would be quicker if Lionel walked. I had borrowed a pair of skis from Francesca with the idea of speeding down each hill and awaiting the mule party at the bottom, but this didn't work, for at the end of each ski run I found my companions had taken a different route and we wasted valuable time trying to find one another. So the skis were strapped to the mule, which promptly bit off the pointed end of one ski and put an end to the matter.

After crossing the river Aventino, running as black as pitch against the snow, we encountered a fresh hazard. The approaches to Civitella were dotted with farms; we passed one every four or five hundred yards. In the doorway of each was a welcoming committee ready to persuade us to drink to the success of the Allies and the death of all Tedeschi. Even though we pleaded pressure of time, we had at least to down a glass of *corto*, a strong black wine distilled, heated and mixed with honey. After the fourth toast I cast my eyes up the route to the ramparts of Civitella and calculated that at least three pints of *corto* lay ahead. My companions were downing it with equanimity and I decided that it would be better to appear chicken than to get drunk. At the next halt, in basic Italian and by mime, I explained that in Scotland it was the custom to pass each glass from hand to hand, as with a loving cup, and thereby managed a sip from each vessel, the remainder of the party happily supping up the balance.

We joined up with Lionel's party at the final ascent into the village and I noted that he was uncommonly cheerful.

'What a splendid hot drink that was,' he said, beaming. 'Was there wine in it?'

'Pretty well pure alcohol,' I replied.

'My God,' said Lionel. 'I thought it had a funny taste.' And he began to hum the last movement of Brahms' first symphony, which was his habit in moments of elation. When he stuck at the seventh bar, which he always did, I assisted him forward and we entered the ramparts of Civitella to the strains of one of music's most Germanic tunes.

Nick was in battle clothes. Gone was the blue suit and the tie and he had not shaved since we last saw him. We told him we would send British troops to Civitella if he would organise the partisans as we wanted. Was he prepared to come under command of British forces and obey orders implicitly? Yes, he was. Then there might be boots and arms for some of his men. Meanwhile, he was to form his forces into four platoons of thirty men each. Two were to be based in Civitella to guard the peripheral road; one was to take up a patrolling base in

145

Map 7

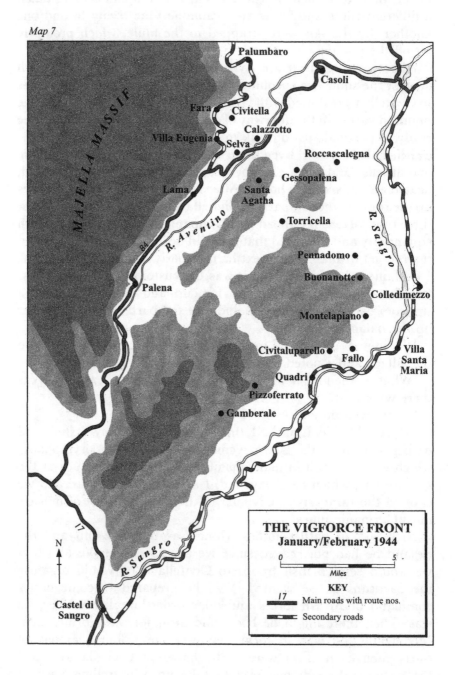

THE VIGFORCE FRONT
January/February 1944

Palumbaro

Casoli

Fara
Civitella
Calazzotto
Villa Eugenia
Selva
Roccascalegna
Gessopalena
Lama
Santa
Agatha
Torricella
Pennadomo
Buonanotte
Palena
Colledimezzo
Montelapiano
Civitaluparello
Fallo
Villa
Santa
Maria
Quadri
Pizzoferrato
Gamberale

MAJELLA MASSIF

R. Aventino

R. Sangro

84

N

17

R. Sangro

Castel di
Sangro

0   5
Miles

KEY

17   Main roads with route nos.

Secondary roads

146

Calazzotto, and the remaining one was to assist a small British force from Casoli to join the partisans in Calazzotto on the next day. A company of the 6 RWK would arrive in Civitella the day after that. He was to appoint commanders for each platoon who would report to Lionel and me at Casoli that night. They would be back before first light. He was to deploy a series of listening posts close to the enemy positions.

As we left Nick's command post on the top of the fort, the courtyard was packed with partisans anxious to show us the deficiencies of their footwear and their arms. Nick averted our being mobbed by calling for silence and making a short speech in which he said we were now brothers-in-arms, and as a combined fighting force we would demolish the Germans and return the Abruzzi to peace and prosperity. This was well received, and the alliance was sealed with yet another glass of the dreaded *corto*.

We hurried back to Casoli to find that the brigadier was already there with a small swarm of staff officers around him. News of the partisans had spread and they had become the most interesting item on a static front where there was not much for a brigadier to do.

Brigadier Spencer was no doubt a good husband and father and probably the very model of a modern brigadier, but he was not the man to fill the role of the late lamented Swifty Howlett, a ball of energy and high spirits, who had been killed by a shellburst on the last day of the Sangro battle. Brigadier Spencer had only one truly distinctive characteristic, which was to preface every remark with the phrase 'Yes I see'. We showed him the four partisans who had conducted us back from Civitella. 'Yes I see,' he said. We showed him their Albanian rifles. 'Yes I see, Albanian,' he said. We showed him the full tactical position on the map and he said 'Yes I see', a dozen times. Finally I said we wanted to form an official partisan force under the command of Lionel, and call it Wigforce. We wanted boots, arms and greatcoats for one hundred and twenty men. We wanted fifteen miles of signal wire, and several other items. At the end of it all the brigadier said 'Yes I see'.

There was long pause and I took the brigade major aside.

'Does that mean yes?' I asked.

'Can mean anything,' he said.

'Can we go ahead?' I asked.

'Depends if Division are keen,' he said.

'What's the likelihood of that?'

'Division will be keen if Corps are keen,' he replied.

'What will make Corps keen?' I asked again.

'I think Corps will be keen,' he said. 'Corps are very likely to be keen. Partisans are good news. Popski's Private Army, you know.'

'But I want to set up this force now, this afternoon,' I said. 'If we don't we'll lose momentum and the confidence of the partisan leaders. Can I do it? And another thing. What is the brigade's patrolling policy? I assumed from the briefing that we should be aggressive. But will you support a really active campaign which may bring reprisals?'

'Give me five minutes on the blower and five minutes with the brig,' he replied.

Lionel and I paced the snow outside the mess door while the due processes of military consultation took place.

'Fools,' said Lionel. 'Fools. Fools. Fools. If they mess this up, I'll never forgive them.'

When the brigade major came out he gestured me inside but left Lionel trudging the snow, almost bursting with steam.

'Aggressive, yes. Partisans – Division seem reasonably keen,' the brigade major said. 'Of course it all depends how keen they are at Corps.'

'Can I at least set up the force?'

'No harm,' he said. 'No harm. Division see no harm in setting up the force.'

'Boots, arms, ammunition?' I asked.

'Boots and greatcoats, yes,' he said. 'Arms and ammunition – it depends how keen they are at Corps.'

'Yes I see,' I said.

Even before the Brigadier had left the mess a notice in Italian was posted in Casoli, announcing the official formation of Wigforce and calling for recruits. Copies were carried by partisans to all the surrounding hill villages and were up by midnight. Queues began to form immediately outside the cinema in Casoli, which was to be the partisan recruiting centre.

We accepted about one man in six. Lionel refused to enrol any ex-officers because he believed the poor performance of the Italian army was due to the poor quality of its officers. We appointed a British and an Italian adjutant in double harness, two sergeant majors, two quartermasters, a squad of six interrogators to smell out the fifth columnists, and a goat named Enrico as the Wigforce mascot. By ten o'clock we had enrolled about fifty men. The next morning (11 January) the queue was even longer and the training of the new recruits began. This was unconventional. Clearly, any attempt at square bashing would be useless, and weapons training was soon restricted to a group of four or five men assembling and stripping the odd collection of automatic weapons for which we had a supply of ammunition. Lionel had some idea of basic training in minor tactics but this proved ineffective, since the partisans could not see the point in make-believe attacks. Why pretend there were Germans in that group of houses? they asked. There were plenty of houses with real Germans inside. We should attack them.

At dusk Lionel's escort arrived and he set off with a mixed force of British and partisan troops to join Nick's forward platoon at Calazzotto. Later he told me that the whole operation had been a model of efficiency, sentries posted on the flanks, guides in position, bridges built and a telephone line laid by dawn joining Casoli, Calazzotto and Civitella. He immediately set up three reconnaissance patrols, one of which he would lead himself.

With Lionel safely on his way and the recruiting process dribbling on into the night, I realised I had eaten nothing for twenty-four hours. This was a common predicament: you became engrossed in a close succession of events and unless you were lucky enough to be in the right place at the right time, it was possible to miss every meal. I sent Rutherford, my lion-hearted batman from Dundee, to the baron's to enquire if I would be welcome.

'I think it will be OK sir,' said Rutherford on his return.

What do you mean by OK?' I asked.

'Jaist that when I said ye were comin' they all started rinnin' aboot,' said Rutherford. 'And there's a lovely cookin' smail.'

I washed. Washing consisted of Rutherford heating a bucket of water on the stove, mixing it with a second bucket of cold water to the appropriate temperature, and throwing it over me as I crouched on the kitchen floor above a water outlet. That was stage one. Then I soaped myself all over with French Fern soap, a present from Sempre Triste, and then Rutherford doused me again, this time more carefully to make sure all the suds were washed away.

At the baron's all was gas and gaiters. A fresh white wine had just arrived from the Sangro valley. There was a sucking pig with a tennis ball in its mouth – some sort of sporting joke for the English. There was a duet from an obscure early Verdi opera sung by the two younger girls with Francesca at the keyboard. She was very much the *direttore* and shouted '*Lento – più lento*', or '*Più forte*', at her sisters, as if in rehearsal. Once or twice she made them stop and go back to letter D or letter A or whatever. It was a sort of masterclass.

When I got up to go I suddenly found Elena at my side. She too was leaving. We went out together through the huge double-winged baronial door and once outside, as we wrestled together with bolts and bars to make it secure, our hands touched and I felt electricity pass between us, a small shock perhaps about the strength of four volts, and then I felt her seize my arm. We swung around to face each other and in an instant we were clamped together in a comprehensive embrace. After a minute she broke away and led me by the hand down the street to a stone doorway. She unlocked the door with a huge key retrieved from the depths of her skirts. Inside the embers of a wood fire lit up a small room which looked as though it had been hewn out of solid rock, with an even smaller chamber running off one end. Sitting in front of the fire and quivering with delight at the return of his mistress sat a large dog of the pointer kind.

Elena pulled a curtain and bent over the fire to bring it to life, motioning me to a high wooden chair by the hearth. I sat with the dog's head on my thigh until Elena reappeared in what looked like a white linen cloak. She laid a rug in front of the fire, now blazing, pulled me to my feet and helped me divest myself of my battle dress. She had nothing on under her shift and soon we were making love on the ground with a ferocity which quite alarmed the poor dog. Elena had to hold him at bay with one arm while grappling me with the other. It was all over in less than five minutes and we lay together panting on the stone floor while the fire crackled and spurted little knots of sparks on to our naked bodies. The dog began to lick us indiscriminately. I raised myself on my knees and took Elena's head between my hands as if to kiss her. But she turned away, pulled me to my feet and disappeared, returning fully dressed with two small glasses of *grappa*. After I was dressed she looked at me again, put a hand on each shoulder and gave me a sharp slap on the cheek. Then she smiled, the first smile I had seen, a maternal smile as if I were a small boy who had been naughty but in rather an endearing way. '*Fanciullo mio*,' she said as she turned me round and pushed me through the street door into the now melting snow.

Well now, that was something, I thought. There she was, a woman about twice my age, a woman who could cast a spell over a man and lead him into a deep dark sexual encounter in a trice. No nonsense about romance, no endearments, indeed we had hardly exchanged a word in the twenty minutes we had been together. To be able to excite me so thoroughly and at the same time to enjoy such evident pleasure herself seemed very satisfactory. To make love with such speed and intensity seemed extraordinary. I thought of all the paraphernalia of love-making in my Cambridge days, the flowers, the letters, the endless telephone calls, the candle-lit dinners *à deux*, and all the social foreplay of my visits to her family, her visits to mine, the shiftily-booked hotel room, then often the disappointment, the disengagement, tears, tantrums and excruciating guilt. This is rather different, I thought, as I walked briskly back to the mess.

Next morning I was awakened by the field telephone. It was Division. General Eveleigh had heard about the partisans and was interested. He would like to come to see for himself. I was dealing with Rutherford's fried eggs when I was called to the phone again. It was Corps. General Dempsey had heard about the partisans. Could he visit? Yes he could, and a date was made amid a plethora of good wishes. 'General sends you best wishes, old boy, and good luck to Ingram.'

'Wigram,' I said.

'Oh,' said the voice, slowing down thoughtfully. 'Wigram. Wigram. The same Wigram who visited 8th Army HQ?'

'The very same,' said I.

'Of the battle school?' he asked.

'The battle school, yes,' I replied.

'And the Sicilian campaign?'

'And the Sicilian campaign.'

'Didn't he – didn't he . . . do something?'

'He wrote an excellent report on the campaign and delivered it at the battle school,' I said. 'In Barnard Castle.'

'Ah yes . . . Ah yes . . . I remember.' And he rang off.

Next was Lionel. He had only just got back. The recce patrols had identified two prime targets, one a group of farmhouses, one a range of caves. Both were occupied by at least a section of German troops. They had examined the ground carefully and planned an attack for that night. He would lead the main attack.

'Lionel,' I said. 'Give over. Let da Selva lead the attack. He's the best partisan NCO you have. Let's see how they cope on their own. You're the commander. You're the boss. You can't walk in front of every bloody patrol that goes out.'

But Lionel would have none of it. He had to set an example. He had to be sure the position was properly cleared.

I told him that Division and Corps had both been on the blower.

'LMGs?' he asked. 'Tommys, stens, ammunition?'

'Not yet,' I said. 'Not a gun, not a round. But they sounded keen.'

Later that day I visited Civitella and Calazzotto as the two RWK companies moved into their new forward quarters. Lionel was already talking of a forward base for patrolling. Calazzotto was too far back and, now that it was occupied by a whole infantry company, it had become part of a strongly held line running from the Majella massif south-east to Gessopalena. We had taken a great bite out of no-man's-land and now Lionel wanted to venture farther forward. He had his eye on a hamlet called Selva two miles down the road from Civitella to Castel di Sangro. Partisan intelligence reported it deserted: it had been pillaged and several of the inhabitants had been shot. Better wait and see what happens tonight, I told Lionel and he was agreeable, partly because he was wholly preoccupied by the problem of squeaking snow.

The thaw was now general below three thousand feet and the snow squeaked and crunched in the noisiest fashion, no matter how cautiously one walked across it. Lionel feared that under these conditions surprise would be impossible and, hopelessly adrift from the practicalities of country life as he always was, he had dreamt up the idea that if the men's boots were encased in a thick layer of grease, the boot would slide through the snow silently, eliminating the squeak and crunch. To test this theory he had obtained, as only he could, two great vats of goose-grease; as I arrived, half a dozen partisans were applying this in generous helpings to their boots. They were somewhat bewildered about the purpose of the grease, but the general belief was that it was some novel method of detecting mines. I took Lionel aside.

'Lionel,' I said. 'That grease is no good.'

'How do you know?' he asked. 'We haven't tested it yet.'

'Lionel,' I said. 'The snow squeaks because it is compressed. Whether you use grease or not the weight of the human body will compress the snow and it will squeak.'

'I don't accept that,' said Lionel. 'If the foot slides into the snow instead of crushing it down, it is bound to be quieter.'

'Lionel,' I said. 'Grease will assist the human foot to slide against solids – wood, iron, stone. It will not help it to slide through snow. Snow will clog on to grease. Grease will be of no assistance whatsoever.'

'I don't accept that,' said Lionel.

There was nothing for it but to demonstrate to Lionel slowly and thoroughly that grease did not do away with snow-squeak. When he was convinced he ordered the vats of goose-grease be sent back to the partisans' mess in Civitella. He thought that if a generous proportion of it was absorbed through their daily diet it might work wonders in building up their resistance to cold.

Back in Casoli I telephoned Lionel to wish him well just before the patrols went out, and then drove up to Gessopalena to visit the company there, returning about one a.m. Sleep was still a very precious commodity and I did not seem to have had much of it when I was called to the field telephone. It was Lionel, talking in his clipped emergency voice. Something very disturbing had happened. He couldn't talk about it over the phone. Would I wait for him in Casoli. He would be over in about two hours. I looked at my watch. It was five a.m. I said I would wait and went back to bed. When I woke up for the second time Lionel was sitting at the foot of my bed. It was a rustic four-poster and, as was the custom in those times, the quartermaster and Rutherford had furnished my room in the albergo in a style appropriate to my status. There was a majestic marble-topped writing table 'lent' by the baron and an impressive ecclesiastical chair, from some church, of the kind suitable to accommodate bishops on state occasions. It stood opposite the bed. Lionel sat on this, blue homburg, cloak, greased boots and all (for he himself had obstinately persisted in this folly). He sipped a mug of tea and his brow looked like thunder.

'We've got fifth columnists,' he said. 'Both positions were deserted. The embers of the fires in the caves were still warm. There was fresh milk in a jug in the farm. Da Selva said that the cows had been milked only a few hours earlier.' He went on at some length with a catalogue of evidence to prove the enemy had only just left the two sites, including the discovery of fresh stools in the caves.

'Stools?' I said. '*Fresh* stools?'

'Excrement,' said Lionel. 'Human excrement.'

'You mean shit? Turds?'

Lionel admitted that this was what he meant. He was always disinclined to use four letter words.

'It could be,' I said, 'that when the German HQ at Palena heard we had advanced our base to Calazzotto they pulled back their FDLs.'

But Lionel would have none of it. The partisans knew it was treachery; some of them claimed to know the names of those who were the traitors. If the Germans had intelligence about us as good as ours about them, it would make our task impossible.

'For God's sake, Lionel,' I said. 'There is bound to be quite a lot of this about. Even though the locals hate the Germans, they are all over the place behind the German lines. Some will give them information to save their skins, some will be tortured.' Lionel was convinced, however, that there were fifth columnists in our own ranks. A telephone wire had been tapped, a paybook stolen and there was further circumstantial evidence.

'Whatever happens,' I said, 'we can't get mixed up in a witch hunt. Once we take sides or show partiality we'll be sucked into all their little civil wars. Look at the scene in Civitella. It's like Paris during the French Revolution. We've got ninety-nine per cent of the population on our side. *They* must root out the fifth columnists, not us. Then we will imprison and try them. We don't want to get involved in local vendettas.'

Lionel agreed, descended from his ecclesiastical throne and we went to eat breakfast in amity. We sent a message to Nick Williams saying we must see him at noon. We phoned Brigade reporting the situation and pressing the case for arms. We inspected the new recruits, who were still pouring in and were now being organised into platoons by locality. It was thought wise, however, to supply the NCOs from different villages; thus the NCOs in the Gessopalena platoon would be men from Civitella and Casoli, the Casoli platoon from Civitella and Gessopalena, and so on.

Lionel had big ideas. He wanted to form a force of some four hundred men, one half of which would hold static positions around their own villages, acting as the eyes and ears of our battalion and forming a light screen across the whole of one front in positions close up against, and in some cases behind, the enemy strongpoints. The other half would be formed into a mobile column to carry out raids deep into enemy territory.

The troops on parade could scarcely have been described as a smart and soldierly body of men, since the consignment of greatcoats which had reached us was evidently destined for a guards battalion and were anything up to a foot too long for our Abruzzi fighters. The problem was solved by shearing off the skirt of the greatcoat to the appropriate length. For headgear they wore the Italian peasant's version of the homburg, the odd British forage cap, cloth caps, black berets or the Italian army's raffish-looking off-duty headgear. They were a ferocious-looking lot and I reminded Lionel of Wellington's dictum as he inspected his troops before battle: 'I don't know what they will do to the enemy but by God they frighten me.'

'They don't frighten me at all,' said Lionel. 'With those ridiculous old World War One rifles they don't frighten me enough.'

We met Nick and paced the ramparts of Civitella with him alone, to ensure privacy. He listened to Lionel carefully. 'We have bastards,' he said. 'Is true. We have bastards. I know.'

'How do you stop it?' we asked.

'I show him with one.' Here Nick drew his hand across his neck, at the same time giving vent to the short gurgling scream of a man having his throat cut. 'If no good,' Nick went on, 'I show him with another.' And here he repeated the performance. 'If no good I go' – and here he cut his own throat rapidly half a dozen times – 'until he shit scared. When he dead,' he added reflectively, 'he no go on. When he shit scared he no go on.' Lionel and I went our ways contentedly, he to Calazzotto and I back to Casoli.

Nick never spoke of the matter again and when questioned gave evasive replies. But we heard from the partisans of certain

155

mysterious murders and, from the way they were reported, we had little doubt that each was a step forward in improving the security of our sector.

CHAPTER

12

L ATER THAT SAME DAY, the thirteenth of January, Lionel set up his advanced base at Selva and within an hour he had an array of reconnaissance patrols probing forward in all directions. As I rode across the valley on a singularly grumpy mule to visit him, I wondered at the resilience of the Abruzzi peasants. Here they were, between two armies, clinging to their patch of land through thick and thin. If they were lucky, their farm would be by-passed by both the retreating and the advancing army; if they were less lucky, they would escape the German retreat and suffer Allied occupation, which meant death to all barnyard fowls and pigs, but otherwise nothing worse than soldiers being billeted on their farms. But if they were really unlucky, they would fall prey to a German foraging party – an NCO and four men who would approach a hamlet or a farm, open fire, drive out the inhabitants, loot every article of value, kill all the animals and set the buildings on fire. This exercise was carried out with varying degrees of savagery.

Sometimes the men would be shot as they ran away, sometimes the women captured and raped. There were plenty of eyewitness accounts of these occurrences and, even allowing for the inevitable degree of exaggeration, it was clear that in our area alone several dozen men had been shot, some by putting a rifle in their mouths and discharging it so that it scattered their brains over the walls and roof of the room where the atrocity was committed. Many women had been raped, sometimes in hot blood as they were hunted down and felled by the German soldiers, sometimes more deliberately when they were imprisoned until the squad had completed the job of looting and burning. Then, as they sat round a fire drinking *schnapps*, the women would be raped systematically. The Germans would drag out a bed or table and four men would hold the woman down by the arms and legs while the fifth assaulted her. The women were often turned free to wander back to the nearest friendly habitation, although some were killed and others were in such a state of shock they died of exposure.

Despite these horrors, the native population struggled on. Everywhere in the country animals were being collected and fed, cows milked, horses and mules captured and returned to their owners. Rebuilding was taking place even under shellfire. One of the most moving images I carried with me from Casoli was that of a continuous procession of women, from young girls to octogenarians, all dressed in black, winding their way up the steep streets from a stone quarry at the base of the village to the houses at the topmost point, where the most damage had been done. Each one carried a large stone resting on a coiled cloth on her head. Occasionally the Germans would drop a few shells on Casoli; when the whistle and crash of the first shell was heard, the whole line would stop motionless and, as if in a ballet, each woman would lower her stone to the ground with a motion of unhurried grace. If a second and third shell came over, the whole line of black would melt into the doorways and narrow passages which made up the honeycomb of an Abruzzi hill town, only to resume the perpetual motion of their exercise as soon as the coast was clear.

One day in Civitella, Lionel and I discussed the art of survival with a group of partisans and their wives. In the early days those who could leave their homes went north or south indiscriminately, depending upon where they had friends or family. Soon it was realised that north was no good, the war would catch up with you again. But some of the richer people still believed that there might be a German victory. The proprietor of the fort, for instance, who lived in the castle within it, had taken half of the family fortune south to Foggia. His wife had gone north to Ravenna with the other half. This sort of insurance policy was, we were told, common enough. We asked about the baron, who owned much of the Aventino valley. Why had he not scarpered? He had more wealth than he could move, they said. He had to sit on it. Wheat, figs and wine kept him in Casoli. He was, it appeared, an object of ridicule and featured in a number of black jokes and little bits of doggerel which they quoted with gusto. Yes, he had been a fascist, but who of his class had not? Yes, he had been friendly with the Germans, but so had all the rich people. Was he a fifth columnist? This must be a joke: he had no loyalties to either side, only to himself. He would sell his daughters to anyone who offered him a safe conduct out of Casoli with his loot.

'You see,' I said to Lionel as we drove away. 'No point in putting the baron in prison.'

'Better inside,' said Lionel, 'he's a tricky fellow.'

As Lionel's patrols began to report back to him in Selva he got a surprise. The German post nearest to him was not in front but behind. Halfway down the road which ran back from Selva to Civitella there was a group of buildings on a high point known as the Villa Eugenia. Here there was a German outpost which could look down on both villages. Indeed, the Germans were seen by our patrol looking through binoculars and marking maps.

Lionel drew up a plan of attack. He would lead a fighting patrol of eight British and ten guerrillas (led, appropriately, by the partisan NCO called da Selva). This force would leave Civitella after dark, make a wide sweep round the bottom of the mountain and attack the Villa Eugenia from the north. Our force at Selva would send cut-off parties up the road to capture the retreating Germans. A guerrilla platoon under one Giovanni Brucelli would follow behind Lionel and occupy the position once it was captured. A 'B' echelon, made up of mules and porters to evacuate wounded and to carry up ammunition and rations for forty-eight hours, was to follow behind Brucelli.

This little foray, the first of many, was described by Lionel in his patrol report:

At 2000 hrs orders were completed and the fighting patrol left Civitella at 2100 hrs. Order of march – Guide – da Selva – Wigram – Brucelli. Good time was made to the top of the ridge through the melting snow and mud and at 2245 hrs the party halted about 500 yds north-west of the objective. A small recce patrol of the commanders went forward and a plan was made to assault in extended order through the thin trees on top of the ridge – British force leading.

At 2300 hrs the assaulting British troops moved forward (2 brens 2 rifles 4 TSMGs) with the guerrillas (da Selva) on the right flank slightly in rear. In a few minutes we were challenged by a voice in German at about 50 yds range. All opened fire and went in. The enemy answered with spasmodic bursts from 2 Spandaus and 2 Schmeissers, tracer being fired from the former. The British force never wavered but went straight in and 3 or 4 of the Italian guerrillas were also very good. The rest of the guerrillas stood off well to the rear and made conditions very dangerous by firing their weapons in all directions and shouting at the tops of their voices. All this must have sounded very terrifying

159

to the enemy and he fled in the direction of our ambush. The position was a large one and it took about 30 minutes to clear a large wooded area and two groups of houses.

I called out for the guerrilla ambush but they were not up as close as they had been ordered to be and said they had seen nothing of the enemy. Unfortunately it was a very cloudy dark night and the many trees gave good cover to the enemy.

Our casualties were 1 wounded – Sgt Manning (slightly) – and 1 guerrilla wounded.

I did not have time to search the area thoroughly and it was very dark under the trees but the following is a report of what I found:

1 dead German Obergefreiter, epaulette green with yellow piping. Numerals 18 have been removed. All personal papers sent herewith. Body carried back to Civitella by Guerrillas under guard.

2 Spandau machine guns (handed to Guerrillas.)

1 Bomb thrower, 2 bombs sent herewith

1 Field telephone attached to a line going in the direction of Corpesante (I have taken this myself)

1 Pistol (have kept this)

The German positions were not in the houses but in small fox-holes cunningly hidden in the wood. It is evident that despite the snow they all slept out in the wood with their weapons at the ready and the whole position was a model of soldierliness: everything in its proper place and very well organised.

As soon as possible Brucelli was got up and put in position. Although they had been well to the rear, many of his men had run away, others talked all together at the tops of their voices, others went round looting. I had considerable trouble with them but finally got one section with a captured machine gun into position at the top of the hill. Later the other two sections got into position covering the road. I used da Selva and my own force as a mobile reserve.

The operation was over much earlier than I had anticipated but I was able to telephone from Selva for the 'B' echelon. This reached us at 0100 hrs. I made a final tour of the position at 0130 hrs warning Brucelli of the possibility of counterattack and ordering him to keep completely quiet, to prohibit all movement by day and to set a trap for any visiting German patrol. I then returned to base reaching here at 0230 hrs.

At 0300 hrs the noise of firing was heard from the direction of Brucelli and at 0415 hrs he visited me saying he had been counterattacked and had withdrawn his men to avoid casualties. He had not sustained any casualties. I telephoned to Selva warning them to keep a sharp look-out and ordered Brucelli to reorganise and be ready to reoccupy the position tomorrow. I will seek to verify his story today but it seems difficult to believe as we still hold Selva and they have just reported again (0830 hrs) that they have seen no sign of the enemy.

(Signed) L. Wigram; major, 15-1-44

P.S. 1100 hrs. Patrol sent out by Sabati from Selva reports Eugenia entirely clear of enemy, all food, arms, etc in position and untouched. He has posted a section on the high point about the houses which will occupy the position until relieved. Have told Civitella guerrillas (Nick Williams) to find a platoon for this task and they expect to be ready this afternoon.

The guerrillas could not, we realised, be described as a good all-round fighting force. As guides and as single sentinels, often keeping vigil in listening posts many miles behind the enemy's forward position, they were invaluable. As standing patrols guarding access roads and tracks, although not inclined to stand for long, they were again valuable because nothing slipped past them and they gave good warning by firing off their weapons or running back to report what they had seen. They could march for seven or eight hours by night over almost impossible terrain without rest. But in attack and defence their methods were unconventional, as I described in a dispatch to Brigade:

In an assault, they adopt a hedgehog formation, as a conglomerate mass moving forward at a snail's pace, all facing outwards and discharging their weapons in the air and sometimes in the ground to the detriment of any troops nearby. As soon as an objective is reached there is an immediate uncontrolled rush for booty. Boots are the main prize. The guerrillas do not speak of killing a German but of winning a pair of boots. They are not above looting our dead if it places them in no danger.

As the reports of Lionel's patrol were forwarded upwards a truck arrived at Casoli unheralded and unexpected. It contained arms, ammunition, more greatcoats, rations and boots. There was one sample set of blue battle dress, more was to follow (it never did). I phoned Lionel. 'Corps must be keen,' I said.

'Greatcoats are no good,' said Lionel. 'Much better use the space for more ammunition.'

An hour or two later the divisional general, Eveleigh, arrived in person. He had the quick eye and decisive manner of a fighting

161

general. We were doing a first-class job. The guerrillas were a first-class idea. He would help in any way he could. Corps were keen. We must hammer, hammer, hammer at the Boche. Push him back. He went to look at the ground from our OP at the top of the town. He sat down at the mess table and studied our dispositions on the map. He thought they were first-class. All generals, especially those with their roots in the infantry, are entranced by minor tactics, finding in the handling of platoons and sections a blessed release from the sterner stuff of a general's life, which is mainly concerned with the movement of brigades, artillery regiments and supply columns, and arguing with other generals. General Eveleigh, like a happy father playing with his son's toy railway, quickly absorbed the salient facts about our front, made a few shrewd comments, told us once again that we were conducting a first-class show, leapt into his jeep and drove off through the mud. It was a stimulating and heart-warming visit, but when I called Lionel to tell him that the bandwaggon was rolling our way, he only said: 'Did you tell him we don't want greatcoats?' For the rest he regarded the support we were getting from Division as less than his due.

That night at the baron's I found something out of the ordinary was going on. When I entered the great hall, it was empty except for Francesca, who led me to a small study ostensibly to show me a Puccini manuscript which was one of the family's treasured possessions. After the inspection of this object, Francesca asked me to sit down on one side of the desk. She seated herself on the other side and, placing her forearms flat along the desk's surface in a deliberate fashion, she addressed me formally.

'*Caro* Forman,' she said. 'You are now a friend of the family. We have a great affection for you and we know that you too have a respect and a liking for us. But you are also an army officer and the representative of a foreign power and my father feels it is our duty to explain to you the delicate position of a landowner and patriot, such as my father is, in the face of the political uncertainties of our times.'

It was in effect a plea not to put her father in prison, although such an eventuality was not even hinted at. It was carefully prepared, eloquent and quite up to the standard of a pleading in the High Court, and as I looked at Francesca's serene beauty I could not help thinking of Portia. Someone in Civitella must have reported our conversation about the baron, I thought; they've got the wind up. After some twenty minutes I interrupted the flow of oratory.

'Francesca,' I said, 'if you go on much longer I will think there is a case to answer.'

She stopped dead, looked at me and laughed.

'Better to protest too much than too little,' she said and then she looked at me seriously and asked, '*Caro* Forman, do you believe or do you not that my father is an honourable man and a true friend of the Allied cause?'

'I believe your father is a highly intelligent Italian gentleman,' I replied, 'who will recognise what is the right thing to do and what is not the right thing to do in any circumstances, no matter how difficult.'

She looked at me, crestfallen, held out her hand and said, 'Let us forget all this. Come to supper.'

That night I made love again with Elena, and indeed from now on I would go to her house on most of those evenings when I was in Casoli, whether or not I dined with the baron. When she was at home she left two stones, one on top of the other, on the low wall by her door. Although we always made love with an intensity which for a few moments seemed to fuse us together, our relationship did not extend into the rest of our lives. She did not ask me whether or not I was married, and showed no curiosity about my home life. She told me that she was a widow. Her husband had a stepson and one day when the father had returned unexpectedly he found her in bed with the boy, whom he attacked and nearly killed. The boy ran away and never returned. Her husband had died two months later of a fever. Some people thought that she had poisoned him. She told me this so that I could understand the suspicion in which she was held in the town and why she appeared at the baron's home only on sufferance. We did not exchange endearments but we began to form a sort of animal companionship which had nothing to do with our bouts of sexual activity. One night when I got up to go she took my army leather jerkin from me and when I returned she had sewn on to it a rolling sheepskin collar. I brought her practical things like cigarettes, which were harder currency than money, and food. I spoiled and petted the dog, treating him with greater tenderness because there was none in my relationship with her.

During the next week Wigforce became a coherent fighting unit. Lionel now had seven platoons based in the forward villages on our front. Beyond them he had a network of standing patrols spreading between and behind the nearest German strongpoints. Beyond these again he had single sentries in listening posts and in German-occupied villages, ready to send a runner back with news of any movement. We had already driven several miles down the triangle that made up the top of no-man's-land. Back at base, Lionel kept a chosen band of guerrillas and some twenty special-ly trained British NCOs and men as a striking force. Each night one or other of the German forward posts would be attacked and harried and sometimes captured. With the return of each successful patrol morale rose, and we had difficulty restraining the guerrillas from taking affairs into their own hands and organising private raiding parties whose aim was more likely to be looting than any tactical gain. They also had a disagreeable habit of exhibiting in the villages the bodies of Germans who had been killed in action. At first we thought this was some kind of celebration of victory, but we later discovered that the proprietors of the body charged an admission fee. We put a stop to this practice, forcibly, and lectured Nick Williams and his fellow commanders on the need for the guerrillas to observe the Geneva Convention no matter how dastardly the behaviour of the other side. This stricture was, however, soon to be forgotten.

From the sixteenth to the twenty-first of January, apart from a visit from the corps commander, General Dempsey – who turned out to be exceptionally keen – and some desultory shelling of our main positions which called for reprisals, my life was mainly vis-iting. At first light I would set out by jeep, on a mule or on foot, and travel through the now clear air along tracks and footpaths to call on our forward positions. It was an exhilarating exercise, moving up under the massive shadow of the Majella, stopping off at depots and rear positions on the way, delivering mail and the occasional newspaper from home to men who were greedy for news of anything outside their tiny window of vision from their fixed position in a village, farmhouse or foxhole. One of the illusions that can afflict a man who spends day after day looking at the same piece of ground is that it is no longer connected with the rest of the world and that his tiny piece of the Abruzzi has floated off from everyday life and become the only island of reality, beyond which there is nothing.

As time passed my affection for the Abruzzi peasant grew warmer. I loved the sound of their language, very different from Roman speech, and their wide range of gestures, some of them elaborate and most of them peculiar to the region. A conversation with an Abruzzoni could take the form of a continuous mime, at first one-sided, but as I grew familiar with the repertoire I too could match words with hand movements to the limit of the most demanding gestures of all which, when offered a second helping of pasta, indicated 'Thank-you-very-much-that-was-quite-delicious-I-could-not-eat-any-more-but-let-us-drink-a-toast-to-each-other' – all without a word spoken.

Although in many ways they had the character common to most peasants the world over – close with money, stoical in the face of disasters (whether caused by natural forces or by war), hard-working, close-knit within families and clans, land-jealous, prone to vendettas and deep hatreds – the Abruzzesi had unique qualities: a form of black humour, sudden outbursts of passion and a generosity of spirit which, once you were accepted as a friend, enfolded you in the intimacy of the family circle. I remember one night eating pasta and drinking the dreaded *corto* in a farmhouse little better than a hut, where the cutlery consisted of knives (one between two), of the kind used to gralloch a stag in Scotland, and half a dozen forks carved by peasant hands from bone. I admired the forks greatly – they had the grace and balance of Minoan antiquity. Seeing this, as the party warmed up, the *signora* offered me the set of forks as a present. I felt I could not deprive them of an essential eating tool and so took just one fork as a gift and a memento.

Next morning a sodden little packet wrapped in coarse black paper turned up at the albergo. Inside were the remaining five forks with an almost indecipherable note begging me to keep them, which I did, returning the next night to sing them a thank-you song to accordion accompaniment, which had a verse devoted to each member of the family and a chorus to the tune of 'O Sole Mio!' beginning, 'O For-che-tta'.

Lionel's relations with the same peasantry were just as strong but different. His Italian was better than mine and he could converse with them about the war in his usual passionate style. A letter home gives some idea of his feelings for the Abruzzesi:

> The Germans in the area have been particularly nasty. They have employed the 'scorched earth' policy. Not only have they destroyed military objectives but every single farm and building for miles around. In some villages not a single building remains. Their method is to close all the doors and windows and then explode a mine inside the house. This blows down all the walls and the roof and usually sets fire to the ruins as well. It is absolute vandalism – serving no military purpose whatsoever – and it has made the Italians so mad that they have become very keen to fight again. I have made many friends among them and have found a lot of them real winners . . .
>
> I speak a lot of Italian now and am beginning to jabber away just like a native. It is a beautiful language – full of music – when you begin to understand it well. I shall be forced to learn English again myself if it goes on much longer. I hope you won't mind having an all Italian husband, but then you're used to changes by now darling aren't you.

From the very first they regarded him as their natural leader and once they had seen him on patrol they recognised that here was a man with a degree of courage and dedication which made even the legendary Al Capone look like a sewer rat by comparison. They were of course right in that Lionel would have stood out as an unusually brave and cool customer in any company, but here, among the freebooting partisans whose strong points were neither steadfastness in battle nor sang-froid in an emergency, he was a paragon. Tales of his bravery and military acumen, many of them mythical, spread rapidly, and even when he visited a distant hamlet or farmhouse women and children would run out to salute him. It was interesting that when he and I were together, although my seniority in rank was known and acknowledged, the partisans always turned to him for an opinion on military matters. They also sensed a judicial quality in him and he was besieged by people with legal problems: a tenant who refused to quit, a farmer whose stores had been stolen by a neighbour during a raid by the Germans. He would deal with such matters as best he could, often while striding between his patrolling base and Civitella, surrounded by a knot of appellants, witnesses and interested parties. To the very end the Abruzzesi had difficulty with Lionel's name which, since the Italian language has no substitute for W, was usually converted into Veegum, Oueegum or even Eegum.

On 15 January I set out at first light to visit Gessopalena. On the way up I heard some desultory firing on my right front but thought nothing of it. When I reached the village I climbed through the ruins with the company commander to see how the local school had survived first the destruction of half the village by the retreating Germans and since then a daily dose of intermittent but accurate shellfire. The school was in the nave of the one remaining church, a building solid enough to resist a direct hit. There were two classes sitting back to back on church pews and separated by a hessian screen. The children seemed to be equal in age in both classes and I asked the teacher why this was so. He told me that one class was the Catholic school under the instruction of the priest and the other was a people's school set up by the newly formed Communist Party, of which he was a member. I saw several children sidle up to a large wooden box which stood at one end of the hessian screen and take something out of it. On closer inspection this turned out to be carrots, which were provided to keep the pangs of hunger within bounds.

'*Queste carote sono cattoliche o comuniste?*' I asked the teacher.

'*Sono come l'acqua,*' he said. '*Senza politica finché non sia bevuta da qualcuno.*'

As I was leaving the church a runner summoned me to the field telephone. It was Lionel.

'The bastards,' he said. 'The bloody bastards.'

'What have they done?'

'Rounded up all the families in Santa Agata and killed them in cold blood.'

A runner had come in to Calazzotto in the small hours and reported that a strong German patrol was moving out up the Castel di Sangro–Casoli road. Lionel put all systems on alert and sent a fighting patrol out to ambush them. There had been no contact, but he had just heard that soon after dawn the German patrol arrived at the hamlet of Santa Agata, rounded up all the men, women and children in the vicinity, locked them into the largest room in the farm and set fire to it. They shot those who tried to escape by putting a rifle in their mouths. Between forty and fifty were reported killed.

'Where is the German patrol now?' I asked.

167

Lionel replied that it was already four miles away and returning to its battalion headquarters. He was calling down artillery fire in the hopes of catching them on the road home. He was beside himself with anger. Shooting a civilian who was thought to be a spy was one thing; the indiscriminate murder of civilians, which we had already seen, was appalling enough, but this was an act of mindless barbarism resulting in the deaths of forty or more innocent men, women and children. We had to do something about it, we had to inform Division and get photographs for the newspapers at home. I should go there myself so that I could be an eyewitness and give a first-hand account to the press. He could not go without cancelling all his patrolling plans for that night.

So it was that later that day in the failing light I found myself with a couple of British NCOs in the centre of a small group of guerrillas moving over some of the craggiest country in the Abruzzi, passing the solitary rock pinnacle of La Morgia and striking down steep valleys to the ill-fated village of Santa Agata. We had no photographer – and anyway, there was no light.

As we approached, the moon rose and I heard – always an uneasy sound – the concerted howling of dogs. There were three of them, sitting black and motionless against a drift of snow which filled the yard of what had been the principal farm, lifting their heads to the moon and howling their hearts out. Between them, sprawled against the snow, lay two dead bodies and behind them the embers of the burnt-out farmhouse still glowed. There was nothing to be done. We left a guerrilla patrol to bury the dead and made our way back to Casoli. I wrote a lengthy report for Division for onward transmission to our war correspondents but it never saw the light of day.

On the following night Lionel visited me in Casoli. The massacre of Santa Agata had had serious consequences. Whereas some of the guerrillas were enraged by the atrocity and determined to be revenged, others, particularly those from isolated farms near the front line, were not so belligerently inclined. Several had shoved off without a by-your-leave. Others had come to him saying that now the snow was almost gone, they had to get back to their farms or their families would starve.

We talked far into the night and decided that if Wigforce were to continue to play a major role we would have to reorganise. Platoons would continue to be based on their local villages and

168

hamlets. Isolated farms would be evacuated. A bounty would be offered on discharge to those who returned their boots and their arms. All hamlets and groups of farms would have their own home guard with at least a couple of rifles to scare off marauding German foraging parties. For the rest, Wigforce would be built up to a mobile column of some 300 guerrillas, and Lionel would consider several options for the best use of this force. I urged him to abandon some plans which seemed overly daring. He really couldn't expect, I said, to win the war in the central Apennines single-handed. General Montgomery wouldn't like it. At this Lionel looked up. 'I haven't thought about that letter for weeks,' he said thoughtfully.

'Wigforce may be a help,' I said.

'I hadn't thought of that either,' said Lionel. I was quite sure he was telling the truth.

CHAPTER

13

DESPITE THE SETBACK of the Santa Agata affair, by the twentieth of January Wigforce had harried the German forces aggressively and without pause. Detachments of seven to ten men holding isolated positions were liquidated, supply columns were ambushed, sentries garrotted or captured and headquarters areas subjected to irregular but violent artillery fire. As a result, the Germans were forced back to a line of major positions too strong to succumb to a partisan attack. No longer did they loot the farms and hamlets. If they ventured out, they were likely to come under sniper fire; now they moved only by night and their only patrols were defensive.

Lionel and I discussed the merits of a set-piece attack on the German line of strongpoints. There was one village in particular, Toricella, which had become the keystone of the German chain and which we longed to liquidate. One day I went up with Lionel and our brigade major to study the possibilities from an OP in Gessopalena. At first Lionel was keen to attack; the brigade major and I were doubtful. Even a night attack would have to be mounted on a battalion scale with at least two companies. The Germans, perhaps thirty to fifty in number, were in an ideal defensive position, manning the topmost buildings on a high comb of rock jutting out from the main part of the town. All approaches were mined and booby-trapped, surprise would be impossible and the casualties would be heavy.

Lionel reluctantly accepted our view, and as we drove back to Casoli he said if we were not to carry out any major attack, the role of Wigforce on the existing battalion front would be static. Active patrolling – yes. Terrorising the Germans – yes. Protecting the local population – yes. But if he could advance no further, Wigforce's role in penetrating enemy positions, its strongest card, was played out. I knew that he had something up his sleeve, and back in Casoli he unfolded a plan for the next phase. He would

170

leave the local elements of Wigforce, some two hundred strong, in the villages on our front to hold and to harry. Their field of activity would stretch from the foot of the mighty Majella on the right to the Sangro on the left. He would lead a mobile force of some three hundred guerrillas and twenty or thirty British up the Sangro valley to penetrate the mountainous middle sector of the triangle which made up no-man's-land.

It was risky, but it was the right thing to do. After a couple of hours of discussion, we agreed that he would work out the plan that night in all the necessary detail.

We then walked across the road to witness an all-male ENSA entertainment, 'Stars in Battle Dress', which featured transvestite activities of the most outrageous kind, breasts made of balloons popping like fireworks, skirts lifted until they almost revealed incongruous male organs, and *double entendres* so thick in the air to leave no room for any pretensions of plot. One pretty boy was made up convincingly as a ravishing dark beauty, and his integrity was respected by the producer in that he never had his trousers fall down, his breasts explode, or his posterior assaulted. His girlish simpering aroused such a paroxysm of sexual excitement in the audience that I feared for his safety after the show. I later discovered that the sergeant major, who had the same thoughts as mine, had provided an escort for the cast from the cinema to the guard room where they were royally entertained by the senior members of the sergeants' mess.

Lionel had slipped out shortly after the show started. It was not to his taste and he wanted to continue working on his plan. The brigade major, on the other hand, had enormously enjoyed the antics of the 'Stars' (who were, as it turned out, very seldom in battle dress) and drove off to Brigade in high good humour.

Lionel and I then faced a problem together. If he led his mobile force up the Sangro, he could no longer remain under my command. The RWK left-hand boundary was several miles short of the Sangro, which lay in the area covered by the 5 Buffs. Lionel wanted me to make the case for extending the battalion front to cover his activities or to swap territories with the Buffs, but I knew both of these plans were hopelessly unrealistic. He did not want to report to the CO of the Buffs, not through any disrespect for him but because it meant a new man who was unfamiliar with Wigforce as the first link in the upward chain of command.

We considered the claims of Brigade as the seat of operational command and of division, but eventually decided that the right route would be direct from Corps to Wigforce. This followed the army tradition that any independent ancillary forces outside the normal divisional structure became 'Corps troops'. Besides that, we knew that General Dempsey and Corps were keen and they were the source of supply for arms and ammunition.

Those in command at Corps enthusiastically endorsed this proposal. Even though I had recommended it, the change in the command was a bitter pill for me to swallow. Lionel and I had developed Wigforce together; from the first meeting with Nick Williams until now – the eve of departure of the mobile column – it had been a joint enterprise. But more important than that, we were ideal military partners: our minds worked in the same way; we spoke in our own shorthand; we complemented and reinforced each other's tactical sense. And I felt that I was a necessary restraining influence on Lionel when he too quickly and too enthusiastically adopted venturesome plans of action. I had more knowledge of country matters (viz. grease on the boots), and was capable of alleviating the effect on him of the more inhuman forms of army orthodoxy.

Unfortunately, Lionel did not reciprocate this view. Apart from our friendship, he saw me as a valuable partner, a useful ally and a reliable commanding officer. For the rest, he treated me as a convenience: someone who would protect him from visiting firemen, see his reports were properly presented, obtain arms and ammunition and generally allow him to conduct his war with as little interference from officialdom as possible. The need for someone to temper his more urgent enthusiasms or to make him question his hastier judgements never crossed his mind. So, two days later, as he bustled about shepherding his motley crew aboard the trucks, he was oblivious of the fact that I was standing by a little jealous, a little resentful, at the same time full of high hopes for him but with a sickening sense of apprehension in the pit of my stomach.

As we leant against the leading truck drinking mugs of char, I addressed him.

'Lionel,' I said, 'there is no need for you to lead every bloody fighting patrol yourself.'

'I only do it when the patrol is critical,' said Lionel.

'You have done it every time so far,' I said.

'They have all been critical,' said Lionel. 'Lesser patrols I will leave to Exell or to de Selva or Bruneschi.'

'Lesser patrols being one man and a dog,' I said. 'Listen to me, Lionel. Don't push it.'

But his attention was wandering because, addressing his owl-like gaze down the convoy, he saw wrong things being done.

'Don't put all the grenades on one truck, Sergeant Raimondo,' he shouted. 'One shell could do for the lot. Spread them over four trucks.'

'Lionel,' I said again. 'Listen to me. DON'T PUSH IT.'

But it was useless. Looking over my shoulder, he yelled: 'And see the Brens are spread equally too. You've got three on the first truck and none on the second.'

He dashed off to supervise the final loading of his column and five minutes later drove off standing up in his jeep at the head of the convoy. He slapped a powerful salute as he passed me, which I returned with interest, but I could see his mind was far away, wondering perhaps whether he should have taken the two-inch mortars or left them behind. And so there was no handshake, no 'Good luck, old boy,' nor any clipped farewell message in the British style. To the last Lionel was wholly engrossed in the matter in hand and had no attention to spare for anything else.

I got a copy of Lionel's first report on the afternoon of 24 January:

> Force reached agreed base at 0330 hrs. Very tired. Route extremely difficult. OP here first class. Villa S. Maria, Civitaluparella, Buonanotte, all reported clear of enemy at present.
>
> Am sending out recce patrols Civitaluparella, Fallo, Quadri, Pizzo-ferrato and Gamberale areas.
>
> Civilians report that enemy patrols visited Villa S. Maria and Buonanotte on 22nd. Small patrols of enemy (12 strong) to take wire and food. Am arranging to station alarm posts in all villages within range of our base (unarmed). On approach of enemy, a runner will be sent to warn us. We will be at 10 mins. notice to move day or night, and should thus be able to ambush any patrols within 1 hrs. range of base.
>
> Have had great difficulty with telephone lines. Country very hard owing to enemy demolitions. About 4 more miles of line needed to get us through. Am sending my signaller with this note tonight, in hopes that he can procure this and lay it tonight.

Definitely NO movement towards here in daylight. We are definitely under constant enemy observation.

'Route extremely difficult' was an understatement. From the point where the Sangro plunges southwards from the landward end of the coastal plain, it runs through an ever-narrowing valley with a high ridge on each side; halfway up the side of the eastern slope Lionel had de-bused his mobile column, at Colledimezzo. This was the most forward Allied position in the valley. From here on it was all on foot, with a mule train following a mile or two behind. At first his course ran near the foot of the valley, which begins to narrow sharply, with steep side valleys, some of them more like ravines, running in from both sides. All bridges were blown and the roads were mined. The Sangro and its tributaries were in flood from the melting snow and several of the crossings were waist-deep.

Some three miles down the valley from his start point, Lionel reached Villa Santa Maria, a village overhung by a towering cliff which rises to an abrupt upward slope, the summit of which is about 2000 feet almost vertically above the valley floor. It was up this wall of stone that Lionel had to find his way, the column often reduced to single file. Even the mules could go no further, so it was man-pack, every man carrying at least sixty pounds and some nearly one hundred. On the very top of the comb of rock which ran behind Santa Maria lay Lionel's objective, Montedelapiano; when seen from the valley, a straggle of houses on the skyline; from the other side, a traditional hill village climbing the eastward slope to the summit and then, as it were, sliced off with a vertical stroke, because below the topmost houses a precipice fell sheer to the valley below.

Once established in his mountain base, Lionel sent out long-distance patrols to every remaining German-held position in no-man's-land, the most distant about ten miles away. Some were held permanently, others visited by strong German patrols whose intentions were not always military, as Lionel described in his report (of 25 January, thirty-six hours after his arrival) concerning the village of Pennadomo which lay due north of him, actually between his base and the Allied line:

Details furnished by an eye-witness at Pennadomo, German raid 23rd – 22 Germans visited town at 0700 hrs and remained all day,

174

leaving at 1830 hrs. Armament 5 Spandaus (brand new) remainder all Schmeissers, except 4. Mostly very young troops, who said they were Austrians, but Germans often say this to gain Italian sympathy. MG posts arranged to circle town, with central Cmd Post on prominent roof. Object of Patrol – loot, rape, drink. 5 girls raped at pistol-point. Most soldiers drunk when they left town in evening. What an opportunity missed!

Am arranging for all towns in area to organise bands to protect their own homes and to prevent further German atrocities. I feel we owe it to them to provide arms if we can. Can use all arms we can get. Plenty of very good man-power available here. If armed would constitute real threat to enemy flanks and left C and might inflict many casualties when he tries to withdraw down only exit road.

Lionel's régime in Buonanotte is described in a report I wrote on Wigforce subsequently:

In his new base Lionel found many new recruits. He reformed and exercised his men by night. All British and guerrillas alike were dressed as Italians. Lionel still affected his black cape and purple homburg. Information poured in. German posts were visited daily by his men who went out alone, sometimes unarmed, sometimes with a revolver, penetrated to the town boundaries and chatted to the inhabitants. He knew the exact strength of the German garrison in every town within 15 miles. He had many cross-checks. Watchers in the forests saw reinforcements and reliefs go up and down the still snowbound roads. A washerwoman would notice the increase of eight German shirts in her weekly quota. The movement of a gun from one position to another would reach him as fast as a man can walk. The sifting of this information was a huge task and this was Lionel's difficulty. He was understaffed. His force numbered some 200 guerrillas and 30 British troops, and he had with him only one other British officer. Leadership was the problem. He could chat to them in Italian and they thought the world of him, for his gallantry had impressed them immensely. Indeed the stories of his prowess grew and his name became a legend. They would do anything for him. Here the chain of command stopped since he was the only officer who could speak Italian. Any officer who could not speak to them in their own language was comparatively useless. Lionel's subordinates then could only be the most trusty and gallant peasants who were reliable in command of a Section or even a Pl. but who could be trusted with nothing higher.

His first major fighting patrol, which he led himself, was against

Quadri, a village on the floor of the valley, on the evening of the twenty-fifth of January:

During the 24th January two recce patrols reported that the small enemy post said to be at Quadri was still occupied by the enemy and not abandoned as hitherto thought. Civilians stated that the Germans formerly in the area and believed to number 17 had gone away on the 23 January leaving the post vacant. On the morning of the 24th the priest rang the church bell for the population to return but on returning they were fired on from one of the posts – a house dominating the town (the doctor's house). It was believed that the other posts formerly occupied were now vacant.

As this seemed a very good opportunity and as it looked as if the enemy were thinning out preparatory to departure I decided to take a fighting patrol to Quadri.

Composition

British – Major Wigram and 12 ORs.
Guerrillas – 2 fighting patrols of 15 men each (Mancini and di Marino).
SBs – 1 British plus 4 guerrillas to carry stretchers.

The patrol left the base Montedelapiano at 1800 hrs. Dark night; no moon, high wind, rain squalls; going very bad owing to melting snow, all streams in flood. Making across country patrol reached Fallo at 2210 hrs. Found clear of enemy and in ruins, with a few civilians still in occupation. From Fallo we followed the rd. to the rd. junc. then rly. line to Quadri. The rly. line and the approaches to Quadri are heavily mined by the enemy and unsafe without a good guide.

Reported enemy posts were found to be empty. Passage through Quadri was very difficult – piles of rubble very high owing to enemy demolitions. Difficult to move without making a noise. On reaching outskirts of the town I decided to go forward with my subordinate commanders to make a close recce. I soon saw the house, a prominent white house dominating the town with a large balcony. Good cover to the rear – ruined buildings. I made the following plan (time 0110 hrs.)

House to be encircled by fire. Pte. Marsh with two brens and two TMCs to cover balcony. Exit at the front. Di Marino to circle right, Mancini to circle left. House to be assaulted from above by British troops led by me.

I allowed 15 mins. for the circling troops to get in posn. then moved to the back of the house, taking cover behind some ruined buildings – distance 50 yds. I moved forward cautiously and was at once challenged by a voice, in German. I replied with a burst of TMC. There was only a very narrow passage between the ruined buildings, for an assault,

176

room for three men only, shoulder to shoulder. Sgt. Harp on left, self in centre, L/Cpl. Jarvis on my right, remainder unable to fire, only to follow up. We opened up with a volley of TMC fire. The German sentries fled round the house after firing two bursts at us from behind cover. We approached the house, all firing as we went. As we wanted prisoners I ordered the cease-fire and shouted out in German 'We are English. If you come out you will be taken prisoner and we will not fire. You cannot escape, you are surrounded.' There was the sound of muffled voices from within, then the door slowly opened and five Germans came out with their hands up. As I was searching them there was a burst of fire from behind me and all our guns and rifles opened up (Italians and Marsh below). In the pandemonium the prisoners became frightened, scattered and escaped, and we had considerable difficulty in rounding them up. We were now in considerable danger from our own fire.

I ran round to the front of the house and tried to find out what had happened and tried to stop the firing. I found that the enemy sentry after hiding behind a wall had fired at us again, and then run round the house and jumped down from the balcony straight into the arms of Marsh and party. He was at once shot dead by a hail of fire from all directions, but by an unlucky chance succeeded in killing Marsh with his final burst. They fell in each other's arms.

After much yelling I managed to order the cease-fire again. I made a search of the house and collected all documents I could find plus the paybook of the dead German. We captured 2 MGs and several other weapons (handed to the guerrillas). We found a telephone line leading towards Pizzoferrato but no telephone to fit on to it.

As there was now a noise of fire coming from the direction of Pizzoferrato, directed at us, I anticipated an early counterattack so I decided to get out (if possible with the prisoners) as quickly as possible. The prisoners yelled with fear when they saw where we were standing, saying that we were in the middle of an AP minefield. They afterwards lifted four mines from under the straw and enabled us to form up ready for the start home.

I had considerable trouble with the guerrillas. They were wild with excitement and trying to lynch the prisoners. I put the prisoners under a strong British guard and started for home at 0205 hrs.

We had a nightmare journey home. Every bridge was blown, all rivers in flood, and often waist deep in water. Piles of wreckage and ruin to negotiate with the prisoners on our hands. We also had to run the gauntlet of enemy posts, lying between us and home and had plenty of opportunity for ambush. We did the journey (11 miles) in five hours twenty minutes, reaching home at 0725 hrs. The whole patrol did the journey home without a halt, arriving home (incl. Italian guerrillas) with all personnel, weapons, and prisoners intact and carrying all captured weapons.

It being impossible to evacuate the prisoners from here in daylight and conditions being favourable for interrogation (prisoners being terrified of our guerrilla stronghold), I did a preliminary interrogation and found all prisoners willing to talk. Their story also tallies exactly with our information from civilian sources.

They say they belong to No. 2 Coy. of the special Aufklarungs-abtelung (motor-cyclists) HQ at Pizzoferrato. No. 1 Coy. believed to be on their left area Pennadomo. No. 3 Coy. on right. Coy. strength 70–80. Commandant – Major Pick (not Rick) at Palena. They moved straight from Volturno front with a short stay for leave (7 days) in Sulmona; reaching this area two days ago. Our party at Quadri were sent to relieve elements of 568 Inf. Regt. (also 30 Div.) who had already departed without handing over leaving the post vacant for 24 hrs. They marched in at night with one guide and were still awaiting details of their duties, from their Oberleutnant, who had promised to visit them yesterday but failed to turn up. They had no maps and no telephone to connect to the wire. The best subject for interrogation is Gefreiter. He is intelligent and willing to talk. The Unteroffizier is sullen but also willing to talk. Fickert is intelligent. Andreas is a Slovene who speaks little German.

Unfortunately these men are recent arrivals and know little. It is very encouraging for us to find that these men were just dumped down anywhere and left to fend for themselves. 4 Soldbucher and papers sent herewith. Soldbuch of deceased is Gunter. Soldbuch of Unteroffizier Hachtel is missing. He says it is in a drawer in the house. Am hoping that guerrilla patrol will collect this today and any other papers in the drawer.

26 January

Morale is very high here. British and guerrillas have had constant stream of men offering to be volunteers and can raise several hundreds if arms are provided. Information is also pouring in and I think that if some further arms could be supplied guerrillas could capture and hold Pizzoferrato and Gamberale, thus threatening the whole enemy supply line and axis of withdrawal. I should like full instructions on this as higher policy is no doubt involved. The guerrillas are very keen to get arms as they seem to fear enemy brutality prior to withdrawal and many towns are totally unprotected.

(Signed) Major L. Wigram

These were ambitious thoughts. Pizzoferrato and Gamberale were the last two major villages in no-man's-land. Although only just lower than halfway down the triangle between Casoli at the apex and Castel di Sangro at the base, the bottom end of no-man's-land was covered in thick forest with few habitations. If the top was chopped off the Germans would have to retreat to the line of the Sangro – a withdrawal of about fifteen miles. Also, their main north–south supply line for the central sector of the Gustav Line passed through Castel di Sangro and to cut this or even to threaten it would be a major triumph.

All this time I was disconsolately kicking my heels at Casoli. Lionel's signals, as the account of the Quadri affair indicates, were full and meticulously drafted. He would usually complete a report by ten or eleven o'clock each morning and if the line was working for speech, they got back to Corps in about an hour. If the line was poor and morse code had to be used, they might take up to four hours. Corps were conscientious in passing the signals to me but, again, the line between Corps HQ and Casoli was faulty and sometimes I would sit in the orderly room for several hours in a fever of impatience, knowing that Lionel's doings of the previous night were known and available to everyone concerned except me. After a few days I could stand it no longer and made the trip to Corps, where I persuaded a friendly intelligence officer to send me a copy of Lionel's signals by dispatch rider as soon as they arrived.

Equally distressing was my exclusion from the planning of Lionel's affairs. I sat in the Casoli *albergo* like a mother whose boy has gone to boarding school for the first time and who worries whether he is remembering to put on his winter woollies and take his cod-liver oil. My concern was Lionel's belief that perfect planning would result in a perfect operation. Even at Barnard Castle, I had taken a delight in throwing spanners into his meticulous calculations.

'It will take seventeen minutes for the platoon commander to reach that spinney,' Lionel would say.

'Suppose he has violent diarrhoea and is taken short,' I would say. 'That would add at least two minutes.'

'The plan has a tolerance of up to three minutes,' Lionel would reply with some asperity.

179

'Then,' I would go on, 'as he is pulling his trousers up he treads on a snake which bites him in the fleshy part of the leg.'

At that point Lionel would probably give up. As in training I kept hurling burst tyres, blown bridges, avalanches and forest fires in his path, so in the real war, when he enunciated a plan calculated to the finest hairline, I immediately assessed it from the point of view of sod's law (which roughly means that any disaster that can happen will happen, plus a few more which are unforeseen). One part of this examination started from the assumption that the enemy had precise advance information of one's plans. How would he react? Another was based on the hypothesis (frequently borne out) that any detached unit will always get lost. And so on.

So I fretted. I visited the forward positions constantly; organised some patrols; one clear frosty day climbed halfway up the Majella to a point well above the height of Ben Nevis, and saw spread out before me, it seemed, about one half of Italy; spent time in Civitella with Nick Williams and his lot; thought frequently of visiting Lionel but dismissed the idea as impracticable; wrote up my patrolling experiences on the Sangro, and paced about the battalion mess like a caged animal. I no longer dined with the baron because I had come to feel that there was something indecent in eating and drinking with a host whose hospitality was dictated, at least in part, by the fear that his guest might send him to prison. Also, Elena had disappeared. When I went to the house one night there was no stone on the wall, nor was there the next night. I noticed that the curtains were drawn all day, and on asking one of the baron's relatives whom I met in the street what had happened to her, he merely shrugged his shoulders and said 'Ha sparita.' I asked him where and he shrugged again. 'A sua famiglia, nella montagna.' When pressed again, he turned away saying 'Non lo so.'

The absence of Elena was both a penance and a relief. I missed the mad excitement of our encounters, for sexual desire can be a torment when suddenly frustrated. At the same time I was becoming a little fearful of her power to make me act as a sort of sexual dummy. Like a puppeteer, she pulled the strings and I jumped. I had become her toy and her creature, and I feared the power she had over me.

I had two personal messages from Lionel which reached me by

a relay of guerrilla runners. The first was to get me to approach Army on the matter of more and better weapons. He was going to mount a major attack on Pizzoferrato. Corps, although keen, were apparently not keen enough. The second contained an outline of his plan to attack Pizzoferrato. He would need support from Corps troops and he wanted me to go over the plan with the GSO to check it through and make absolutely sure he was going to get exactly the support he needed. The message form was crumpled and bloodstained. It was dated 30 January, but it arrived in Casoli on the afternoon of the second of February. Evidently it had had a difficult passage. I looked at the clock. Lionel's fighting force was due to leave base in less than two hours. It was too late to do anything.

That evening I pored over the map and marked up Lionel's route and that of his supporting troops. Would there not be minefields here and here? Surely the Pizzoferrato garrison would have an outlying section here and sentries on the crestline opposite the town here and here? Lionel would have taken account of all these possibilities, surely. But what else? I was impressed by the audacity of the operation, but it was hazardous. Looking out of the window at the bright flicker of moonlight between the scurrying clouds, apprehension began to gather in my stomach and chest like a physical thing. I went to bed wakeful and uneasy.

CHAPTER

14

O<small>N THE FIRST OF FEBRUARY</small> Lionel wrote to his wife:

I am still without further news of you and am simply aching for a letter. There are difficulties about the post just now so I'm not unduly alarmed – only very disappointed.

Spring is already here in this part of the world. As I write this it is as warm as a June day, with the sun shining brightly and the snow melting hard. It is the sort of mountain climate one would pay a lot to enjoy in peacetime on one of those winter cruises, but one does *not* enjoy it now although one should.

I see a lot of Italians still – particularly their small village life now. They are absolutely primitive here – just as they were hundreds or indeed thousands of years ago. I went out to a meal last night with the chieftain of a local village. When I asked him how long the family had occupied the house he replied 'always' and I couldn't get any other answer from him. He had the usual large family – 5 daughters and 3 sons – rather smaller than usual in fact. In the small villages when there is a feast the women are not allowed to participate. They prepare the meal in the kitchen and serve it but don't appear otherwise at all. The feast consists of spaghetti, followed by two sorts of meat course (one after the other) a vegetable course, then cakes and wine. You drink ten or twelve glasses of wine if you are polite. I am getting very fond of Italian wine. I used to hate it at first but it grows on you. I can drink a lot of it now without feeling the least bit tight so you had better start practising too.

I am counting the days till I get home to *YOU* and those wicked infants. I take long looks at all the little children here whenever I can. They are very nice but I never see any to equal ours – never. They haven't got the secret or haven't had the right pattern to work from I'm afraid.

All my love darlings and do write lots and often.

At 1800 hours on the evening of 2 February Lionel led his party out from his base at Montedelapiano. Once clear of the town, a screen of guides and scouts fanned out in front, then came Lionel himself, walking in the centre of a knot of runners and messengers, next Lieutenant Guy – the only ex-Italian army officer to be admitted to Wigforce – leading two platoons of guerrillas, then the British contingent, some twenty-six strong, a hand-picked assault platoon of guerrillas followed led by Lieutenant Exell, the only available British officer in the Corps who could speak Italian, and finally a squad of sappers, in all a force of about one hundred and fifty men.

The column marched across country for about an hour until they reached a village where they met with a body of sixty Italian commandos, whose task was to follow up the attack and consolidate the position after the assault. These were mountain warfare troops who had fought in Albania and Abyssinia, but never against the Allies, and as reward for this they had been allowed to keep their identity and were now fighting on our side. They were to leave the village at 0200 and reach Pizzoferrato at 0600. Routes were checked and watches synchronised.

The main party set off, travelling across country to avoid the minefields laid across the roads and major tracks. The moon, at first intermittent, came clear of cloud at about midnight, but progress was slow, partly because the advance guard frequently had to test for mines. By 0400 hours on the third the main party arrived at Pizzoferrato.

The village of Pizzoferrato lies on the neck of a narrow ridge which juts out from the downward sweep of a wooded hillside. A towering rock rises up at the extremity of the ridge and dominates the village and the whole valley beyond. This column of rock, about two hundred feet high, is precipitous all round; and access to its top is by a spiral ledge chiselled out of the stone face which, as it nears the plateau on the summit, passes through a small cluster of houses. The lowest of these buildings (the Third House) was a range of cottages, the next was the Second House, a farm building standing about thirty feet above the Third House. Above that again was the First House, a substantial affair clamped against the cliff face with five storeys on the outer side and three on the inner. It followed the line of the cliff round eighty degrees, one end being almost adjacent to the topmost enclosure on the rock which consisted of a walled courtyard with a chapel (the main feature of the whole protuberance) standing on the skyline.

Map 8

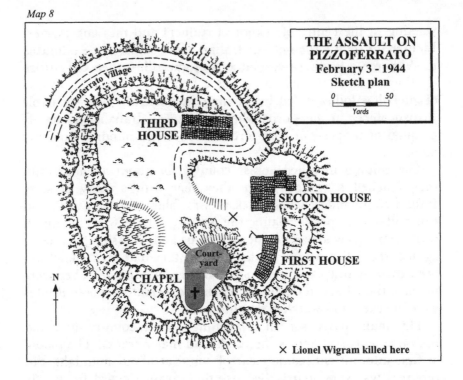

**THE ASSAULT ON
PIZZOFERRATO
February 3 - 1944
Sketch plan**

0   50
Yards

To Pizzoferrato Village

THIRD
HOUSE

SECOND HOUSE

Court-
yard

FIRST HOUSE

N

CHAPEL

× Lionel Wigram killed here

This little complex had been closely observed by the guerrillas over the past week. It was occupied by a force of between thirty and fifty Germans who were almost wholly isolated from the village below. They had a troop of artillery about half a mile north-east of the village and the remainder of that same company was in possession of Gamberale, a village about two miles away.

Lionel dropped off the sappers near the enemy gun positions and told them not to move until they heard the main attack under way, and then to rush the sentries and sabotage the guns. He paused at the base of the rock and went forward with Guy and Exell to check the position. Everything conformed exactly to the model used in planning the operation.

Lionel and the British contingent surrounded the First House; Exell and his hand-picked partisans the Second, and Guy's two platoons the Third. By 0445 all three parties reported they were in position. Guy then sent two men forward to the Third House which they reported unoccupied. He brought his two platoons up the rock and joined Exell's force surrounding the Second House.

Up to this point, although the moon was too bright for comfort,

184

surprise appeared to have been maintained. As the whole force lay in an agony of silence ready to attack, a German sentry opened the gate of the First House and walked forward towards the point where Lionel lay. When he was about fifteen yards away Lionel leapt to his feet and shouted in German: 'You are surrounded by a large force. Put up your hands. We will treat you well. We are British.'

The German sentry threw down his rifle, put up his hands, and walked steadily towards Lionel. Lionel went forward with two guerrillas to take him prisoner. When they were a few yards apart, the sentry flung himself to the ground. A shot was fired from the ground-floor window of the house which killed Lionel instantly. At this the whole party opened fire. For half an hour the two upper houses were subjected to a hail of fire from the attacking force. Exell forced an entry into the ground floor of the Second House, but the Germans barricaded themselves on the first floor. It was not possible to rush the First House because the small inward frontage was heavily mined and booby traps could be seen in the main doorway.

Suddenly the Germans opened fire. The effect was devastating: they had clearly marked the position of our men in the moonlight and had refrained from returning fire to achieve surprise and kill the maximum number in their first fusillade. Our party withdrew behind cover but kept up the exchange, with both sides shooting and taking cover as best they could.

At 0530 a party of about fifty Germans arrived at the base of the rock from Gamberale. They advanced up the causeway and attacked the partisan platoons in the rear, causing casualties. Lieutenant Exell was wounded and took no further part in the action, and at this point the Allied force began to disintegrate. The British and some partisans retreated yard by yard and rock by rock towards the chapel. The guerrillas lower down began to slip away over the edge of the cliff. Nevertheless, the shooting continued remorselessly. As the daylight gained strength, our men began to offer better targets to the Germans. After some hours the remaining British and guerrilla forces on the top of the rock decided to withdraw into the chapel, barricade the door and sit it out until the arrival of the commandos, who were already well behind time.

It was in the chapel that the last horrifying chapter in this action was played out. The British and Italian forces, now short of ammunition, leaderless and surrounded by wounded and dying comrades, found they were unable to fire outwards from the chapel's windows which were too high from the floor and for which there was no firestep. All exits were covered by German marksmen. The Germans blew in the windows and lobbed stick grenades through them. They also contrived a fire position from a ladder against one of the windows. By firing a Schmeisser from there they forced the men inside to cower against the back wall, where they were easy targets for grenades thrown through the rear windows. The last desperate defenders of the chapel gave up shortly after 1000 hours. Several of the guerrillas were lined up against a wall and had their brains blown out; the rest of the force were taken prisoner.

At 1100 hours the commandos arrived. Their guide had lost his way and then allowed them to run foul of several mine-fields. There was nothing they could do; the battle was over. Throughout the day sporadic firing continued as the guerrillas retreated down the rock and away across country. At 1800 hours a German party left Pizzoferrato for their battalion headquarters in Palena station, some ten miles away. They took with them the wounded Lieutenant Exell, twenty British prisoners, many also wounded, some severely, five guerrilla prisoners and over a score of civilians whom they suspected (some rightly some wrongly) of being partisans.

Many of the guerrillas stayed in covering positions below the rock for a second night and on the morning of the fourth, the day after the battle, they formed a patrol and found one remaining German in the town, whom they took prisoner. In the First House they found twenty dead Germans. The British casualties were five dead (including Lionel), one officer and twenty other ranks wounded and prisoners, eleven guerrillas known to be killed (probably many more whose bodies were removed by local people), five prisoners and an indeterminate number of wounded. (Any wounded man who could walk or be transported was given shelter locally until he was well enough to return home.) The guerrilla patrol reported that Lionel had been buried where he fell, in front of the First House. A small white cross, with his name inscribed, had been erected over his grave.

CHAPTER

15

I SPENT THE MORNING AFTER THE Pizzoferrato raid hanging around the field telephone in the Casoli orderly room. At best I expected to hear something between ten o'clock and noon, at worst by two o'clock. But the hours came and went and when I had heard nothing by half-past two, I rang Corps. They had heard nothing. They had been in touch with the signaller at Buonanotte. He had heard nothing. They were perplexed. I was not so much perplexed as fearful, knowing that no news was likely to be bad news. If all had been well, Lionel would have got through somehow. As the long afternoon wore on, assumption gave way to certainty and I prepared myself for the worst. At about five o'clock the sergeant major put his head round the door. 'Guerrilla to see you, sah,' he said and without meeting my eyes he ushered in the shambling figure of one of the Civitella partisans. He was out of breath and distressed and panted out his message.

'*Major Wigram morto, molti partigiani morti, Inglesi tutti morti.*'

He had no further or better particulars. The message had come by guerrilla grapevine, a system of runners between points where for a few miles the civilian telephone system was still working. This was faster than a relay of runners, but only just. As I was questioning him, Corps came on the phone with much the same message from our signaller at Buonanotte. Major Wigram was dead: the whole force had been killed or taken prisoner.

There would soon be guerrillas returning to base who would know more. I sent a signal to all the forward companies to bring in immediately any returning guerrillas who entered their sector. At about seven o'clock the first one came back in a jeep from Gessopalena, then another three, and then more, until there were a dozen men waiting to be interviewed.

Over the hours up to midnight I pieced together the story of that fatal morning. Some of the accounts were contradictory, some irrelevant and some devised to exonerate the messengers,

187

most of whom had run away. By the time the last man left the room I had a pretty full picture of the whole affair.

I could not sleep. Lionel dead. How could he have fallen for that ruse? It had been used on the Sangro and we had discussed how to cope with it. He had taken a risk at Quadri and it had come off. Now he had taken one too many. Why had Exell not set fire to the Second House and smoked the Germans out? Why had Lionel not taken the commandos with him from Faro? To let them go separately was asking for trouble. Then I answered each question – Lionel walked up to the sentry because he thought he was in dead ground from the house. Perhaps his killer had not shot from a window but had been concealed outside – the Germans had spotted the British force earlier and set a trap. Exell could not fire the house because his troops could not get out without being killed. The commandos could not leave with Lionel because half their detachment had not arrived and they had to wait for it. Then I asked all the questions over again and found new answers which raised more questions: why, for instance, had the Germans buried Lionel and left twenty of their own dead in the First House? But always my thoughts returned to those moments when Lionel called out, 'You are surrounded by a large force,' and the bullet of death which followed it. This scene played in my mind over and over again, sometimes in slow motion, sometimes in that strange eerie light which in films is known as 'night for day'.

Then, in the small hours, guilt. My Scottish presbyterian upbringing always left me open to attacks of self-accusation, and now I succumbed to an overwhelming sense of remorse. Lionel, my friend and in many ways my hero, the leader of a movement which had reformed infantry tactics, who had dared to explore the prohibited territory of morale in battle, who had inspired hundreds of officers like me with a new professionalism and a new belief in our ability to beat the Germans, this man had been killed in a *Boy's Own Paper* adventure in the mountains of Italy, in an action which in the context of the whole front was totally unimportant. And I could have stopped it. The fact that he was under the command of Corps was irrelevant. I had worked as his partner in devising and building up the toy army of Wigforce, a dangerous toy, and one which had caused his death and the deaths of many British and Italian young men. *Mea culpa*.

There is one sure antidote to the morbidity of the small hours, and that is to stand vertical, to dash cold water on the face, and to imbibe a pint of scalding hot tea, preferably fortified with Johnnie Walker, while inhaling a Capstan full-strength cigarette. To hell with it, I thought, whatever he was doing, wherever he might be, Lionel would have fought Germans. Nothing would have kept him away from the sharp end of war. And since General Montgomery in his infinite wisdom had pushed Lionel into the shallows of warfare, where I too happened to be, we could do nothing other than what we were trained to do. Fight the enemy – fight the enemy until you do for him or he does for you.

But this mood did not last. For the next few days I went through my visiting routine like an automaton, with a fixed smile and an apparently cheerful address, but inwardly I was absorbed by the dull, thudding, insistent replay of the last hours of Lionel's last patrol.

By the seventh of February the Germans had evacuated Toricella, Pizzoferrato, Gamberale and all the no-man's-land which lay within the original triangle between Castel di Sangro and Casoli. Whether this was brought about by the efforts of Wigforce, or whether those efforts did no more than accelerate a retreat which was part of the German plan, we could not tell. Meanwhile Wigforce had quietly melted away. I called in the forward companies to consolidate on Casoli, leaving only a screen of guerrilla outposts up against the now distant enemy, and prepared to hand over the battalion front to our successors, for we knew that we were to join the 1st Army in its assault on Cassino.

On the ninth of February we set out to cross the Apennines, but were blocked by a second snowfall and did not arrive at Villa Ventura until the sixteenth. Here Paul rejoined the battalion and I reverted to my status of second-in-command. We moved up in readiness to attack Cassino but the weather was against us and every day the codeword reached us, 'Bradman will not bat today'. We marvelled that any staff officer could believe that such a transparent message could fool anyone; certainly by the time we learnt that Bradman would bat today (16 March), we felt there could not be a single German commander who did not know the identity of the mighty Don or the significance of his going in to bat. But batting at Cassino was tough and,

189

when Paul sent me up to hold the castle on the lower slopes of Monastery Hill, it became even tougher. On the morning of the twenty-third of March, I was leading a counterattack out of the castle against a German force only about sixty yards away when I saw a smoke canister from a supporting New Zealand battery land in a shellhole. 'Lightning never strikes twice in the same place,' I yelled to my batman Rutherford. 'Let's get in there.' But we were no sooner in than lightning did strike again, in the shape of a second smoke canister which landed on, and shattered, my lower left leg. By impressing some stretcher-bearer members of the neighbouring Indian Division, Rutherford managed that night to lower me, still woozy from a heavy intake of morphine, down the precipitous cliff to the town below. But every time a shell fell the bearers dispersed and poor Rutherford had to recruit a fresh squad. Later I was told that my leg was amputated in an Indian field hospital at the base of the rock. I have fleeting memories of a seemingly endless nightmare trip in a field ambulance with five other wounded men, all of us screaming for water, of which there was none.

In the base hospital in Capua, sometimes delirious, my thoughts returned to Lionel. Cassino had driven him into the background, but now the tragedy of Wigforce returned with a vengeance. I was lucky: an infantry officer had only two options in World War Two – death or being wounded. Virtually none survived intact in the front line through the North African campaign and Italy. I was lucky to be wounded and lucky again in that as septicaemia spread up my limb, I had access to plasma and penicillin. Penicillin was new. There was only enough for a few dozen cases, and as an officer of field rank I was one of those who got it. Other ranks died. But Lionel was unlucky. A bullet through the chest. A neat circular hole at the point of entry in front, a gaping jagged chasm nine inches across behind, a typical Schmeiser job. If the German who killed him had been a foot off centre, Lionel would have lived. If he had hiccuped as he shot, if Lionel had stumbled, if Lionel had put one of the guerrillas in the centre instead of himself. If the New Zealand smoke canister had fallen two feet short it would have killed me. Lionel would be alive and I would be dead. But that wasn't destiny. It wasn't planned by anyone Up There. It was luck, pure bloody luck, so shut up and stop churning it round and round. Another whisky. Another shot of morphine.

Hold the pretty nurse's hand.

Two weeks later I was one of a dozen wounded officers aboard a private yacht converted to a hospital ship. Once out of the Mediterranean we struck foul weather, but after a ghastly week we lay up in the still waters of the Bristol Channel. By this time the natural reservoir of strength which had sustained many of us through the first shock of seeing a part of one's body shattered, the loss of blood and the spreading septicaemia, was running out and we slumped back into a semi-concious limbo until the infection began to ebb and we could take nourishment again.

I was in this low state when one day I found Lionel's wife Olga by my side. So far as I can remember, she was a petite woman who spoke to me gently and sweetly about Lionel. I had of course written to her as soon as I knew of Lionel's death and she had replied, but now she wanted to know everything he had done from the day of joining the 6 RWK. This I was quite unable to provide; some things I could not remember, some things I could, but the effort of recounting them was too great and sentences would drift off into silence as emotion and fatigue overcame me. We made an odd couple, the widow dry-eyed and alert, interviewing the returned soldier incoherent apparently from grief, his cheeks wet with tears. Some weeks later I wrote her a full account of Lionel's doings in Italy and we continued a desultory correspondence for some months. I never visited her, perhaps because subconsciously I wanted to forget the whole thing, perhaps also because of a residual feeling of shame and because I wanted the war out of my life altogether.

As I gained strength I had other visitors. Polly took up residence in a nearby hotel and sat by me for as many hours as a tolerant ward sister would allow; my sister Sheila arrived, scarcely recognising in the crumpled bed-bound individual the strapping Argyll officer who had taken leave of her just under a year before. She brought my dog Robin, now the monarch of Dumcrieff, who instantly won all hearts and was allowed to sleep that night at the foot of my bed.

Once recovered and able to hop about on crutches, I rejoined Paul, now the commandant of an officer training unit at Bournemouth, and worked under the consultant psychologist to the army on a series of training experiments. A brilliant and eccentric man, he willingly took aboard my account of Lionel's main tenets in the matter of morale and infantry organisation in battle, and this led to an assignment for me to compile the new army manual on the principles and practice of instruction for the infantry. This was a labour of love; once again I embodied in it a large element of Lionel's philosophy, indeed probably too much, because my manual had only a short life, the War Office replacing it as soon as they could with a document which paid greater respect to orthodoxy.

As I was in the later stages of completing this work, I was asked if I would go to the Royal Military Academy at Dehra Dun, where for over a century the British had trained in their own image officers for the Indian army. My job was to assist the handover of the academy from the British army to the Indian, who would henceforth train their own officers. I jumped at the chance and for several happy months instructed Indian instructors in the lessons I had learnt at Barnard Castle and in the field in Italy.

Back in civilian life, in 1947 I returned with my wife-to-be, Helen, to Casoli and Civitella. We were royally received. There was no transport available in those days except UNRRA trucks, so we were provided with two splendid white horses, Cesar and Cesarina, to make the journey to Civitella. On arrival we learnt that Nick Williams had been killed in a brawl in a brothel, but Achille Gattone was active in presenting me with a request to the king, signed by three hundred ex-guerrillas, for financial recognition of the great services they had rendered the Allies. For the next five years a similar document was to reach me annually in London. A monument was to be erected to the guerrillas in Toricella. Could the name of Major Wigram be inscribed with those of the partisans? Certainly, I said. He would be honoured. The baron entertained us to dinner.

Time and lack of transport did not allow us to visit Pizzoferrato on that occasion, but in 1966, as part of a family holiday, I made a pilgrimage to the rock, the First House and the chapel. Lionel's grave had disappeared, his body removed to the Allied war cemetery on the Sangro, but the walls of the chapel had been left exactly as they were when the British force finally capitulated. Behind the altar there was a crucifix surrounded by the pock-marks of Schmeiser bullets, but itself untouched. Beneath it was the inscription:

THIS CRUCIFIX
WAS MIRACULOUSLY UNSCATHED
BY THE FURY OF THE ENEMY
BEING RENDERED IMMUNE
FROM THE STRUGGLE AND STRIFE
FEB 3   OF LIFE ON EARTH   1944

A miracle I could have done without, I reflected, or would gladly have exchanged for the lives of those who were butchered against the chapel wall.

I visited the partisan monument in Toricella which carried the names of sixty or seventy local inhabitants who had been murdered as well as those of the guerrillas who had lost their lives. The face of the monument had been defaced by tar. I asked in the village why this had been done, but no one was willing to give an answer. Lionel's name had not been included.

In September 1990, after I had remarried, I paid my last visit to Pizzoferrato to take photographs to illustrate this book. Nothing had changed except that there was now an account of the battle, inaccurate in some details, typed, framed and hung in the apse of the chapel. My wife Moni had asked for the chapel to be opened but got a negative response. Only when I went down and talked about the British major who had been killed on that site did the mood change. I was escorted, almost carried, up the rocky path to the chapel door (for I have difficulty in walking) and the events of the morning of Lionel's death were told to me once again. They were still vivid in their memory. This time, as I surveyed the scene, I felt at peace, perhaps because in the process of recording the story of Lionel Wigram and of Wigforce I had exorcised a memory which had haunted me for nearly half a century.

APPENDIX

I

In May 1943 Lionel Wigram was posted to Allied Forces HQ in North Africa. He bore with him the following letter to General Alexander:

From: Brig. H. W. Houldsworth,
Commandant, School of Infantry.

Tel: *Barnard Castle 275, Extn. 1*

The School of Infantry
Barnard Castle,
Co. Durham.

1st June 1943

My dear General,

The bearer of this letter is Lieut. Colonel L. Wigram who has been mixed up with Battle Schools and Battle Drill ever since your first conception of this teaching. He became the first Commandant of General Utterson-Kelso's original Battle School in the 47 Division and when the GHQ Battle School was formed he came here as Chief Instructor. When the School of Infantry started he became Chief Instructor of the Battle School Wing. During the past three months he has been filling the appointment of GSO I Research at this School. He has now been posted overseas and I am informed by the War office that he is going to your theatre of war to the 2 i/c Pool with a view to command.

Wigram is a most outstanding person with the quickest and most fluent brain I ever met. He has, without question, done an outstanding service to the army but in so doing he has incurred the prejudice of many Senior Officers in the country chiefly on the grounds that he was putting across the whole case without any battle experience behind him. He had of course been given a very free hand in the past but there are very few who could have put the whole thing across with such marked ability and success as he has achieved.

Wigram naturally has a great ambition to gain experience and to do some fighting. He has had little experience of commanding anything and I am not prepared to say how he would do in this respect but he has the kind of versatile brain which can turn itself to anything and produce the goods at the other end.

I feel you will be interested to hear of his arrival in North Africa and there is no one who could tell you more of our doings here or of our requirements. I also feel that if there should be delay in posting him to a Battalion it would be greatly in our interests and in the interests of Infantry Training at home, if he could have some freedom to move about and obtain information about certain points of training over which we still are gropping [sic] in the dark.

Yours sincerely
(signed) H. W. Houldsworth

General the Honourable,
Sir H. R. L. Alexander, GCB, CSI, DSO, MC,
Allied Force HQ.,
NORTH AFRICA

Lionel was posted to the HQ of 78 Division, to whom the brief was passed that he should 'have some freedom to move about and obtain information about certain points in training'. He went ahead of the division in the first wave of landings in Sicily and rejoined it some days later when it disembarked. During the campaign he had a wide range of experience (which he describes in his report) and he finished up as acting commanding officer of the 5th Buffs in 36 Brigade. At the conclusion of the campaign he wrote a report and dispatched it on 17 August 1943 to Brigadier Kenchington of the Directorate of Military Training British North African forces, who forwarded a copy to Brigadier Cooney the DDMT at the War Office, with the following note (which includes a heartfelt appeal for help):

In haste on journey. Wigram has seen a lot in his six weeks and done well. I think its well worth the journey to let him spend a few days at his old School saying how experience has modified his teaching views.

Remember however – I'm sure you will – Alex's caution about not altering things on one man's or one general's experiences. We are getting in some considered views very shortly as *at last* they have agreed to our going forward to collect, compare and sift views at all levels.

SOS. Lack of equipment and welfare amenities at enormous Base Draft Trg Units is threatening morale badly and unless you can make WO send equipment *earmarked* for trg and perhaps persuade Gen Jardine's branch those dumps in the wilderness are a place with special need for morale – unless all this I think the winter will not be a good time to keep tails up.

The text of Lionel's report is as follows:

Dear Brigadier,

As requested I am appending* a report of the lessons of the Campaign in SICILY as they have occurred to me. As you know owing to the kindness of the Div Comd I was allowed to come over to SICILY as an observer at the beginning of the Campaign, subsequently rejoining 78 Div on its arrival. As a result of this I was able to see some eight or nine different Bns in action, and to study and compare their various methods. I was also able to meet a very large number of old students from BARNARD CASTLE of all ranks. I was able to discuss all the points I am making below with a large number of officers with considerable experience in battle, and I find that there is general agreement. As you know it also transpired owing to the fortunes of war that I found myself at different times commanding a Section, a Platoon, a Company and finally a Bn, and I was thus able to get first hand experience of many of the matters to which I refer.

1. ATTACK BY INFILTRATION

The Germans have undoubtedly in one way scored a decided success in SICILY. They have been able to evacuate their forces almost intact having suffered very few casualties in killed and wounded. They have inflicted heavy casualties on us. We all feel rather irritated at the result, well as we have done.

Why has this happened? One hears it said on all sides that the country is mountainous and difficult, and therefore ideal for defence, impossible for attack. In my view this is a completely erroneous impression of the country. It is true that the country is mountainous but it is everywhere close. Every hill is covered with olive groves, plantations, standing crops etc, and in addition the system of irrigation by deep ditches, high stone walls and a great number of ditches and wadis makes the country perfect for individual infiltration. It is quite easy for the Germans to defend by maintaining a very thin screen of MGs and gunner and mrtr OPs sited on the reverse slope of the hills and to get magnificent cross-fire shoots both by day and by night. If we attack such positions frontally even with Hy Arty Supp we play right into his hands. He maintains his screen until the last moment inflicting heavy casualties, then as our attack pushes in, pulls out to take up a further position in the rear. So we find invariably that he has gone, and the small number of dead bodies found and the small number of prisoners taken tell their own story.

*In its original form this epistolary opening runs straight on into the body of the report.

To my mind we have not yet *in our training* put into practice the lessons learnt in the Battle of FRANCE, and more especially in the battles of MALAYA against the Japs. In MALAYA our own position was very similar to that of the Germans in SICILY. We had prepared our withdrawal from hill to hill expecting the Jap to attack us. He did nothing of the kind. By employing minute parties of specialist tps armed with TGs and MGs he filtered through the cover by night in ones and twos and was able every morning to establish road blocks in our rear to shoot up our tpt and communications, to pick off OPs and W/sets, and so to disorganise us that we were compelled to withdraw in disorder from position to position without getting a sight of the enemy. His tps who carried out this work suffered very few casualties.

I think that the whole key to our future success in the coming battles of EUROPE will lie in the organisation of similar forces. From now on the Germans are going to fight a series of rearguard battles wherever they happen to be. If each Bn could produce one or two Pls trained, I suggest, to work in threes, each group of three carrying one MG and one TG and each being prepared *to work entirely on its own*, the problem would be solved. As soon as contact is gained these tps would be sent out at dusk and would be in position behind the enemy by first light. This would invariably compel the enemy to withdraw.

I make the following points in regard to these suggestions:

(i) I am convinced that we have been too ambitious in trying to teach each soldier the art of infiltration. Even fanatics like the Japs and Germans found that only a few men could be trusted to do this job, and they have always left it to specialists. It is an impossible ideal to hope to train the Army as a whole in it.

(ii) yet our men can do this job. Instance the Bn I am at present commanding, at RIVOGLIA Bn HQ was being constantly menaced by enemy snipers and MGs hidden in the rocks and trees at the foot of Mt. ETNA. I sent off a young Pl Comd to deal with the matter. He first of all tried to use his whole Pl but subsequently picked four men and with them fought an individual infiltration battle against the Germans which lasted the whole day. The result of the battle was as follows – Our casualties nil, Germans 3 killed for certain, 6 prisoners captured. German equipment captured – 2 heavy MGs and large quantities of sniping gear. I saw these men when they returned, they said they had been very frightened at first, but as the day wore on and they realised what rotten shots the Germans were they got a feeling of superiority and towards the end were thoroughly enjoying themselves.

I think that every Pl could find a few men like these.

(iii) All the evidence points to the fact that the Germans at any rate in SICILY do not withdraw on a timed schedule but 'under pressure'. There is no recorded instance of them standing to fight to the last round and to the last man. They always cleared out as soon as they were really menaced, and the morale of those captured was decidedly low. This strengthens my view that they would clear out even more quickly if attacked from the rear (or merely threatened from the rear).

(iv) It has several times been suggested that the same object could be achieved by infiltrating whole Bns round to the rear. This may be so, but I do not think it would be nearly as successful and it would result in heavy casualties as the German always protects his flanks by MGs and gunner OPs. I do not think that even a Coy or a Pl could do it successfully except on very favourable grd.

(v) Until we have these little groups trained I do not think Comds have any option but to continue the present costly methods. The matter is just one of *training* and I am sure it would only take a few days. I would very much like to have the opportunity of training and organising a force of this kind. There are all sorts of small points – camouflage, admin, comns etc.

2. ATTACK – BATTLE DRILL

It was my chief concern to see the application of Battle Drill to battle and I watched it very closely. I have come to the conclusion that a number of revisions are necessary if we are to deal with realities.

There is nothing wrong with Battle Drill in theory, but it presupposes that you have a Pl team in which every individual knows his job and his place, and in which every man is brave enough and experienced enough to do as he is told. Of course in practice you have no such thing. Probably about half the Pl really understand the Battle Drill thoroughly, and as I shall show below in any case quite a number of the men in the Pl cannot be relied upon. I have, therefore, come to the conclusion that Battle Drill as at present taught is very useful training, and will give first-class results when applied by regular Bns who have practised it for many months, but we need something very much simpler for this war.

I want first of all to describe how Pls are fighting at the moment. Attacks are invariably carefully prepared, the tps go forward under arty concentrations or a barrage. When the barrage lifts (if the enemy has not gone) he opens up with his MGs, and it is here that the Pl battle starts and it is here that the battle itself is lost or won.

In very rare instances Pl and Coy Comds have applied some sort of Battle Drill to knock out these enemy MGs. Where they have done so they have invariably succeeded in taking the position with very few casualties.

But, in the very large majority of cases, no sort of Battle Drill is used. No attempt is made at Fire and Movement. The positions are taken by what I call 'Guts and Movement'.

The battle goes something like this:-

Enemy MGs open fire, the whole Pl lie down except the Pl Comd and three or four gutful men. Five or six men start making tracks for home, meanwhile the gutful men under the Pl Comd dash straight in to the enemy position without any covering fire and always succeed in taking the position. In some instances some positions are taken by as few as two men, and every Bn Comd will confirm that it is always the same group of nine or ten who are there first, and on whom the battle depends.

I have personally seen this method of attack used in all, except one, of the battles in which I took part, and this explains one of the mysteries I have never been able to solve before – that is the saying of many experienced soldiers that 'you must never allow men to lie down in a battle'.

This method of attack is peculiarly British and from the point of view of sheer courage it really has no equal. I am convinced however that we can find other and better methods, and I make the following observations:

(i) Some Comds say that this method is successful with few casualties. This is true if you speak of casualties in quantity, but it is far from true if you speak of casualties in quality. The Pl in action is almost invariably twenty-two strong and of whatever Regt good or bad, every Pl can be analysed as follows:-

Six gutful men who will go anywhere and do anything, 12 'sheep' who will follow a short distance behind if they are well led, 4–6 who will run away.

I have discussed these figures with many people and they all agree, although there is some slight disagreement on figures. These figures are roughly accurate as shown by the number of Court-Martials for running away that follow every Campaign. Every Bn has between forty to sixty and there are, of course, many others who aren't caught.

Looking at these figures it will be seen that the group from which casualties cannot be spared is the gutful group, yet I would say that casualties in this group are often 100 per cent per month. We must find a method of fighting which is more economical.

(ii) Battle Drill or Fire and Movement is not applied because in its present form it is too complicated, and it presupposes that when a Section is told to do a thing that it will do it whilst in actual fact, as the above Pl figures show, they will probably do little or nothing.

What we need is an extremely simple Battle Drill which takes cognisance of the fact that there are only 4–6 men in the Pl *who can be absolutely relied on to do as they are told under enemy fire.*

The following is my suggested drill:-

(a) *Night attack behind arty concs or barrage* (commonest standard stroke employed out here).

The Pl of 22 men is divided up as follows:-

1st group – All the riflemen under the Pl Comd.

2nd group – 3 Bren groups (3 men to each gun) comd by the Pl Sgt.

3rd group – two-inch Mtr team follows up in rear of group 1.

The leaders of the above three groups have absorbed three of the reliable men in the Pl. The other three reliable men will act as 2nds in comd to take over if the leader is killed or wounded.

The method of movement is simple as the Pl is handled as a Section.

The rifle group will be in fairly tight night formation (patrol). (This is essential to make sure that nobody drops out.) The Bren groups will be in a similar formation and the two groups will move side by side (preferably Bren groups a little to the rear) with a gap of about 50 to 100x (according to the visibility between the two groups). The two-inch mrtr group keeps about 50x in the rear of the Rifle group.

As soon as the barrage lifts and the Rifle group is fired on, the Rifle group goes to ground. The Pl Sgt (who can really be relied on) at once gets his three Brens into action shooting at the enemy MG or MGs. This will invariably silence the enemy guns for the time being. I have made particularly careful observation on this point and have checked it up with a large number of Pl Comds. As soon as our MGs open up the Germans (who are always using tracer) stop. I think they do this because they are nervous or in order to observe our fire. They always keep quiet until we have finished our hate, then as soon as there is a lull they open up again. One almost never sees or hears Spandau and Bren firing together at the same time. It is always one followed by the other. Even inaccurate fire from our Brens will quieten the Spandaus until we have finished firing.

As soon as the Brens have quietened the enemy MGs the Pl Comd gets on his feet, persuades all the rest of the riflemen to do likewise, and leads them straight into the enemy position under cover of the Bren fire. He may tell the

Mrtr to put down a bomb or two also if necessary. He will nearly always be able to make the enemy position in a single bound as the Germans, as a rule, hold their fire (particularly at night) until we are within 200x. If he cannot make it in a single bound he will have to lead his men forward into cover, open up with his two-inch mortar and get his Brens forward in this manner. This will complicate the operation but will rarely be necessary.

(b) *Day attack with Arty concentrations*

Same method of grouping, but groups move much more dispersed, men being at 5x intervals. If forward movement is across country likely to be covered by enemy fire the Pl Comd tells the Pl Sgt to position his Bren groups before moving himself, and the Pl advances by Fire and Movement handled as a Section in every way.

(c) *Day attack, little battle without Hy Arty concs* (e.g. A single Coy sent up to picket a height.)

All Pls in the Coy will be organised as suggested above, and the leading Pl will move forward as described in (b).

If the leading Pl comes under fire from more than one enemy MG post it will be regarded as pinned and the Coy Comd will deploy the rest of his Coy round whichever flank offers the best cover. This sort of battle requires the most inf skill, and it should be practised at home as I think it will be often needed.

NOTES

(i) There is this further practical point on grouping the Brens collectively. In hilly country the speed of the Bren is far different from the speed of the rifleman with the result that it almost always happens that when the riflemen are caught under fire there is a frantic scream for the Brens who invariably are found to be a long way in the rear. With the system advocated the Pl Comd can watch the progress of the Brens so that he does not get out of touch with them. It may be argued that the Section Comds should be able to do this but, in fact, they are not able to do so.

Team work between the Pl Comd and the Pl Sgt is about 10 times more likely to succeed than team work between the Sects – that is my strong point for this very simple drill.

3. BATTLE INOCULATION

The Battle Schools have not gone far enough into this important subject and have missed the big point of it.

Even tps who have been in quite a number of battles are unable to distinguish between Bren and Spandau fire, between the whistle of our own shells and those of the enemy. They go to ground as soon as there is any noise of firing, although it is not directed at them. This often disorganises an entire battle, especially at night.

Comds come back to find their men, but they are seated at the bottom of deep holes and their Comds cannot find them and, because of the noise, they do not answer when called. This problem of offrs and NCOs losing all or a substantial part of their men in night attacks is a very real one and it happened in all the Bns I was with at some time or other. Tps coming up from the rear e.g. tpt, A tk guns etc, ordered to be up for consolidation at first light were particularly bad – there were often considerable delays because of the mere noise of firing.

It is only fair to say that the German appears to be the same. The noise of firing keeps him quiet for a very long time.

(a) I suggest that at all Battle Schools there should be the following *daily* Battle Inoculation. Every student to listen to the noise of the Bren, Spandau, Schmeiser and Tommy-gun.

(b) Advancing men to have firstly fire not directed at them, then directed over them, so that they acquire sufficient skill to know whether or not *they* are being shot at.

(c) It must be impressed on the men *every* day that they have got to learn the difference between the mere noise of battle and fire directed at them. They have got to learn to keep moving fwd as fast as possible *despite any noise* so long as they themselves are not the target.

4. INCENDIARY AMN

Events in this Campaign have proved that despite very heavy shelling a small remnant of the Boche will stay put. It is this small remnant that causes all the trouble. I have seen a lucky shot from a 25-pr set the ground on fire. The Germans immediately went although they were well dug in. I am sure that one of our best weapons is the three-inch mrtr smoke bomb used as a lethal weapon, that is fired directly at the enemy so setting the area alight with the burning phosphorus.

If we could throw some inc amn in our 25 prs we should have no further trouble with the Boche, and I suggest that something on the lines of the RAF oil bomb would be most effective. We can't blast him out but we could easily burn him out.

5. BDE ORGANISATION

This is already out of date and I hope the authorities at home realise it. The Bde Supp Gp is probably all right so far as the MGs are concerned although every Bn Comd to whom I have spoken would prefer to have the MGs in the Bn. The remainder of the Bde Supp Gp is unnecessary and quite useless for the following reasons:-

Four point two-inch Mortars

Very inaccurate – not as quick into action as 25 prs. There is nothing they do which the 25 prs do not do better. If OPs are difficult to come by they are yet another group of people occupying valuable space.

When suitable targets presented themselves they were far out of range, or could be adequately dealt with by the 25 prs. During a three-day battle when I was almost continuously at an OP, the 4.2 mrtrs fired no rounds during the whole period.

They have been used to thicken up fire when concentrations are being put down, but as there is no shortage of guns it is rather a drop in the ocean to add 4.2-inch mortrs to, say, 6 Fd Regts and 2 Med Regts. When they are so used they can be very dangerous as they are not accurate enough to do barrage work. During one attack of this kind we were continuously shelled by something very heavy on our own side and we all thought that this was the 4.2-inch mrtr (this may be doing them an injustice).

20 mm A/A

General Montgomery said at the beginning of the Campaign 'I have no intention of starting the land battle until I have won the air battle.' This is obviously the policy which will be continued and as a result the 20 mm A/A is a complete anachronism. These guns were ordered at a time when our Forces in N. AFRICA were without adequate air cover and were suffering severely. This picture has now changed. These guns have hardly fired a shot and I suggest we cannot afford to tie up such a large number of men in a defensive role of this kind, whilst the inf remain desperately short in other ways.

I suggest that the bodies saved by doing away with the 4.2-inch mrtr and the 20 mm A/A guns should be used in the following manner:-

(a) to provide an establishment for Pls of Specialist Infiltration Tps as referred to above.

(b) to increase the size of the Section which is still always woefully short in actual fact when it gets into battle.

6. TRAINING AT HOME

My principal object was to get careful first-hand notes of actual battles with maps, copies of orders, details, history of events so that our Training Schools at home could base their training on reality. I have kept very full notes of all battles I have seen, and feel at home these battles can be practised on similar ground and the lessons learnt with an accuracy which it has not been possible to achieve in the past. I think that the Campaign in SICILY has really been ideal from a training point of view. We have had every kind of battle – the advance to contact, the prepared attack on a big scale, the Pl and Coy battle, the pursuit and even the flank protection role. In addition we have been able to study the German methods of conducting a rearguard action in detail.

7. MISC POINTS

(1) *Value of Smoke*

Smoke has been little used in the Campaign, I feel that it might have been a great deal of use. It was used very successfully in the battle of RIVOGLIA by your Bde as you know.

(2) *Drawing Fire*

If the German sees a tank or some smoke he fires everything he has got at it always. This gives us two very useful openings:-

(i) a diversion

(ii) to locate his positions

I have tried out both these ideas successfully. They are old lessons but worth repeating.

(3) *Patrolling*

When ordered to send out patrols to regain contact with the enemy who had retired we tried out the idea of sending with them an 18 Set, borrowed from one of the Coys, which was in communication with another 18 Set close to the gunner OP. Whilst the patrol was moving out (in daylight) I manned the OP and carefully registered all likely places where the enemy might be. As soon as the patrol came under fire they wirelessed back to me and we at once brought down the fire of one Fd Regt on the suspected place. This was always effective in silencing enemy fire, and it enabled the patrol to move forward about two miles and to occupy a good position forward of our line for 36 hrs without sustaining casualties.

(4) *A Tk guns*

It is almost a universal custom out here to group A tk guns under Bde collectively, and to make the Bde A tk regt comd responsible both for their training and their handling in war.

This method works extremely well and it relieves the Bn Comd, who has very many other things to do, of the job. Everyone says, also, how much better gunner A tk gunners are than the inf, and I would suggest that these facts be recognised and the guns organised on a Gunner basis entirely.

The present system creates numerous admin difficulties as the guns are handled by Bde, but administered by the three separate Bns.

(5) *Three-inch Mortars and Carriers*

These were hardly ever used throughout the Campaign as the country was quite unsuitable for Carriers (movement off the rds was impossible), and the three-inch mrtrs invariably found that targets offered were out of range.

Our three-inch mrtrs (5 Buffs) did not fire a single rd throughout the Campaign.

(6) *LOB*

Whatever we say about it at home the facts are that a Bn leaves a certain nucleus out of battle.

This usually comprises the 2 i/c, 2 i/cs of each Coy, and about six NCOs or men per Pl. This practice should also be recognised at home, and Bns handled in training minus these percentages.

The size of the Sec should be increased if possible to allow for it as the present size was determined on the assumption that there would be no LOB.

(7) *Panic and Hysteria*

When heavy shelling or mortaring starts it is not unusual to find some men here and there who lose complete control and start to clear out. These men are invariably known beforehand. Their actions may often have the most demoralising effect on the whole Pl, which would otherwise behave very well.

I used to think that it was right to make chaps like this go into battle and take their medicine like everyone else, but I am quite sure now that I was wrong. They are too dangerous and can do too much harm.

Nearly every Bn has now come to this conclusion. They know they have about, say, 20 men who are definitely unreliable and they leave them right out of battle. This will now have the effect of greatly reducing the number of Court-Martials in this Campaign but it has not really solved the problem. I feel that a Bn Comd should be able to get rid of men like this simply by certifying that in his opinion X is not suitable for front-line inf fighting.

(8) *System of Reinforcement*

I do feel that this militates against highly skilled inf methods. Men are first dumped into reinforcement pools, then drafted anywhere. If this system is essential, it very much strengthens my case for specialist infiltration tps.

8. TAKING THE LESSONS HOME

The Div Comd has agreed to allow me (subject to tpt difficulties) to use the present lull to go back for a few days to explain the lessons and to bring out training both in N. Africa and in England into line. Would you be kind enough to let me have your own frank comments on the above together with any additional points so that I can be quite sure that we are really training on the right lines.

Yours
(Sd) L. Wigram, Lt-Col.
Comd 5 Buffs, 36 Bde
CMF

In the Field
16 Aug 43

III

Lionel duly visited Barnard Castle, lecturing there and passing on no doubt everything in his report and probably more. But meanwhile there was consternation at the War Office. At the foot of the memorandum from Kenchington to Cooney quoted above there is a note scrawled in pencil 'type two copies in normal current report form'. Perhaps the author of this instruction had not read the report, for the next available reference dated 5th September runs:

> Herewith Wigram's report – expurgated as I suggest it should go in Current Reports. I have sidelined in red on one copy of the original the too outspoken bits but I think it has not destroyed the report as a prevocative [sic] document.

The senior officer to whom this was addressed passed the matter upwards with the following note:

> *DMT*
> 1. This is Wigram's paper as prepared for Current Reports. It has been bowdlerised and, although very controversial, would I'm certain make an excellent issue.
> 2. I think we might note in the Foreword that 'Many of this officer's opinions are NOT accepted by C in C North Africa. They are, nonetheless, of great interest as being those of a junior officer who had made an intensive study of minor tactics at home before his first experience of active service. They will promote thought and discussion but are to be regarded as contrary to our present doctrine' or something like that.
> 3. I think it would be a pity if we should fear to publish this paper especially as 'Current Reports' goes only to Bde Comds and certain schools etc.
> 4. You may wish to consult IGS.

But at the next level there was disagreement:

> *DDMT*
> I think we better omit this from Current Reports until at any rate we get further reports from AFHQ which have been promised within 10 days or so.
> I have spoken to C in C 21 Army Gp, who also disagrees with many of Wigram's views. And I think we shall only stir up a storm, and perhaps put Current Notes into disrepute, if we include now any of these controversial matters. This will, if agreed to by Alex, be just as valuable in a month's time.

The DDMT agreed:

DMT has decided *not* to publish this yet – not for three weeks anyhow
– to allow the storm now raging round it to die down!

6/9

What storm? To our eyes today Lionel's report seems eminently honest and
sensible. In his letter to Brigadier Houldsworth (see Appendix IV) Lionel
claims that 'some kind friend' had written to the commander of 78 Division
(General Eveleigh) giving a distorted version of his views, 'suggesting he
(Eveleigh) should be sacked' and 'running down General Montgomery'. No
doubt the staff of 78 Division had passed this gossip on to Army HQ, who
would by now be thoroughly alarmed and asking the War Office that the
report should be suppressed.

At the foot of the memo of 6 September there is a note by a Major
Rickett 'B/F at end of month', and sure enough on 29 September Lionel's
report surfaces again:

GSO1
You wanted this hornet's nest brought forward at the end of the month
when it was hoped that the storm might have died down a bit.

DMT speaks of checking these views with other reports which apparently had been promised. Two reports have since come in:

(a) ME Instructional Circular (draft) on lessons from SICILY
(b) Major Johnson's reports (NOT approved by Army).

Major Johnson's report mentions the main points by Col. Wigram
but this cannot presumably be taken as confirmation of his views.

ME Instr. Circular does not mention the controversial points and,
as far as I know, Col. Wigram's views still remain those of himself and
Gen. Eveleigh* only.

Rickett
29 Sept 43   Major GS

Major Rickett
We have plenty of material for Current Reports to go on with. We had
better not publish 'Wigram' until we get rather more official corroboration
than Johnson's report.

30/9
initialled (illegible)

And that was the end of the matter. So far as is known Lionel's report
never saw the light of day.

Incidentally the nature of the 'bowdlerisation' throws an interesting light
on the psychology of the Directorate of Military Training at the War Office
midway through World War II.

---

*This is a poser. Lionel in his letter to Brigadier Houldsworth (see Appendix IV)
says it was alleged by 'some kind friend' that his report recommended that General
Eveleigh 'should be sacked'.

For instance Lionel had written:

Every platoon can be analysed as follows:
Six gutful men who will go anywhere and do anything
Twelve 'sheep' who will follow a short distance behind if they are well-led
Four to six men who will run away.

The War Office bowdlerised version has changed this last sentence to 'Four to six men who have not got it in them ever to be really good soldiers'.

Subsequently Lionel continues:

I have discussed these figures with many people and they all agree – although there is some slight disagreement on figures. These figures are roughly accurate as shown by the number of Court Martials for running away that follow every campaign. Every battalion has from forty to sixty and there are, of course, many others who aren't caught.

And the bowdlerised version: 'I have discussed these figures with many people and they all agree with me in general although there is some slight disagreement on the exact proportions of each type of men.'

The whole of the section critical of the organisation of Brigade HQ is deleted and the culminating stroke of the bowdleriser comes on the last page where Lionel's heading 'Panic and Hysteria' is deleted and the single word 'Misfits' put in its place, followed by the deletion of the recommendation that 'unreliable' men should be left out of battle. This Lionel thought would have the effect of greatly reducing the number of Court Martials. Such men should be certified as 'not suitable for front line fighting'. What Lionel was proposing here was no more than the open recognition of what was the informal practice in most front-line units.

While the War office was plagued by the difficulties of deciding what to do with Lionel's report, he was bearing the consequences, as described in a letter to Brigadier Houldsworth, the Commandant at Barnard Castle, written on 23 November 1943 while he was out of action and sick at Termoli during the battle of the Sangro:

6 RWK
CMF

Dear Brigadier,

I expect you will be wondering what has become of me! I am still alive (just) but it is rather a gloomy story.

I got back quite safely and quickly and took up my new appointment as a 2 i/c. The Bn had lost a lot of officers in the Sicilian Campaign so there was much hard work to be done – training – and we all got down to it. The CO was one of the best – very clever and with a real flair for soldiering. After a short while we settled down very well together and became the best of friends.

Well, then came the bombshell. Some kind friend who claimed to have heard my lecture at the School wrote a letter to the Divisional Commander to whom I had been attached saying that I had severely criticised him in my lecture, had suggested that he ought to be sacked, had run down Genl. Montgomery and the 8th Army etc. – more in the same strain. Of course the Div Comd sent this on to Genl Monty with his own comments and I was summoned into the presence. I had no idea why I had been sent for, was not given the opportunity of saying anything in my defence – merely told what I had done – all accepted as true – that I wasn't fit to be a 2 i/c – my appointment cancelled – and posted as a coy comd to 6 RWK – all this on the very eve of battle.

Well naturally I felt as sick as could be. I think I've worked as hard and as honestly as anyone in the Army – at least I've tried to. But it is such a wicked malicious world.

However I found my new CO and all his officers such a wonderful lot – so keen and enthusiastic – that I was soon able to drown my sorrows. I went into the campaign commanding a rifle coy and felt happier than I had done for years. I got a lot of new experience – just the sort of experience I needed. Unfortunately I succumbed to malaria followed by jaundice a few days ago – so am writing to you from my sickbed. But I expect to be quite better very soon.

When I left Army HQ and made a mild remonstrance I was told that my case would be reviewed in a few weeks time – and I expect this review to take place shortly. My CO has already put in a very strong plea on my behalf – also my late CO – and the Brigadier has been most sympathetic and helpful throughout. So I am writing to ask you – as you know all the facts and the personalities so well – to ask you whether you would be kind enough to tell Gnl. Montgomery the truth. You heard every word that was said and you will remember how careful I was not to mention any names or to criticise anybody. The whole pathetic concoction is a most damnable lie but obviously Gnl. Monty will believe it until he is told otherwise.

I am very sorry to drag you into this affair but you have always been such a stickler for justice that I'm sure you wouldn't wish me and my whole reputation to suffer merely for trying to do my job. But would you when you write please not indicate that your knowledge of the affair comes from me. I have been forbidden to communicate with the School other than through official channels – and although this letter relates to purely personal affairs I would rather not risk being told that I had blundered again.

For the same reasons I sent a message to ask Brig. Cooney not to publish the battle notes I had prepared. It hurt to do this, but the atmosphere is such that I had no alternative. Any 'lessons' will merely be regarded as criticisms of the comds in the battle and the results visited on my head. I hope that neither he nor the DMT will think that I have let them down and if you have an opportunity of explaining to them I should be most grateful.

Well that's about the end of my tale of woe. The only thing for me to do now is to follow the maxim 'actions speak louder than words'. That's what I'm going to do to the best of my ability and my only object in writing this letter is to clear my good name and get myself a fair chance. That's all I ask for.

With kindest regards to yourself and all at the School.

Yours
Lionel.

APPENDIX

V

The debate I had with Lionel in my OP on the banks of the Sangro about sending a letter upwards towards General Montgomery preceded the letter to Houldsworth (Appendix IV). After his death, on going through his army papers, I found the following:

Brig. J. Howlett, DSO
36 Inf. Bde.
Sir,
        Subject: Termination of my appointment as a 2 i/c
At the conclusion of my interview with the Army Commander on the above subject the MGGS informed me that the Army Commander would be prepared to review the case in two or three weeks time if the Divisional Commander would raise the matter when next at Army headquarters.

    I tried to convey this message to the Divisional Commander on returning from Army HQ but was unable to see him.

    I accordingly have the honour to request that my case be now reviewed and to submit the following points for consideration:-

1. When going home I went under a written War Office order. I was not at that time an officer in the 8th Army and any lecture I gave was clearly explained both by the commandant and myself as an expression of one man's view only. No names of units were given. At the conclusion of my visit I was given a letter from the War Office stating that I had done 'very valuable work' for them. They raised no complaint with regard to any of my work.

2. My object was to recommend simplifications in the training at home in order to fit it more closely to battle conditions. In order to do this I had to give some actual battle experiences both of my own and others. I had no intention of casting, nor did I cast, any reflection on the magnificent work performed by the 8th Army and I am deeply sorry if any such impression should have been given.

3. I would respectfully submit that it is unfair and unreasonable to punish me severely for a sincere, if misguided, attempt to do my job to the best of my ability, at a time when I was not under command of 8th Army.

4. When leaving England I brought a letter from the Commandant School of Infantry to General Alexander asking for previous work on my part to be taken into account in giving me a job out here. This letter has still not been opened. If I am to be held guilty of any crime

I put forward the plea that any previous credit to my account should be considered before a punishment is inflicted.

5. The Battalion to which I was posted 5 Northamptons is now in battle. I had just settled down with them. It is not easy after having been a Lt. Col or a GI for nearly 2 years to grow fresh roots and start again as a Company Commander at the age of 36. My late CO is fully prepared to take me back if permitted to do so.

6. I have learned my lesson and request that my case be now reviewed.
   I have the honour to be sir,

Your obedient servant,
(Signed) Wigram
Major

The letter was never sent. But Lionel had taken my advice. It was much shorter, covering only two sides of a sheet of paper. The abject tone of the original draft had been modified. It was addressed to Swifty Howlett who was killed on 29 November, and so was probably written a day or two after our discussion.

APPENDIX

VI

There is no doubt that the treatment meted out to Lionel by Montgomery was monstrously unfair, seriously undermined the teaching of battle schools and set back the armies' approach to infantry training for the remainder of the war, as is clear (despite his protestations) from the following letter from Brigadier Houldsworth to me in June 1944:

My dear Denis,
Forgive my delay in acknowledging your letter of the 8th June and the most interesting enclosures which you sent, but I have been in the North for ten days connected with the 'Salute the Soldier' campaign.

Firstly I am so sorry indeed to hear about the leg. Poor Denis! That is wretched bad luck and you have my deepest sympathy. I understand, however, that they do produce the most remarkable legs in these days, and a chap with your vitality and enthusiasm will soon overcome that disability.

Your notes are a great work and are most interesting. You will appreciate of course that we have received particulars of most of them some time ago through Brigadier Kenchington, and in the same way, we have received copies of at least some of the patrols carried out by your Bn. It is, however, good to have a complete copy of these things here and they will be of value.

You will also appreciate I expect, that we have advanced tremendously since you were last here, the courses generally have improved 100 per cent, and we have embodied all the latest points in the teaching of 'Essentials in Infantry Fighting' which is our main purpose.

I am interested to hear that you were working in close touch with Lionel Wigram. I shall always have the greatest admiration for the drive and efficiency which he put into all his work, and without question he was a very brave man in every sense of the word. We have no copies of the pamphlets which resulted from his Sicilian tour. As you may know, these caused something of a sensation and in fact they did immeasurable harm to this school and I don't think that General Montgomery has forgiven us even now. Of course we had no responsibility for them whatever, but I am afraid that Lionel's connection with the school was enough for the Higher Commanders.

So far as the films are concerned, I am passing this matter over to George Boalch who knows Mrs Wigram, and he will write to her about those which either show him or hear him giving a commentary. I should be very glad and interested to have a copy of the account which you have written of Lionel's regimental service in Italy because, as I have said, I

212

have a very warm corner for him and I am told he was a most gallant officer in battle.

Things are much more difficult here now as, for the time being, they have pulled away our demonstration troops, which knocks the stuffing right out of our somewhat unique methods of showing on the ground practically everything which we teach. It will, however, be very nice to see you whenever you are fit enough to come here, and I hope by then we shall have recovered from this interim period.

Yours ever
(Signed) Harry Houldsworth

Harry Houldsworth could get no copies of Lionel's pamphlets 'which resulted from his Sicilian tour' because these were never published. His view that 'they did immeasurable harm to the school' is therefore mistaken.

It was not any pamphlet nor indeed Lionel's report itself that 'did immeasurable harm', it was nothing more or less than gossip – some of it irresponsible, some of it malicious – all of it based on misconceptions, which led to the downfall of the battle school movement and the wholly unmerited disgrace of the bravest and most brilliant soldier it was my lot to encounter throughout World War II.

APPENDIX

VII

Lionel's death was reported in the *Evening Standard* of 5 February 1944:

THE STORY OF LIONEL WIGRAM
by Leslie Randall

A shot fired in a night action on the Italian front has killed one of Britain's greatest 'amateur' soldiers.

He was Lionel Wigram who in the days before the war figured in the news as a highly successful young Mayfair solicitor who was one of the principals in a deal running into millions of pounds: the purchase of the vast Cardiff estate of the Marquis of Bute.

Since then the public have heard nothing of him, but thousands of soldiers knew him as the originator and organiser of the battle schools, where the British Army has been forged into the superb fighting instrument it is today.

Lionel Wigram was a captain in the London Territorials when Britain went to war. He started, and was the first commandant of the original battle school on which all the others have been modelled. He introduced realistic battle practice, with live ammunition and all the smoke and noise of war.

His Book

He wrote the book on Battle Drill which is now the standard manual for the training of infantry. He was specially promoted from major to lieutenant-colonel by General Sir Bernard Paget when the new system of training he had devised was adopted throughout the Home Forces.

Few men have done more to lay the foundation of victory than this citizen–soldier who revolutionised the system of preparing the Army for battle.

Lionel Wigram was 37. It was on the day after his birthday that he died fighting with the Eighth Army. He was shot through the chest in a night attack on a village while leading a band of Italians he had raised and trained.

He left the School of Infantry (as the GHQ Battle School was renamed when it was taken over by the War Office) to go out and take part in the campaign in Sicily as an observer. He went where the fighting was fiercest, and took a camera with him into action to get pictures of the battles. Then he flew home and gave talks, illustrated by his own pictures, at the War Office and the battle schools on the lessons of the campaign.

To gain more first-hand experience of war he returned to the Italian battlefield. There was no vacancy to command a battalion, and so he reverted to the rank of major. When he left England he spoke no word of Italian. He soon mastered the language and set himself the task of organising Italians.

'Lionel organised and commanded them as only he could,' one of the officers who served with him has written. 'This force has been doing most valuable work and it was actively engaged with British troops in the battle in which Lionel was killed.

'By his ability to speak their language and to see their point of view he made himself the personal champion and hero of these men. They feel his loss as a personal loss.'

Gallantry

'You know of Lionel's immense success in revitalising the training of the British Army, but you may not have heard so much of his gallantry in action. He was an officer of exceptional courage, wit, absolutely no thought of personal danger.'

Lionel Wigram was the son of a Sheffield business man. He won a scholarship to Oxford. After he qualified as a solicitor he rapidly built up one of the most lucrative practices in the West End. He was a director of a number of companies. His rise was spectacular. Before the war when he was 32 his income was estimated in the Londoner's Diary to be £30,000 a year.

He was devoted to his wife and their three young children, and their home life at Moray Lodge, a big house on Camden Hill, he bought from Anne Lady Harmsworth. But from the first days of the war he put aside all his business interests. He went into strict training. He was resolved to make himself fitter and tougher than any Nazi.

Battle drill as the preparation for modern war was the inspiration of General Alexander. In a memorandum written after the evacuation of Dunkirk the general elaborated the need for a new system of training.

Impatient

Lionel Wigram, as a staff officer at a divisional headquarters, read the memorandum. It fired his enthusiasm. He was impatient of delay. He drew up a plan to give practical application to the principles formulated by General Alexander. He was determined that action should follow.

It seemed crazy for a junior officer of the Territorials to set out on a crusade to revolutionise the training of the British Army. His friends advised him that he could not possibly hope to succeed. But he was not deterred. He set to work with all the energy, drive and imagination that had made him such a 'live wire' in business. But he could never have succeeded without the encouragement and support he received first from his divisional general and then from General Paget. His divisional general sanctioned the experiment of a divisional battle school. He appointed Lionel Wigram commandant and gave him every opportunity to put his theories into practice.

The enthusiasm of the instructors and the students was terrific. The school was an immediate success, his fame spread.

General Paget, GOC-in-C the South-eastern Command, paid a number of visits. He was so impressed by the new, realistic training that he issued a directive that it was to be adopted throughout his command. The Canadians took it up. Others followed suit. And when General Paget was appointed C-in-C Home Forces he formed a GHQ battle school and

215

had local schools established for every division of the Army in training in Britain.

Now battle schools have sprung up in almost every land where soldiers of the United Nations are in training.

Never Tired

An officer who was closely associated with the development of the battle schools said to me today:

'Lionel Wigram was one of the most remarkable men of our time. His energy was astonishing. He worked and trained like a demon, but I never once heard him say he was tired. The word was not in his vocabulary.

'He began battle school training at a time when invasion was still expected. Most soldiers were thinking in terms of the defensive. But Wigram always preached the doctrine of the offensive.

'He inspired loyalty to such an extent that his band of young instructors worshipped him.

'I know he had plans to gather these young men round him after the war in big commercial enterprises – not just for the sake of making money, but with the object of doing good with it.'

And a week or so later his obituary appeared in *The Times*:

MAJOR L. WIGRAM
Pioneer of New System of Battle Drill
Major L. Wigram was killed early this month while leading a detachment of Italian irregulars on the Eighth Army front.

Lionel Wigram will be remembered as an outstanding pioneer of the new system of battle drill that is now accepted as an essential part of British infantry training. It is given to few war-time soldiers to exert such a wide-spread influence on tactical teaching. He was 37 years old and the son of a Sheffield business man. Before the war he had already achieved marked success as a London solicitor and company director. He held a commission in a Territorial battalion of the Royal Fusiliers, and, inspired by a paper on tactics written after Dunkirk by General Alexander, he found an outlet for his imagination and organising ability as commandant of the first divisional battle school to be instituted.

It was then appreciated by relatively few people that the old methods of drill were out of date and that infantry training, by the use of live ammunition and other realistic devices, should do more to prepare the soldier for the conditions of modern battle. A battle school already existed in the corps then commanded by General Alexander, but Wigram, who was fortunate in the warm encouragement he received from his divisional commander, was able to put many of his own ideas into practice, and with the help of a team of young instructors it was not long before all the junior officers in the division had undergone a course of 'battle inoculation'. A tough, exacting course it was, to which in time all the weapons of modern war were added, but it was impossible to visit the school and not feel its exhilaration and purpose. Wigram wrote the book on battle drill, which, with few modifications, has become an official manual, and when the Commander-in-Chief (then General Paget) decided that every British division should have its battle school he appointed him with the rank of lieutenant-colonel as commandant of the GHQ school for the training of instructors.

216

Battle drill had come to stay, and Wigram's work was largely done. He declined offers to serve in a similar capacity in Canada and India, and went out to Sicily as an observer to see at first hand how the new training methods could be improved. Later he returned to Italy, where, after learning the language with characteristic skill, he applied himself to the training of Italian irregulars, a party of whom he was leading when he fell. Shortly before the war he was nominated as prospective Conservative candidate for Pontefract. He leaves a widow and three children.

VIII

In *The Times* of Saturday 3 March 1951 there was a retrospective appraisal of the battle school movement.

THE INFANTRY REVIVAL
Origins and Influence of the Battle Schools
From Our Special Correspondent

Two articles in *The Times* some time ago on the revival of the British infantry reawakened a lot of interest in the 'battle schools' through which during the last war the modern revolution in infantry training was achieved. Much light has been thrown by correspondents and others on the origins of the battle school movement, about which there have been certain misconceptions.

Contrary to an impression widespread during and since the war, the schools owed little to the peculiar methods of training of the raiding units formed in 1940 which became known as Commandos. The new style of training for the infantry proper developed on parallel but different lines from those found suitable for producing bodies of fighting raiders. The beginnings lay partly in a memorandum written in 1940 by Field-Marshal Lord Alexander (then Lieutenant-General Alexander), after his return with the Army from Dunkirk, emphasising the need for more realism in the weapon and tactical training of British infantry to enable them to meet the formidably efficient Germans with greater confidence. This made a strong impression on many infantry commanders throughout the Army.

The First School

Among those most impressed was a brigadier who returned from Dunkirk. This officer had survived a long fighting experience on the Western Front. As a battalion commander in 1918, close observation of German infantry front-line methods during the enemy's last and almost successful offensive had convinced him of the possibilities of well-trained infantry. The performance of the German infantry in the battle of France, 1940, strengthened this view. On assuming command of a division in 1941 he established what he called a 'battle school' for infantry junior leaders of the division in Ashdown Forest. Among his young officers was Lionel Wigram, of the Royal Fusiliers, a citizen soldier who had been much struck by General Alexander's paper and, being possessed of unusual imagination and energy, was full of ideas of his own, which he was able to put before his wholly sympathetic divisional commander. He was appointed commandant of the new school, with the rank of major.

The combination here was ideal; the general had an unsurpassed first-hand knowledge and experience of infantry warfare, particularly the German methods; the younger officer, then unblooded in war, had the youth and fire, the vision and the persuasiveness needed to inspire young soldiers whose hearts and minds then were set on wiping out the humiliation of the British Army's bolt from the Continent. Wigram developed a new system of 'battle drill' out of his preliminary conferences with the divisional commander, and collected a team of enthusiasts whom he trained as instructors and infused with his own faith and zest in the task of restoring infantry values and effectiveness.

Discipline in the Field

Battle drill was designed for the translation of the discipline of close order drill on the barrack square into the extended order movements of the battlefield. It was recognised that close order drill had been, in effect, the battle drill of the old days of short-range weapons and close order fighting. Foot soldiers therefore were now taught, by sections and platoons (the front line sub-units), to fall in and 'tell off' man by man according to his individual duty in battle and to his fixed place in standard little battle groups; and they were later exercised in standard field movements in which each man must know and keep his place in relation to the others as precisely as possible.

The movements, in which attention was concentrated chiefly on the offensive, were designed mainly for filtering through enemy positions by 'flanking' to right or left or as 'pincers' by a combination of both with frontal attack. All the movements were done 'at the double' and accompanied by the full and proper use of the various powerful weapons (including mortars) of the sub-unit at the successive stages of the advance. 'Fire and movement' – rapid movement – were the essence of the new infantry attack.

For realism, and as a sharp reminder to men to keep their heads down while in action, picked marksmen stationed near the 'enemy' positions in the exercises fired live tracer ammunition from rifles and light machine-guns over the heads of the attackers. Other battle noises were produced by exploding thunderflashes and charges of guncotton.

This was the physical stuff of the training worked out together by the divisional commander, Major Wigram, and his staff and their pupils on the early courses at the school. The field exercises were the expression of something even more important, a great new elevation of the spirit and outlook of the infantry soldier, to which everything said and done at the school contributed. The greatest prominence was given there to the German dictum that infantry is the principal arm; it bears the main weight of battle; it suffers the heaviest casualties: all other arms support it.

The sense of power and purpose and the exhilaration imparted by the dynamic Wigram and his staff to the officers and other ranks who for a time came under their influence was tremendous. Inspired by it, men willingly ran and crawled and jumped and climbed, fasting and thirsting from dawn to dusk, and found a certain stern joy in the harsh yet somehow not entirely grim routine of their life in Ashdown Forest. Soon the school was beginning to attract men from other divisions of both the British and the Canadian armies for training as instructors.

219

Fortunately for the school, and ultimately for the whole British Army, the GOC-in-C South-Eastern Command at that time, Lieutenant-General (now General Sir Bernard) Paget, had been an infantry soldier. He had served in the Oxfordshire and Buckinghamshire Light Infantry, the regiment whose two battalions formed the major part of Sir John Moore's famous Experimental Brigade of light infantry and rifles in 1803; he had a lively appreciation of the meaning of the new reforms. From his first visit he was a keen supporter, and when at the end of 1941 he became Commander-in-Chief Home Forces he ordered the establishment of divisional battle schools on the same lines in all Home Commands, and also initiated the GHQ Battle School, opened at Barnard Castle early in 1942, to produce the instructors for the new schools.

An early appointment made by General Paget at GHQ was that of a Major-General of Infantry, Home Forces. This was a complete innovation for the British Army, and it was soon followed by the establishment of a new Directorate of Infantry at the War Office. Later on the GHQ Battle School at Barnard Castle was transplanted to become the present School of Infantry at Warminster, a further new development in the British Army.

Under General Paget's vigorous direction the school at Barnard Castle was started with Lieutenant-Colonel Wigram as its chief instructor. A series of striking demonstrations of infantry tactics and fire-power was staged for the benefit of high commanders and other representatives of the British and the Allied armies. The principles and methods taught and the outlook fostered among infantrymen at that school and, through the instructors trained there, inculcated into the British armies everywhere, were a large influence towards the final victory. Lionel Wigram himself met an untimely end in February 1944. He was killed in action on the Eighth Army front in Italy, while leading some Italian irregulars and putting into practice lessons which he had taught with so much enthusiasm and effect at home. His name will live in the annals of the British infantry.